youtube.com/@TheHoofGP

www.thehoofgp.myshopify.com

BRUISED SOLE / GRAEME & ROBERT PARKER

# BRUISED SOLE

*The Unfiltered Story Of The Hoof GP*

**Graeme & Robert Parker**

First published by The Hoof GP in 2024
Laigh Kirkland, Wigtown, Scotland
www.thehoofgp.myshopify.com



Cover photograph by Andy Foreman

Publishing services from Lumphanan Press
www.lumphananpress.co.uk

Paperback ISBN: 978-1-0685215-0-8
Ebook ISBN: 978-1-0685215-1-5
Audiobook ISBN: 978-1-0685215-2-2

Typeset in PS Fournier
Printed by Short Run Press, Exeter, Devon, UK.

*This book is a memoir. It describes the author's recollections and honest opinions of events and experiences which happened over time. Some names have been changed, some events have been compressed, and some dialogue has been recreated from memory.*

*Readers should note that this book contains references to family violence, physical injury, bereavement, suicidal ideation and mental health issues. These are included to describe real life events, and to raise awareness around these issues.*

*For Ash, Kiki, Bam Bam & Maddie –*
*You are my strength.*

# Contents

# Preface

When I was twelve, my parents took me to a clinical psychologist. I'd started having intense bouts of anxiety and distress. When I was fifteen, my father was found dead – floating, face down, in a river – the unfortunate discovery of a woman out walking her dog on an otherwise unremarkable Sunday morning. I spent the next fifteen years thinking he'd been murdered. When I was twenty-seven, an old friend unwittingly stopped me taking my own life just by phoning me out of the blue. If she knows that now, it's only because she's reading this book.

Surprised? This isn't a misery memoir, I promise. It's not a self-help manual and it's not an alternative *Trainspotting* for shit-kickers. I want you to enjoy the book. I'm a positive person and I have a *good* life now, but that hasn't always been the case. For anyone who follows me on social media, it's important to understand that my Instagram, Facebook and YouTube posts are upbeat and fun, but they're *not* my real life. They're a curated, perfected, amped-up-to-eleven version of my life. The edited highlights.

My life may look perfect to some people from the outside. Believe me, it's not. No one's is. I've been lucky in a lot of ways and every day I'm grateful for that. I suppose what I want to do here, in telling you my story, is to burst the bubble I am complicit in creating. Too many people worry that their lives don't live up to what they see in their social feeds, despite not seeing the true lows of the poster's day-to-day reality. It's tempting to equate success with happiness, but comparison really is the thief of joy – it's a twenty-first century disease. None of us are immune to it. Including me.

If I can help break down that wall, even a little bit, if just one person reading this reassesses their self-perception, relative to what they see on their phone, and if I can help dispel some of those negative emotions, then this book will have been worthwhile.

This isn't the sanitised version you see on Instagram. This is my real life.

# Introduction

I'm Graeme Parker, and I'm a hoof trimmer. That sounds like I'm introducing myself to the most niche self-help group in the world, doesn't it? It's not a sentence I ever thought I'd say, but not for the reasons you might think.

I'm a famous hoof trimmer. That's not a sentence I thought *anyone* would ever say. Who would have thought that being a famous hoof trimmer would ever be *a thing*? But here I am – a hoof-trimming, cow-whispering, viral, social media sensation. I'm guessing none of that's news to you, if you're reading this book, and that you probably first encountered me online. If this book is your introduction to the random (and frankly wonderful) world of hoof trimming, brace yourself!

Every day, around a million people click on my Hoof GP videos. Some are looking for drone footage of the epic Galloway countryside I live in; some are interested in the goings on in my day-to-day, family life; others happily get lost in the weirdly hypnotic business of shaping and healing cattle hooves. I still can't quite get my head round it all.

These days, I love my life. I feel like the luckiest man in the world. Every morning, after a healthy slug of coffee, I hook on a cattle crush, climb into my pickup and drive out into the kind of landscape normally featured in films and fairy tales. I live with my beautiful wife, Ashley, our two boys, Keir and Campbell, and our French bulldogs, Mia and Steve, on a smallholding, overlooking the stunning Wigtown Bay.

Wigtown sits on the Machars peninsula, in Galloway – a small spit of land jutting out into the Irish Sea. Galloway is in the southernmost tip of Scotland, with a hammerhead peninsula tacked on to the far end like an afterthought, and that kind of fits. Wigtown is a special place. Yes – I'm biased, but I took the long way round to figuring that out. Sometimes you have to go away before you can really find home. If you're wondering about the name, Wigtown, it has nothing to do with hairpieces.

Our only close neighbours here are non-human: brown rabbits, deer, foxes, pheasants every colour of the rainbow and sheep who frequently escape their fields and really should know better. More on them later. In the late summer and early autumn, Canada geese fly over our house in tight v-formations, honking their way to the warm shores of the estuary. It's quite a sight, but it's nothing compared to the sunrises here: purple and blue one day, red the next, orange the day after.

You can sense the history here, just from driving around. If you head west a few miles, across the top of the Machars and down the twisting, bouncing blacktop that leads to the village of Kirkcowan, the countryside opens up to rolling hills that look like they've been CGI'd and mysteriously crowned by the prehistoric Torhouse stone circle. Local legend has it that King Galdus – a man who supposedly gave the Romans a good hiding when they rocked up here – lies underneath the three stones in the middle. Legend also has it that he's buried twenty miles away in Cairn Holy. Historians would tell you that he probably never existed. But no one has ever actually bothered to excavate it to find out.

The stones themselves date back to the second millennium

BCE and predate Galdus and the Roman invasion by at least a thousand years. What we're dealing with here is a stone circle that seems to be linked to the winter solstice, that may or may not have something to do with the druids and might have something to do with an ancient Caledonian freedom fighter who probably never existed. There's so much history in just one set of stones that no one can agree what happened here, but it's still not important enough for anyone to dig or scan, archaeologically.

This is Wigtownshire in a nutshell: a forgotten place, the junction between Scotland, Ireland, England and the Isle of Man, packed with history, myth and legend. It's an outlier – an autonomous region that wasn't fully absorbed under Scotland's rule until the mid-thirteenth century because no one could tame it; a place where people still leave their doors open half the time; a place we refer to as 'The Shire'. I was strangely proud when I realised the local nickname had made it into Wikipedia.

The Shire forms the western part of Galloway. They say Galloway is like Scotland in miniature, with beaches, marshland, moorland, and mountains to the north. Galloway takes its name from the Gall-Ghàidheil: the 'Stranger Gaels'. The Gaels in question were strangers because they had mixed with the invading Vikings. That's why we have these strange old names here: Wigtown; Whithorn; Torhouse. One of the theories about the place name Wigtown is that it was originally Viktown; the 'vik' being old Norse for water inlet. The last ruler of the area, Alan, Lord of Galloway, died around 1234, but this place still feels like its own nation state, and I love it. I'm proud of being from this strange old part of the world, where people still see things slightly differently.

The Shire might not look special to outsiders, beyond

the obvious beauty of the scenery, but it's the stuff below the surface that counts. When you let someone out at a junction, for example, they thank you properly, because they know you will probably meet again. It makes no sense to be rude. Even if you don't know the person, the chances are your friends or family do. I'm not saying everyone is always nice but there is the sense of a proper country community here.

For years prior to moving back here, I lived in a city, surrounded by lights and noise and people, twenty-four-seven. I've never felt more alone. Here, I'm lucky to spend time with family, and friends I seem to have known forever. The remoteness means that when you do see someone, you're always in a better mood for it. The way things are here, you'd struggle to walk along the main street in Wigtown without a good few people saying hello and asking how you are. It's a different pace of life, with less hurry and more living.

You can't get away with much, because everyone knows your name, your face, and the skeletons you might normally expect to hide at the back of the cupboard. When I was younger, this level of visibility was too much. It unsettled me that every trip out the door all but guaranteed some kind of unintended social interaction. I felt like I had to put on a face for the world. I found home limiting – the lack of jobs, the lack of nightlife. I moved away for the bright lights and what I thought I was supposed to want.

These days, I love being recognised here. It's not hard to pick me out. I'm the guy driving the Tonka toy, pulling the shiny black cattle crush (picture a sort of steam-punk bondage-wagon, if you haven't seen it in my videos). In 2020, Ashley and I bought our smallholding, complete with cottage, and slowly began making it our own. It was the culmination of a dream for me.

I've been filming and posting videos on YouTube since 2019. It started as an add-on to my business: a side gig. But, like so many things in my life (as you'll find out), it quickly got out of hand. I put together a few short clips to educate farmers and people working in the industry about hoof care. Things kind of exploded from there. The Hoof GP now encompasses everything in my life: my wife and the boys, a whole load of cows, farmers, and people I run into along the way. At the time of writing, I have over 2.3 million subscribers on YouTube, and 2.2 million followers on Facebook. I'm the world's number one agricultural influencer.

How did all this happen? In 2014, I was still freeze branding cattle. I swore then I would never become a hoof trimmer. Not a chance. But the world has a way of streamlining your plans and life has thrown me a few curveballs. If someone had told me ten years ago that I'd be where I am now, I would have laughed politely and made a mental note to keep an eye on them.

But please don't get the wrong impression. Over the years, I've gone through some pretty big challenges, mentally and emotionally, especially where my family are concerned. I don't generally like to dwell, but as I hurtled towards the milestone of the big 4–0, I started to feel like that was as good a moment as any to pause and reflect on how far I've come, to get to this point. I've gone through some especially strange and tough times, and these have had an undeniable impact on who I am today. I *am* in a happy place now, but getting here has taken some doing, not least because I suffer from ultra rapid cycling bipolar disorder. It's a condition I struggled with for a long time, and it nearly ended my life. For a lot of the time, I didn't know what it was, but these days I have the right medication to keep it in check. And that's just *one* of the challenges I've faced.

I may look like I have things sussed out, like I have the perfect life, but things haven't always been this rosy.

I'm not the person you think I am.

This book is the honest, warts-and-all, skeletons-in-the-closet story of how I became the Hoof GP. I don't generally spare my own blushes, but I do try to spare the blushes of others … most of the time.

So, grab a sickly-sweet cup of coffee and a doughnut or three, get comfortable, and buckle up.

This one gets bumpy.

# Chapter One

I position myself in the optimum place on the concrete floor. Then I think better of it and move. I do this a few times before I get it right. I'm in the workshop and things are slowly coming together.

I'm surrounded by vehicles: pick-ups, a McLaren 600LT, a BMW M6 in a colour best described as GREEN and a Porsche 911 GT2 RS – a car I've been dreaming about for a long time. There are two cattle crushes, one in black and red and another in GREEN. My work bench sits in a corner, surrounded by a full range of red Milwaukee power tools – part of a sponsorship deal. Fast cars, trucks, power tools and a haven from the world.

All good things for me.

The walls of my workshop are lined with flags people have sent me. I want to get as many as possible into shot. All those people going to all that effort. The least I can do is get them on screen. No pressure. When I've decided on a less than perfect starting point (because nothing can ever be as perfect on screen as it starts out in your head), I do a last, mental check. What do I have to say? I have no idea what I'll *actually* say. That's the point, the buzz. But there are a few things I want to say.

I used to have a few beers before doing this. Ok, when I say *a few,* I really mean two. And when I say beers, I mean fruit ciders, but it's all relative. This used to be terrifying. I used to have bullet points printed on A4, so if I went too far out of bounds, I'd have a structure I could use to claw my way back. Those days are gone.

With my checklist done, I take a deep breath, click on the *create* button and then hit *live*. The rush is still there. I'm not thinking about my dentist appointment, or my VAT return, or how good my hair looks (the answer is always 'awesome' by the way). I am present. In the moment. Will tonight be the night I choke? Will I dry up and say nothing? Will it be the night I say the wrong thing and get cancelled?

There's a fifteen second latency when you're 'live'. You don't get any feedback telling you if anyone's there for that first, seemingly endless pause. The toughest thing is not giving in and asking, 'can you hear me?' Doubt can make you do weird things. I've ended up sharing my screen before.

And now ... I'm talking. The comments start to appear on screen, moving downwards, too fast to read at first. But I'll catch up. I feel like I fit in here, now, better than anywhere I ever have before. I never felt like I fitted in at school. I've never really felt like I fitted in in many places since. In some ways I think I got that from my dad. He never really found his place in the world.

My mum and dad were a strange sort of mismatch, with very different personalities. I think it worked really well when it worked at all, which certainly wasn't all of the time. They shared a sense of humour, a dedication to hard work and, in the beginning, a common sense of purpose. They came from very different backgrounds, which never seemed to bother either of them, but I don't think it was the same for some of the people around them.

My dad Ian's family were – it turns out – a bit of a mixture as well. My full name is Graeme Milroy Glen Parker. I have the same middle names as my father, my grandfather, and my two brothers. I proudly passed the middle names on to my sons, Keir and Campbell, when they were born. As you can imagine I took a bit of stick for the 'Milroy' bit at school, mainly from people who thought it was a first name.

Milroy is one of the oldest surnames in Wigtownshire. A relative of mine, John Milroy, was one of the Wigtown Covenanters, and he was executed for his religious beliefs during The Killing Time. A stone in Wigtown churchyard, less than half a mile from my front door, commemorates both this and the deaths of the Wigtown Martyrs, two women – Margaret McLachlan and Margaret Wilson – who were tied to stakes and drowned in the incoming tide for their refusal to swear an oath declaring King James VII as head of the Church of Scotland. Margaret Wilson was only eighteen years old. The Martyrs are a huge part of the history of Wigtown, and you can read about them in *The History of the Sufferings of the Church of Scotland from the Restoration to the Revolution.* I pass that churchyard every day, and you can see it in a lot of my videos. It's a beautiful, dishevelled, stone-built place. The ivy-covered ruins of the medieval church still stand in the background.

The Milroys themselves leave a paper trail going back to the seventeenth century, and more than one of my ancestors came to an abrupt and early end. John Milroy, a tailor, impaled himself on his own cutting sheers while crossing the River Tarff, on stones, near the settlement of Kirkcowan. Centuries later, history repeated itself, far closer to home than I could ever have imagined, and it would change the course of our lives.

The family were in the Kirkcowan area for another two and

a half centuries and stayed in the rag trade. They founded a waulk mill – a water-driven mill – on the Water of Tarff in 1779, and then a carding mill, to separate the wool. They became very wealthy in the process.

People used to say that you 'went out of the world and into Kirkcowan'. You still do. I should know. I used to live there, in the shadow of all that history, driving past the two towering brick chimneys of the mills every day. You can see my old house in Kirkcowan in some of my early videos. I used to wonder where that saying came from. I thought it was rooted in the quiet, other worldly nature of the place, but it turns out you used to have to leave the main road to get there. It's a simpler explanation, but Kirkcowan is still weird. I'm allowed to say that, by the way.

The business shut down in 1954, with no real market for the high-quality goods they produced after the war. They made woollen blankets, so the invention of the duvet probably didn't help! The family were strict Free Presbyterians. My great grandmother, Jessie Milroy, was a bit different, by all accounts. She had been rendered 'lame' – a term we no longer use – after falling off her horse, some time in her twenties. These days there'd be medical treatments and modern walking aids to help her, although knowing me I'd probably stick her in the crush and see if I could do something about it. Back then, she carried an ebony cane she'd happily hit anyone with if she felt like it. In photos she looks a lot like my grandad with a wig on, dressed from head to toe in suitably austere black attire.

After her accident, the family sent for a local doctor. John Glen Parker was a young man who had moved to the area from the big smoke, otherwise known as Glasgow. Exactly what happened next is a mystery and probably would have been covered up, given the sensibilities of the time, but one version of events is that Jessie's brother, Willie, saw something take place between the two of them – in the orchard – that shouldn't have. At that point it was decided that there would have to be a wedding. I'm guessing there was at least one shotgun involved.

My granny used to tell me that she went to Kirkcowan to see my grandad's family before they were married. Her future mother-in-law, the imposing Jessie, drove her out into the woods with a picnic basket, pulled up at the side of the road and got out. I know the spot well, it's near a hamlet called Barrachen, open on one side, with trees on the other. Jessie whistled, and a wild looking man scurried out of the forest, grabbed the picnic basket from the boot of the car, and tore off again. He was some kind of cousin and lived in a shed out there. When he died, they went to clear out whatever things he had. When they opened one of the drawers it was full of glass eyes.

If the Milroys were quirky, John Glen Parker was, and remains, an enigma – mainly because no one knows anything much about him. A genealogist traced our family tree back and discovered that his father, Robert Parker (we're not massively original with names in our family), was born in a workhouse in Cumberland. Going to the workhouse was the ultimate humiliation in Victorian England. It was where people went if they were destitute, often working back-breaking jobs and gruelling hours for food and board. Robert's mother probably went there because she was unmarried and pregnant. As was the way in the workhouse, mother and child were separated and Robert was apprenticed to the mills when he was old enough. It sounds grim, thinking about it – like something out of a Dickens novel. I can't imagine being separated from my kids like that. But Robert did okay. He found his way to Scotland, where he settled, became a foreman in a cotton mill and married a woman called Jeannie Glen. My other middle name comes from her.

Their son John is listed on a census as an 'apprentice mill tenter' as a teenager. Tenters worked textile mill machines with hooks. It's where the expression 'on tenterhooks' comes from. And yes, I had to look that up. Every day's a school day. Ten years later, he appeared on another census, as a doctor. How does that even happen? It's a long shot now but it would have been unthinkable in those days. However he did it, he somehow made it in the world of medicine, married an heiress and ended up with a sizeable practice in Bradford.

He seems to have clung on to his roots though. Family legend has it that the Labour Party was formed in his house in Bradford. He was a life-long friend of Keir Hardie, so I guess it's entirely plausible, but, like everything else with the man, it's a mystery. My grandad couldn't or wouldn't tell anyone about his own father. His history seems to have been erased through some still-unknown sense of shame. That's partly why we called our eldest son Keir. That, and Keir Mill is a place I used to work, although I never thought about the mill connection at the time. We called our second son Campbell. I used to work a lot in Campbeltown, on the famous Mull of Kintyre, and we thought it would be nice to name him in the same way, to tie the two together.

John Glen Parker and Jessie bought a hobby farm called The Knock. Knock translates from Gaelic as 'small hill', and that's a good description – the farm rose up in the centre, with the old house standing on the horizon for miles around. He built roads, drystone dykes and a cairn he used as a hide for watching birds that still stands today. He was clearly always handy. My paternal grandad followed in his footsteps, career-wise. He was privately educated at Dollar Academy in Stirling and later became a GP himself, a few years after his father died.

My grandparents met in Edinburgh. She was at Edinburgh College of Domestic Science, or the 'dough school' as it was called, learning how to cook, and, if you believe my grandad, on the hunt for a husband. Her father, Sir Charles Fitton, held a military cross from the First World War and we have no idea why. He would later serve as a Lieutenant-Colonel in the Home Guard, in the Second World War, and pick up an OBE there, before going on to be knighted for political and public services in the North Riding of Yorkshire. The military cross is one thing, but the OBE and the knighthood are just showing off. I think he was in steel, back in the days when people were 'in' things. If Grandad thought *he* was posh, he was in for a shock.

I don't think he got on well with his in-laws. My grandad served in the Royal Navy as a medical officer on a ship. He and Granny had set a date to get married but at short notice he got word of needing to sail for a beach in Normandy. It was June 1944. Yeah, that's right. He was headed for the D-Day landings. This didn't bode well for the nuptials. When he phoned to postpone the wedding, there was a bit of an angry conversation. His future father-in-law demanded to know the reason, Grandad said he couldn't tell him, and my great grandad resorted to the age-old 'don't you know who I am' line of attack. Grandad reportedly took great pleasure in putting the phone down on him.

My mum Christine's family were a bit more normal. Her dad's family, the Nimmos, have lived in Wigtown for generations. My grandpa Nimmo grew up in the family draper shop, which seems to have been a good business until some dodgy accounting by his older brother meant that they had to sell up. My great grandpa had a springer spaniel that sat in the window of the shop all day, emerging at the end of each day to tell everyone it was home time. The family business left a big impression. My grandpa could sew anything, and frequently did. He kept a Singer sewing machine next to his armchair after he retired, had a keen interest in how anyone was dressed, and was always fixing something. Sometimes he'd have a go at something electronic, take it apart, put it back together and wind up with some leftover parts and a radio that still didn't work.

He grew up in the flat above the shop. It's a grand, granite, Georgian building with huge sash and case windows at the front. These days it's pretty well known as The Bookshop – Scotland's biggest second-hand book shop. It has even featured in a few books. The owner, Shaun Bythell, wrote *The Diary of a Bookseller*, about his life there. He's since followed it up with another three books. His former partner, Jessica Fox, wrote *Three Things You Need To Know About Rockets* – a memoir about coming to Wigtown from America after she visualised herself working in a second-hand bookshop, by the sea, in Scotland. I suppose I've just stuck it in another book now.

Grandpa Nimmo was a hard worker. He was a civil servant and eventually ended up as the court officer for Wigtown, in the days when it had its own court. These days, the court is centralised, like everything else in the west of the region, in Stranraer. But, back then, the local court was in Wigtown's County Buildings – a vast pink Gothic revival mock-chateau which dominates the centre of the town. Grandpa's job meant that he had to live in the premises. He was always fixing or tidying something, even though he wasn't actually supposed to.

He was a slight man, with a full head of white hair. He wore a suit, complete with a hat, pretty much every day of his life, even after he retired. He was proud of being, as he saw it, the best dressed man in Wigtown. People used to call him Tonto, after the character in *The Lone Ranger.* He was well-known for coming to the rescue, helping anyone out when they needed it.

The Grange of Cree is a place I work a lot, these days, and the owner is a regular customer of mine. The farm sits on low, flat, fertile ground leading on to the salt marshes in Wigtown Bay. It's about a five-minute drive along the road from where I live now. It's also the place my granny Nimmo was born, but she didn't live there for long.

She never knew her real name until she needed her birth certificate, well into adulthood. She was supposed to be called Sheila McKie. McKie is another old Galloway surname and dates back to Robert the Bruce and two brothers who supposedly saved the king from harm while out hunting with him. One of the brothers shot a raven with an arrow, and brothers being brothers, the other followed up this feat by shooting two ravens with the same arrow. Their family crest either appears as a raven with an arrow through its head or, you guessed it, two ravens, with an arrow going through both heads. You can see a version of a crest on gravestones in Newton Stewart to this day.

When my granny was a baby, the family were settled at the Grange of Cree, my great grandfather being a 'gentleman farmer' in those days. In 1930, when Granny was born, there was a lot more manpower involved in farming, with farm hands and servants doing the bulk of the work. These days, with mechanisation, tractors, quad bikes, milking machines, and even robots, one farmer can do what would have been the work of four or five people. Back then it was a different way of life. Things would have been slower, and farmers would have been a bit more separate from the daily grind. But John McKie was no gentleman, as it turned out. No one these days knows the real ins and outs of it for sure, but whatever happened, the end result was that my great grandmother was pushed down a staircase and seems to have been left for dead.

My great grandfather left the farm straight away. They had five kids between them, and he took the oldest, Jack, and skipped town. My granny was a month old at the time. Before he left, he registered her birth, in the name of Jessie Sheila McKie. Granny wouldn't find out about the Jessie bit until she got married, at the age of twenty-two. She always hated that name.

John McKie washed up in the Northeast of England, on a new farm, with a new name: John Davidson. That would have been a lot easier to do in 1930, but it seems his parents supported him. None of his children, besides the eldest, ever saw him again.

My great grandmother recovered fine, physically. Everyone told her to stay where she was, at The Grange of Cree, that the farm was where she belonged, that she had four of her children to support, and that she had to be strong. She just couldn't see things that way. She was heartbroken at the breakdown of her marriage and the loss of her eldest son, so she decided she had to leave. There used to be a photo of her on Granny's mantelpiece. She looks a lot like my mum.

She moved into Wigtown, to a newly built, two-bedroom council house in The New Road. My mum would later be born on the same street. It must have been a tough existence. Her in-laws told her they would help but they never did. She had lost her home, her husband and her income from the farm, and she had four kids to feed. Her solution was to take in paying lodgers. I can't imagine how that must have worked, with four kids and two strangers. And, as well as the lodgers, she took in washing as another source of income.

This move into single parenthood would turn out to be an eerie foreshadowing of my mum's own experience, when my parent's marriage eventually ended.

Granny grew up quickly, living in the house in The New Road. She worked as a nanny, coincidentally, for some mill owners in Newton Stewart, then later as a school cook. There was a fourteen-year age gap between my her and my grandpa, which definitely showed. My mum told us that Granny was the more modern parent. She would explain *why* her kids shouldn't do something. Grandpa's reasoning was more along the lines of: 'Because I say so'.

Granny was an outspoken character who always seemed to be laughing and had a knack for saying things people didn't expect. My mum told us that they were having dinner one night with a cousin of Grandpa's, who was telling them about her marriage and what she thought the secret to that was. Her husband had been blind, and she felt that their having to rely on each other was what had made them so successful as a couple – a kind of co-dependency, in a good way. Granny, who loved a gin and tonic, told everyone this was nonsense and that the secret to a successful relationship was, as she put it, 'the physical side, because if everything else goes to hell, you've still got that'!

They always seemed to be happy, but they worked incredibly hard. Every night, after finishing their day jobs, they would go to work in a pub called The Fair Seat, in a village called Sorbie. It's another place nearby where I frequently work with a regular client.

They lived in a council house for the start of their marriage, with their kids being born there – a fact Mum is still very proud of. In Scotland, following on from the First World War, there was a project to build what the government called 'homes fit for heroes', and you can still see a lot of the houses from this era around Wigtown. They worked to give their kids holidays and to increase their standard of living, to send my uncle, John, and my mum off to university, in a time when that wasn't really the done thing.

Granny once got very angry with a local guy in the pub, someone who had a reputation for just always being there. The man took her aside one evening and said, 'do you mind if I ask ... how do you do it?' She couldn't understand how this man didn't appreciate that it was all down to hard work. That, and not spending all your time and money in the pub.

While my mum went to the local high school, picking up the qualifications she needed to take her to Glasgow University, my dad was on a very different trajectory. His parents had settled in a small market town in North Yorkshire – a lime-stone-built market-town called Malton. Malton is beautiful. It looks like something out of a Constable painting. My grandparents' own lives had involved public school (the UK name for private school, which is both confusing and contrary) from an early age. That kind of education and getting through a world war gave them a sense of distance from everything, probably out of self-preservation, more than anything. Dad said when he was a kid and he wanted a hug, he'd climb into the maid's bed.

They sent him to a boarding school at the age of eight. I can't imagine that. When my kids were eight years old, I missed them if I was home late, never mind away overnight. But that was the way of the upper middle classes in 1950s Yorkshire, and they weren't about to rock any boats. Dad was sent to a local school first, and then at the grand age of twelve, he was shipped off to Loretto, a fairly exclusive public school in Musselburgh, a few miles outside Edinburgh. Dad used to love telling stories about that time in his life, about having too much money, about escaping to London for the weekend, about tricks they played on teachers and the canings they got in return.

One particularly laid-back teacher was taking a group for prep (a sort of homework for when school *is* home) one night in a big hall. As the boys worked, the teacher walked up and down the middle of the hall, between the rows of desks. What he didn't know was that a group of pupils, well aware of his walking habit, had decided to use it to their advantage. As he reached the centre of the hall a set of bells rang behind him.

The teacher birled around. 'Who did that?'

No one spoke. The silence and the tension grew. Behind him, at the other end of the hall, a second set of bells rang out. He turned again, to catch the perpetrator. More bells sounded behind him. He turned again. More bells. 'Who is doing this?' he demanded.

Silence.

'If no one admits to it I'll cane the lot of you!'

In the end, he lined up a hall full of pupils, and began doing just that, but being so laid back, he didn't actually really hurt anyone, so some of the boys decided there was no harm in some extra caning. As he got to the end of the line, he was getting tired and thought he saw some familiar faces. More than once, he was heard asking, 'Haven't I caned you already?'

Another time, this teacher arrived in the hall to find his Messerschmidt bubble car on the stage.

Dad told these war stories with a sense of relish and a liberal helping of implied bravado. In reality, the brutality of boarding school life in the fifties and sixties had way more of an effect than he ever let on. He eventually escaped from Loretto and ran away to Kirkcowan and the Waulkmill, where my auntie

Molly (a fearsome character who was a headmistress, and who I always remember frequently feeding us biscuits and telling us wild stories when I was a kid) let him stay. She phoned my grandparents, who had no idea about any of his school worries, or what he was studying or wanted to do. Auntie Molly was horrified.

He eventually left Loretto and went to a technical college in Scarborough, much nearer home, sat his exams and got into Glasgow University to study aeronautical engineering. He wanted to fly, so he quickly joined the university air squadron. He got his pilot's licence before he got his driving licence. That had less to do with his skill as a pilot than his terrible knowledge of local roads.

Dad sat his first driving test in Stranraer, in The Shire. Stranraer was at that point a port town, with ferry links to Ireland, which have since moved a few miles up the coast. There wasn't a lot else there, apart from farming, and a sixteenth-century castle that sits in the middle of a square surrounded by some slap-dash mid-century architecture (I'm guessing there were kickbacks involved). There was no reason for Dad to have spent much time there. It was a town he didn't know well, so when the instructor said, 'Take the next left,' he did – straight into someone's driveway.

His dream was to qualify as an aeronautical engineer and join the Fleet Air Arm, the Royal Navy's air specialism, as a pilot. His other dream was to run The Knock, the family farm my great grandad Parker had bought all those years before. At some point, someone told Dad that the Fleet Air Arm was set to be disbanded. Around the same time, Grandad told him he could run The Knock, or study, but he couldn't do both.

Grandad had bought the farm at some point in the 1960s,

having a sentimental attachment to it from his own childhood. Later, in his early fifties, my grandad was going through a midlife speed-wobble that would eventually see him 'drying out' in a specialist rehab facility. One night, he was stopped by the police while driving. When they asked him if he knew he was on a one-way street, he told them that he had only been driving one way. This did not go down well. Unluckily for Grandad, the breathalyser had just been brought in and he had the dubious honour of being one of the first people to be charged with drink driving on the evidence it provided. He wound up with a driver and things slowly deteriorated from there until he was 'sent away' for a while.

He had bought the farm from his brother, and then evicted his other brother, who was actually farming there. Now he expected my dad to drop out of university and pick up where he'd left off. As demands go, that's a lot to place on the shoulders of your twenty-year-old-son. Dad did probably the only thing he thought he could: he dropped out of university and went to train on another farm so he could take over at The Knock. He would spend the rest of his life being called a drop-out for his trouble.

Mum, on the other hand, went to Glasgow University to study modern languages: German, French and Spanish. Her dream was to work for the diplomatic corps and travel the world. Glasgow in the 1970s must have seemed fairly exotic. She lived in the West End and went to places like The Ubiquitous Chip, a trendy haunt frequented by people like Billy Connolly. One night, she was sitting in a bar when a woman asked, 'are they teeth yer ain, hen?'[1] At one point in time, it used to be

1. Scots, meaning: 'Are those teeth your own, love?'

said that some people in Glasgow got dentures as a sixteenth birthday present, to avoid having to pay for dentists as adults. Whether that's an urban myth or not, Mum's teeth are very much her own. She's added a bit of Greek and some Russian to the French, German and Spanish over the years, and still loves learning about new places.

When she was still at school, the young farmer she was going out with at the time said he wanted to introduce her to a friend one day and took her to a rocky farm down by the shore in Monreith, around ten miles away from Wigtown. When they arrived, they saw him from a distance, in a field, standing behind a wall. It looked a lot like he was responding to a call of nature. Awkward.

The English guy in question was tall, with curly red hair and a very seventies moustache. I don't think she thought much of him the first time they met. She was probably discouraged by what she thought was an abrupt introduction, but, over the next few months, they met again, a few times.

Mum worked at Castlewigg, a hotel in the Machars, miles away from any town. Dad became a regular customer. She says she thought he was a bit annoying, with his dubious tache, unkempt hair, and the kind of dress sense that only someone trapped in the world of privilege and private education can truly master. When everyone else was wearing flared trousers and had long hair, Dad turned up in drainpipes, sporting the kind of hairdo that Sideshow Bob would be proud of.

Eventually Mum must have given in, and they got together.

# Chapter Two

I was born in Dumfries in October 1982, the fourth of my parents' five kids. Growing up, I didn't feel like I had a best friend at school. That's a strange thing to say, I suppose, but I counted myself as lucky. I had four of them at home on Barmeal: Robert, James, Kirsty and Susan.

Robert is my eldest brother. We all call him Bob. He's very creative and the nicest guy in the world, but so laid back he's permanently on the verge of tipping over. There's a family joke about him being indecisive. Our theory goes that if a car comes while he's crossing a road, he's likely to be run over while deciding which way to run. He bounces when he walks and has ideas about being an author. He's written three unpublished masterpieces and used to be a stand-up comedian, even though he's quite introverted. Bob doesn't know this, but I admire him hugely and wish I had half the qualities he does. He's an amazing father, and the life he has built for himself and for his family is impressive. (He's also my ghost writer, so he does know this, and you can take all this with a *big* pinch of salt.)

My next eldest brother, James, is three years older than me. He's like an armed forces cliché: 6'4" in height, fit and strong. When he was at school, they used to call him 'straight face', on account of his seriousness. He spent six years in the RAF. From a distance he looks pretty buttoned up and regimented but follow him around for long enough and you'll get a different picture. He's a sculptor. He has all the airs and graces to cut it in the art world and around his wealthy clients, but when I phone him up, he usually answers me with, 'What do you want, you little ...?' (I'll let you insert your own expletive here) He's one of the most reliable people you'll ever meet. He's like a father to me now and we're very close. When he was younger, he nearly became a professional golfer but took the military route instead. I think he's always felt like it's his responsibility to look after everyone and he acts like the eldest, even though he isn't. These days, you can usually find him building big installations and sculptures in glass, stone and metal. When he was training to join the RAF, he used to go running in the mornings. A local guy, Andy McKie, a man known for his well cultivated moustache, Russian style hat and sense of humour (and who may or may not have shot two ravens with the same arrow), saw him one morning and shouted, 'Run Forrest! Run!'

We've called James 'Gump' ever since.

My sister Kirsty is two years older than me and my closest sibling by a long way. We've always been trouble when we're together. Like James, she has a dark sense of humour. She works with my mum, in the family coffee shop. She's always polite and friendly and has been compared to a Barbie doll in the past but don't let any of that fool you. We all know the truth. She's a wrong 'un.

Kirsty and I were trouble when we were younger. We went on holiday when we were teenagers, and we refused to come home. My poor mum wound up paying for later flights in the end. We got very drunk on the last night. I think I was sixteen, so Kirsty would have been about eighteen. A group of local youths chased us down the street. I feel like I'm old enough to call them youths now, although that's maybe stretching it a bit. Back then, they were just a vague threat, but we had to run. We made it back to the apartment, but they hung around outside. They refused to go away. What we needed was a cunning plan. We raided the kitchen cupboards and cobbled together what we had. Eggs would have been perfect, but we didn't have any. We pelted them with spoons. They didn't come back.

I can't lie to Kirsty, which can be inconvenient. I just blurt out whatever's on my mind. But I always have, and I hope I always will. That's the thing about having a big sister. You've got someone two years ahead of you who can make things seem that bit better just by listening.

My little sister, Susan, is a year younger than me. We're close these days but in the past we were terrible for winding each other up. I don't really know why. Maybe because we are the two youngest and were always home together when the others were at school, but she's my little sister and I'll always love her.

Craig, my hoof-trimming apprentice, sidekick and sparring partner, is married to Susan now. If you haven't seen my videos, just picture Igor in any of the Frankenstein films, with a comb-over, an unhealthy love of fantasy TV shows and an Ayrshire accent. If you don't know what an Ayrshire accent is, think of Shrek and dumb it down a couple of levels. (Sorry, Ayrshire!) He knows I'm just kidding. Craig and Susan have six kids between them. They're all lucky to call them parents, and I'm lucky to have them in my life.

I've always been the fast talker in the family. I once cut Susan's hair so badly that my mum had to give her a crew cut afterwards. It was quite an achievement, considering we only had safety scissors. If it makes me sound any better, I did eventually turn the scissors on myself. On this occasion, my hair did not look 'awesome', and for the next six months Mum had to put up with people telling her what a lovely little boy my sister was.

Thanks to my styling skills, I was in for a serous row. Mum says that when she started shouting, she ran out of breath. At that point, I blurted out the words, 'Mummy, you're as beautiful as a pink flower.' That derailed Mum's train of thought long enough for me to abscond. I don't really remember it that well, but I can believe it. My mouth does get ahead of me sometimes.

We grew up on Barmeal Farm. My earliest memories are of farming: sitting on the back of my dad's quad bike, waiting. I think I must have been about five. I can still remember the sound of the engine, revving from a low-pitched growl to an angry snarl, the whine of the gears, the sizzle of puddles hitting hot metal, the smell of baking mud. When we reached a gate, I would jump off, then open and close it as Dad drove through. I was the best gate-opener – and closer – in the world. To me it was the most important job in the world, and getting it right was everything.

I would face backwards, hanging on as tight to the quad bike as I could. I would curl my toes up in the end of my wellies, so they didn't fall off, and as my feet dangled in the wind I had to remember to keep to one side, to avoid the heat from the exhaust. There were no niceties. There was no talking. That wasn't a bad thing. It's just that work was work.

We would drive, slowly, through herds of cows with young calves. This was our universe. It wasn't a romantic thing, and I don't think I was particularly aware that we owned any of it. It's just that everything around us was agriculture. It's a happy, cosy thought, looking back. I never believed it was a perfect existence, but it was perfect for me in many ways, and I always knew I was going to be a farmer.

Until I wasn't.

Barmeal *was* my true home, though. For years, after we left, I dreamed of buying it back. I suppose you'd say we had a homestead lifestyle there. Locations don't get more idyllic than ours was. The approach was down a bumpy track that cut through a lush, green world – a patchwork quilt of a landscape, arranged between dry stone dykes. You'd glide through trees, round the mill pond, and emerge into a time capsule.

The house was massive, or it certainly seemed that way then. It was built sometime in the eighteenth century and sprouted some additions down the years. It sat comfortably in its own mini forest, a white sentinel in its territory. There had been a tennis court at the back, in a grander time, and my mum and dad unearthed what was left of it, lifting stones and cutting back weeds over the course of a summer, until they had a lawn the size of a football pitch.

It was the place we played football, badly. The place my dad used to hit golf balls before sending Kim, our cocker spaniel, to fetch them. She was good at that. She wasn't quite so good at dropping them when she came back. She was far too keen on parading around, her dalmatian-spotted body arched to one side, tongue hanging out at a jaunty angle, tail going like she was trying to take off. You had to shout 'dead!' to get her to give anything up. She was a gun dog and treated the balls as proudly as a duck or a rabbit she'd caught.

My most vivid memories of Barmeal Farm are of the bonfire nights we used to have. In the UK, the fifth of November is the anniversary of the date Guy Fawkes' 1605 Gunpowder Plot was foiled. It was a plot to kill the Protestant king in the Houses of

Parliament and reestablish Catholic rule in England. There's no religious significance for most people, now. I think these days it's more about bringing in the winter after Hallowe'en, with a big fire, plenty of sugary treats and explosions in every colour. I remember the bonfires, the effigies of the 'Guy' on the top, the toffee apples, the rockets in tins. There were spinning Catherine wheels my dad nailed to wooden stobs (or fence posts, if you're not from Scotland). Most of all, I remember creeping back there the next day, desperate to see the scorched remains and the brightly coloured paper of the spent rockets. We shouldn't have been there. The fire would still be smouldering, and we were always told there was the chance of something going off.

On UK television in the 1980s, they still showed weird and usually terrifying 1970s safety films, related to everything that could kill you, during the ad breaks. Most of the death traps featured were things we grew up with, or near to. We learned that fireworks almost certainly meant injuries, that tractors were the work of the devil, and you should never fly a kite near an electricity pylon – just in case you were considering it. Whether we were safe or not, curiosity was a constant factor in our miniature world.

Most of all, I remember the companionship I grew up with, with my four siblings. It meant there was always someone to play with. We were like comrades in arms. Literally. Most of our games involved some form of physical conflict. There was the always-popular game of 'war' which did exactly what it said on the tin. The particular type of war depended on whoever devised it at the time, or, as we used to say, whose game it was. The unifying theme was the long list of casualties. Like the time we had to pause a battle when we found a rusty old oil drum and Kirsty asked if we would roll her down a hill in it. The sound of her screams, fading in and out as the barrel rotated, is unforgettable – that and the amount of begging we had to do to get her not to tell Mum.

There were farming games, too. One of my earliest memories is of playing in the front garden at Barmeal, in a self-contained area where we kept lambs in the spring. Pet lambs were a recurring thing growing up. The ones that were lost or got separated from their mothers, for whatever reason, got the five-star treatment from us Parker kids. Twice a day, we fed them warm formula milk from old bottles with rubber stoppers and red teats on the end. I can remember the warmth of the bottles in my hand and the sweet smell of the milk. The worn-down labels on the bottles let you know they'd started out full of Gordon's Gin, Johnny Walker or Famous Grouse whisky. Looking back now, it doesn't surprise me there were so many of those around.

We had various lambs, named with varying levels of imagination through the years: Larry Lamb, Gutsy Gertie, and one named after someone at school who always thought he knew best. The lamb that sticks out most in my memory was called Tiny. He was anything but tiny. He loved his milk, and he leveraged his growing bulk to maximum effect to get to the front of the queue. I can remember standing in the small garden at the front of the house, with Kirsty and all these lambs, and thinking 'this is our farm', as if it were to scale.

At the end of the house there were trees in all shapes and sizes: tall firs, ancient oaks, and a greengage tree with the sourest fruit in the world. Mum once tried to dig into the earth round that tree, just to tame some of the wildness and plant a flower bed. She accidentally unearthed a set of stone steps, spiralling down to the lawn. There was a sense of history all around. Some of the trees had fallen over, and their root systems, unearthed, hung in mid-air, leaving ready-made hideouts and fox holes for children like us, hell bent on combat.

My brother Bob made himself a tree house in one of them. It wasn't the most advanced thing in the world. It mainly consisted of a ramp and some old baler-twine running between the branches, as (pretty useless) guard rails. I don't think I'm over-protective, but I'm not sure I'd let my kids up there.

I remember being on my scooter. I must've been about three years old. I approached the ramp leading up to the tree house. The red wheels moved back and forth, along loose, rocky earth, and I prepared to make my run. The ramp ran from above a drop; a small cliff, formed by one of those upended trees. From there, it ran over a gulley, straight up into the branches of the tree. It couldn't have been more than a two-foot drop, but when you're three years old and you're on a baby-blue plastic scooter, modelled in the shape of a rabbit, and the bunny's ears are the handlebars, everything looks bigger.

I do have a memory of being warned not to do it. That had no effect. In one family member's version of the story, Bob whipped the ramp out from under me and watched me fall to the ground, probably cackling as he did it. In Bob's version, I just missed the ramp. Neither of us really know what happened next. Bob says all he can remember is telling me not to do it and then me coming back from hospital with bandages. He has a suspiciously blank bit in the middle ...

What *I* really remember, and what probably means the most to me, is the way we've all talked about it over the years. Family versions of events get darker and more convoluted with every telling. This particular tale makes one of us out to be a bigger sadist every time – and it's not me! That's how it works with us. We've learned to behave this way over time. There's no situation that can't be drastically improved by taking the absolute piss out of each other, and, when we're together, nothing's off limits. It's a conversation with the brakes off, a verbal game of war, and it's rare that anyone wins. We've evolved to be that way, partly because we've wanted to, and partly because we've had to.

The Kiltie brothers, Andy and Norman, were a permanent fixture at the farm. They worked for my dad for years; gruff men with moustaches and crash-helmet haircuts who always seemed to be drinking red cola. They were hard workers with endless patience and senses of humour. They were my heroes. I still run into them now and again and we always stop and chat. Andy usually opens with the line, 'Me help. Me help,' because that's what he used to get from me every time he saw me when I was a kid. The Shire is a small place, and I still work with their nephews, in different places across the region, most weeks.

The sheep pens were at the front of the house, along with the big, red, tubular steel gates we used to swing on, the dipper, and a whole load more memories. In front of that was a vegetable garden. I remember the orchard and picking red apples down in there. It seemed like we were cultivating something year-round. My mum grew vegetables: carrots, beetroot, dark red potatoes. There was a hen house at the bottom and a load of what was probably just wasted ground. As kids, we'd try to collect eggs without being pecked and dig up vegetables to make soup when we had the time.

The scariest place I knew was the mill race. The farm had an old threshing mill. They'd taken the water wheel away years earlier, when the mill fell out of use. Dad drained the mill pond when he moved in, deciding that young kids and water were a bad combination, but you could still hear a stream of water draining through the pipe that ran from there down to the race. What remained was a twelve-foot-deep, stone-sided pit. It might as well have been bottomless. It seemed to lure me in. I was terrified of it and of the sound of the running water as I got nearer.

In what would prove to be a pattern of unfortunate decision-making, my dad fell in there one night, after a drunken misadventure. He spent hours trying to climb back out.

He had a lucky escape that time.

# Chapter Three

Dad was an interesting character. He would proudly tell people he was five feet eleven and three quarters tall. It's one of the more unusual boasts I've heard, and being from a farming community, I've heard some fairly unorthodox things put out there as claims to fame. The culture here can be strange if you're not used to it.

When I started my business, I bought a van from my brother, James, for £700. I still maintain he got a good deal. It said 'James Parker Fencing' on the side, so he had free advertising for a start. He once parked it in a local supermarket carpark, and was prowling around inside, probably looking for steak, knowing him, when a voice came over the loudspeaker system. 'Would the owner of the James Parker Fencing van please come to customer services?' 'That'll be me then,' Gump said to himself. I love it when he gets caught out in situations like that. I can't even remember what vehicular infringement had prompted the naming and shaming, but it couldn't have happened to a nicer guy.

When I owned that van, the alternator belt went one night on my way home. After what I like to think of as highly creative work with some cable ties (there were sixteen or seventeen of them), the belt was fixed, or fixed enough, I hoped, to get me home. It stayed like that for the next three months, until I broke down on the Dumfries bypass and had to be rescued by my friend, Robert Geddes. The best way I can describe Geddes is that he's a bit like a Scottish version of Chuck 'The Sherminator' Sherman, from the *American Pie* films. I could tell you a hundred stories about him, at least ninety of which aren't fit for public consumption.

I eventually bought a pick-up truck, as you do when you have a good excuse, like eventually needing to pull a cattle-crush around. I was proud of my new purchase. It was a serious piece of kit. It was a Mitsubishi L200 Animal, for any fellow pick-up anoraks out there. I was so proud of it. I was desperate to add my own branding. It needed to be something that said: 'hoof trimming', something that projected a strong image, so I had a rampaging bull emblazoned across the bonnet. Don't tell me you wouldn't do the same if you could justify it. The bull was what I suppose you might call *sanitised* in its appearance. For months afterwards, whenever I turned up at a new farm, I was met with the same statement: 'That bull's got no balls'. In many ways, that comment shows the culture round here, where brutal honesty is the preferred means of communication.

I don't think my dad ever really grasped that mentality. He used to complain that all most people wanted to talk about were the three Cs: cattle, cars and casual gossip. I'm not sure if I would agree with that these days. Some of my friends have more varied interests than you might imagine. That's in a post-internet age though. Life here would have been more boxed off in the seventies and eighties, with only three TV channels as a window on the world. I've always liked cattle and cars, but I can see why you might get a bit cheesed off with casual gossip. I've been the victim of it a few times now and it doesn't bother me, but I can see how it affects people around me.

I think the perceptions of others profoundly affected Dad. Farming was a big wake up call for him. He knew farmers, back home in Malton, but they were arable farmers, and that's a very different game to livestock farming. There's a lot more money in it, for a start.

Dad had only ever spent time on family holidays in Wigtownshire, before he started farming here. The family had a holiday house – The Neuk – in Monreith, the village that borders The Knock. It was an old, terraced cottage, with maybe three rooms originally. As with most houses round here, people had added to it over the years. The roof at the back was made of tin and made a real racket whenever it rained, which, on the west coast of Scotland, is a lot. His extended family spent time in the area regularly, usually sailing and enjoying the beach.

That sounds like a pretty privileged existence. From that perspective the farm must have had a novelty value for him – something that would have quickly disappeared when he got there and had to grasp the reality of farming on a rain-lashed, rocky outcrop, far from friends and the closest thing he'd ever known to home. For me, The Knock was the family farm, other than Barmeal. It was a big part of my identity. For my dad it was a romantic idea. He felt enormous pressure to turn theory into practice.

My great grandparents had bought the farm as a holiday place, and somewhere to retire to. For them, it never needed to be worked as a going concern. That was the fundamental problem. When they bought it, they'd had a choice between The Knock and The Isle Farm, one of the best working farms in the area. So, why choose The Knock? Simple. It had the best view. My great grandmother used to say you could see seven kingdoms from the old farmhouse: Scotland, England, Ireland,

Wales, the Isle of Man, the kingdom of the sea and the kingdom of Heaven. You can take the girl out of Kirkcowan ... etc etc.

I think Wales might be a bit of stretch for the naked eye, but the rest are there in force on a clear day.

The farm had been owned by the Maxwell family, known principally for the naturalist and author, Gavin Maxwell, who wrote *Ring of Bright Water.* There's an otter memorial to him on the headland next to Monreith beach, near the place he exercised his own pet otter. The Maxwell estate encompassed a large part of the surrounding area for centuries.

Most Scottish farmhouses are built in front of the farm buildings. It means you have to pass them if you're on your way to do some sheep rustling. The Knock is the other way round. You pass all the farm buildings before you come to the farmhouse itself. Why was our farm back to front? In a word, smuggling. The whole of this coastline was rife with it for a long time. The house was built in the strangest way you've ever seen, half on top of a rock, with a clear view to the sea on three sides. It doesn't look like any of the other farmhouses in the area either, with its low roofline, hunkered down against the winds that batter it from all sides. Under the stairs there was a brandy hole – a decent sized rectangular hole in the ground used for storing whatever contraband was in demand at any given time: brandy, port, tobacco – anything the government wanted to tax heavily, there was a market for. Local legend has it that there is a tunnel under the house, leading through the fields and down to the beach. It's a pretty far-fetched notion, or it would be, if I hadn't seen a wooden archway disappearing under the house and into the hillside.

The farmhouse itself is derelict, now. About as derelict as it's possible to be. It's more or less a pile of stones, and we've seen it gradually degenerate over the years. You can still see the arch, as the wood, plaster and slate all rot and sink into the ground, but it's unreachable. It was completely abandoned in 1957.

John Glen Parker, my great grandfather, died in 1942, without leaving a will. That meant that everything went into trust with the family's bank. The family then found themselves in the strange situation that the last of them to die would inherit everything. They set about trying to break the trust to avoid that, but it took time. Meanwhile, the bank refused to let them spend any money. The house fell apart as a consequence, and my dad later found himself running this back-to-front farm with no farmhouse, living in his parents' holiday cottage and being in the way whenever anyone was there on holiday, which was a lot of the time. When he married my mum and they started a family, he had no choice but to buy a bigger farm, with a bigger house: Barmeal. That meant taking on a serious debt and a lot more responsibility, which would ultimately prove to be my father's undoing.

Despite its considerable size and all that financial commitment, Dad was in his farming element at Barmeal, but it was him who made the decision to sell it; a decision made with the heart. Some people say there's no room for sentiment in business and I can understand that. Maybe I'm the exception that proves the rule. I'd like to think that channelling my love for what I do into my business has generally made a positive impact on the way I run things, but I've seen so many other people run into problems.

It's probably obvious from the boarding school choices and the holiday-home ownership that my dad's parents were upper-middle class. His father was a GP who came from money but hadn't inherited any of his own. When Grandad's brothers,

Bobby and Billy, and his sister Alexandrina (known as Lexie) were all at medical school in Edinburgh, they had staff to look after them. That seems ostentatious, thinking about it now.

Grandad didn't have any of that privilege when he eventually made it up there. Times had changed by then and he lodged with a woman on a floor of a sprawling Victorian villa on Mayfield Road in Edinburgh. He claimed she 'got pregnant by a sailor and had to sell up'. He had a way of telling a story, my grandad. He was a small, bald man with a bit of a belly who loved a drink. He looked a lot like Mr Toad from *Wind in the Willows*. Drove like him too. Maybe that's where I get it from. His stories would start out innocently enough but always ended up with someone dying in an unusual way – like the biker that passed him in a traffic jam who struck another car and consequently disembowelled himself on his own handlebars. Or someone or something getting 'blown to bits, in the war, of course', or someone getting pregnant. There were a few awkward silences but not many dull moments with him.

Dad was always under pressure to succeed, to make his own way. Grandad had done that himself through lack of choice. His father had died before he'd finished medical school, so Grandad had a good education that was nearly complete, and he struggled on despite his lack of inheritance. At one point, he came home for his brother's wedding on an old motorbike. He didn't have enough money to buy a present, so he had to sell the motorbike. Then he had to borrow a bicycle and cycle the hundred and twenty odd miles back to Edinburgh, along old roads that cut through the heart of the Galloway hills. These are roads I know well, now. They're some of my favourite to travel – running through some of the most scenic landscapes I've ever seen and on towards my favourite bit of tarmac, The Dalveen Pass. It's a twisting, challenging stretch of road that clings to the slopes on one side of an impressive valley through the Lowther Hills, connecting the north of Dumfries and Galloway to Lanarkshire.

Whatever struggles Grandad experienced were very much the first world problems of the day, but they left a bitterness. By the time he felt he'd made it, he was in his late forties and seems to have become jealous of his tall, good-looking son, who would and should have had every opportunity, but for his own father's resentment. In the end, Dad sold Barmeal after falling out with Grandad.

Dad's drinking was at least partly to blame. My grandad had a habit of making bitter comments. Nothing was ever quite good enough. As well as being a GP, he was the senior partner in the family farming business, which by that time included Dad, and Barmeal. It was a sprawling three hundred and sixty acre stretch of good land that Dad had drained and cleared over time. He'd blasted and dug out ditches to reclaim as much land as possible. All he did was work in those days. He was obsessed with cattle breeding and the effort he put in paid off. Market days were his main preoccupation. They were like a drug to him. The cattle market was in Newton Stewart – a small town, nestled in the Galloway hills, twenty miles away, and the place I would eventually go to high school.

For livestock farmers, market days are the high point of the year. I can still smell the sawdust. I can hear the auctioneer's machine gun chatter, like a foreign language to me, punctuated by the bang of his gavel. I can see the farmers, dressed in their Sunday best; my dad had a pair of brown Chelsea boots he always referred to as 'market boots'. I think farming people in The Shire generally do. The Crown Hotel, directly over the road from the market, was a secondary hub, heaving with agricultural types like us during lunchtimes. They would cover the hallways in plastic to protect the carpets from the muck dragged across the street on boots. The whole place had a utilitarian feel to it on those days. There was a buzz, with the success or failure of people's financial years hinging on what happened there. Imagine your worth being decided in a room full of strangers on the bang of a wooden hammer? Immense pressure, but the potential of a big payday.

The price of the livestock was listed by the pound, and that was always my dad's primary focus, the thing he really cared about. His whole year was geared towards this one goal – getting the highest price per pound of beef, or, as he called it, topping the market. He was a well-regarded cattle breeder and that meant he often did get the best price.

On those days, he would phone home with the news, eager to impress Grandad, only to be dismissed with a telling off for being boastful. I can't imagine what that must have been like. Dad was many things, but he was always interested in what his kids did, what they thought and what their ambitions, hopes and dreams were. To be dismissed, firstly as a drop-out and a failure, and then as a braggart for succeeding in the family business, must have been a serious kick in the nuts.

In order to make a go of the business and to have a house for his growing family, a house The Knock could not provide, Dad took on Barmeal. He paid £150,000 in 1979, equivalent to around £850,000 in today's money. That's a massive amount of debt to take on when interest rates are low, but they'd grown throughout the 1970s, and in November 1979 they hit 17%. With that kind of pressure, the regular digs and the feeling Dad often had that he didn't fit in, things were always going to boil over between them.

One night in 1988 when they'd both had too much to drink. Grandad made one too many stupid digs and Dad took it personally. He probably went away and brooded over whatever had been said. Then, he ended up having to calve a cow that went into labour and I'm guessing – angry at his father's high-handed attitude – he'd turned up at the door of The Neuk, in the wee small hours. He insisted that Grandad help him calve the cow. Maybe it was anger that motivated him in the beginning or maybe he was just drunk and enthusiastic and angry that Grandad wouldn't go and do this thing with him – he was a doctor after all. Whatever happened, there was some kind of confrontation and that was the end of any real relationship they had.

Grandad turned up at Barmeal the following day and told Dad he had to buy him out of the business. Without the funds, or any means of raising the funds, he was in a dire situation. If this sounds to you like the kind of father–son spat people have and then resolve I would usually agree, but that's not the way it worked with those two. No one backed down. The only compromise reached was that my grandmother took on some part of Grandad's share in his place, and there was an agreement that meant Dad could buy her out for a nominal sum if she died. It was an agreement that would eventually prove to work both ways.

Short of cash and looking for a way to buy his father out, my dad did the only thing he could and sold some of his precious land at Barmeal. It must have hurt. The farming business meant everything to him. He'd worked so hard, in such difficult times, to build it, and now he had to carve it up and give pieces away.

He had one farm, The Knock, a rocky inhospitable place, with a crumbling, derelict farmhouse and a tiny worker's cottage, and Barmeal, with its lush, green pastures and a house anyone would be proud to call home. Viewed from the outside, it should have been an easy decision, but not when you add sentimentality into the mix. The Knock had been in the family for generations. My grandad had bought the place for his own, sentimental reasons. He'd had the old farmhouse redesigned and intended to retire there, then pulled out, blaming Dad for 'not making it pleasant enough'. Dad could sell Barmeal, with its grand house and its easily farmable land, at top dollar, or he could sell the family farm, the place he'd dreamed of farming since childhood; his grandfather's dream; his father's dream. He chose the first option. He knew if he didn't, he'd ruin his relationship with his father forever.

It must have been an impossible decision and I can't say which way I would have gone.

The plan seemed a solid one, at first. He'd sell the bits of Barmeal he needed to, keep some of the better fields, move the family to the worker's cottage at The Knock and build an extension. Dad was keen, energised; he must have felt like he was striking out on his own again. I didn't have much experience of The Knock up till that point. It was a farm about two miles down the road, something we owned that – as kids – we occasionally went to when we were moving cows or sheep, but it had its own beach and that was new. It's a beautiful, rugged, unforgiving place. I can see why every generation of the men in my family have fallen in love with it over the past century. You can walk out onto a headland, scramble over an old moat and stand in the foundations of a prehistoric fort, overlooking the endless blue grey of the Irish Sea, towards the Isle of Man and the Mountains of Mourne in Northern Ireland. You can look down onto secluded beaches, places we had barbecues and learned how to swim. You can pull sea bass and pollock from the jagged black rocks that stick out into the sea. The sound of that sea hitting those rocks is a distinct part of my childhood; something that evokes memories of laughter and probably me pushing the boundaries of my parents' comfort zones.

It might seem illogical to be in a place of such beauty and yet be in any way unhappy. In Dad's mind, before he took it on, he was honest enough to say he had a 'romantic view' of farming there. But the wind is harsh, the winters are long, and there's not much in the way of company.

I have no real memory of moving to The Knock. Once the decision was made, we were sent down to Yorkshire to my gran's house to let the adults get on with it. I don't think any of us kids viewed the move as positive or negative, at first. I just remember the gradual realisation that we had swapped a fantastic life for a dismal one, living on top of each other in a tired cottage that had been badly renovated in the 1970s.

At Barmeal, there were big parties, full of grown-ups and laughter. At least, that's how I remember it, through fond, childish eyes. I remember one fancy-dress party when I was very small where Mum and Dad played host to a Saudi guy called Salem. One of Dad's friends worked for him. He was part of an oil dynasty and regularly spent time in the UK. I think my dad's friend might have been his UK fixer. He had cars and homes here. At one point his chauffeur ran off with his Rolls Royce. He even stole the alloy wheels from his other car, a Ford Granada, and left it up on blocks. Salem calmly told his fixer to put new wheels on the car and keep it.

He asked if he could go shooting in Scotland and Dad's friend brought him to our house. He was an unusual addition to daily life, this guy with the strange accent, the dark glasses and the moustache. There seem to have been a lot of people with moustaches around then. Mum made pork pies, which were very obviously not halal, and he kept eating them. When she tried to tell him what they were, he just wagged his finger and said, 'Beef pies'.

When my parents hosted this fancy-dress party, the only evidence we saw were the costumes – a Roman centurion helmet here, a bunny girl outfit there and an emu costume in the corner. Salem left behind a bracelet for my mum as a thank you. It was made in three colours of gold.

Now that I recall it, what kind of party was that really?

In 2001, shortly after the planes flew into the World Trade Centre, newspapers ran stories about Osama Bin Laden, telling the world who he was and where he came from. In one of the pictures, he was seen with his older brother, in London. 'That's Salem!' Mum shouted, when she read the story. He had been the head of the Bin Laden family but was killed in 1988 while piloting a light aircraft, a few years after his trip to The Shire.

After the move there were no more parties, and gradually, no more visits. Unbeknown to us at the time, our return from Yorkshire to our new life at The Knock marked a boundary line between 'before' and 'after'.

Life got a lot stranger, after.

## Chapter Four

There's an image that lives in the back my head. One I'll probably always have, like scar tissue – it serves a purpose but it's messy.

There's a tabletop, covered in papers, business plans, ideas – like hopes and dreams, drawn up, quantified, then cast aside, as each plays out in the dreamer's head and others emerge to bury them. Used mugs and plates heighten the sense of chaos, accessorised with the obligatory, overflowing ashtray. It's a mess infused with frustration and hopelessness in a room that reeks of cheap whisky and discontent. If the road to hell is paved with good intentions, these are the blueprints.

This isn't something I conjured up in my mind's eye. This is where my dad lived. It's *how* he lived. I wonder if he ever realised he'd gone too far. Maybe after the affair, maybe after it ended his marriage, maybe during the time he spent 'inside', or maybe when he made his final, inescapable fuck up. Maybe, as he lived out the falling dream a lot of us have, reality finally bit. The inertia and the drink cost him his best years, and eventually, everything good in his life. Maybe it was a relief for him to know the gig was finally up, to realise that all those unanswered questions about what the future might hold had been resolved in one final, unstoppable move.

But I'm jumping ahead of myself here.

Dad was an intelligent guy. Maybe too intelligent. You don't study aeronautical engineering if you're just any old fool. Money can't help you fake that. But sometimes it was as if he were overpowered, like he had too much juice in that mind. It was like putting four hundred brake horsepower through the front wheels of a mini and watching them spin. His brain was impractical. He was well known for breeding good cattle, but he was living in a hellhole, trying to maintain his reputation on a rocky, boggy, gorse-bush-ridden wasteland.

Selling Barmeal had been a necessity.

As the saying goes: 'You can't eat the view'. The Knock was a nice idea – the whole hobby farm fantasy – if only it were just a hobby farm, and not an endeavour your livelihood, family and future depended on. In retrospect, Dad probably suffered from the same rapid cycling bipolar disorder as me, but he was never diagnosed. He had a hell of a temper. His mood could turn on a sixpence. One minute he was happy and joking, as though he hadn't a worry in the world; the next he'd be screaming, intimidating everyone around him – including the adults. He was a big guy, with red hair, a loud voice and a sharp tongue at times. If you annoyed him, he'd quickly put you in your place and he didn't care too much if he made you cry in the process. I've heard relatives from down south say he was too sensitive and maybe that's true, but he seemed to have difficulty in understanding anyone else's point of view. He also retained a pathological need to please his father, despite everything that had gone on.

After my father died, my grandfather admitted that he suspected he'd been bipolar. Who knows if it could have made any difference, but it would have been nice if he'd said something sooner and recognised it as an issue. It might have been more meaningful, coming from a GP. Maybe he felt it would be more harmful to pin the stigma of diagnosis on his son in times when mental illness was treated much more harshly. Maybe he was trying to hide things. Or Dad was. I suppose we'll never know. Whatever his reasons, he knew something wasn't right, but refused to do anything about it.

Grandad's theory was that it all started after an accident.

When he was younger, Dad got himself into trouble a lot. He did short-sighted things. He had an impulsive and sometimes compulsive side. His alcohol-assisted plunge into the mill race wasn't his earliest or only misadventure. He once blew himself up, trying to get a bonfire going with some petrol. That earned him singed eyebrows and a few days in bed. It's a stunt I would replicate later, and you can see the results in some of my videos.

Another time he went out on a pedalo boat, on holiday in Spain, with his sister, my auntie Lindsay. He pushed her into the water, and she started screaming, telling him she'd been stung by a jellyfish. He didn't believe her at first, but by the time he let her back on the boat, her back was a red, raw mess and she was in excruciating pain. He casually told us about it one day, saying it had earned him a beating with a golf club. So, he wasn't without his own trauma, but the impulsiveness of his reckless streak, combined with the urge to dedicate himself to certain things – flying, for example – suggests he may well have been bipolar.

I used to be like that when I was younger. I excelled in some areas and screwed it all up in others.

Dad had a fairly sceptical approach to health and safety, and danger in general, as an adult. On one occasion, he was cornered by an angry bull and had to make his escape by climbing over its back. Another time, he was kicked by a cow and decided to escape by vaulting over a five-foot steel gate. What he didn't know was that the kick had damaged ligaments around his knee. Things got a lot worse when he landed on it. That particular incident earned him a stint in a full leg plaster, unable to move and do much but drink vodka and pontificate.

The accident that probably had the greatest impact on him – other than the one that ended his life – happened in the early 1980s at Barmeal when I was really little.

Silage time is a big event in Galloway, with people working crazy hours in an effort to stay ahead of the weather. Silage is grass, cut and stored away in the summer, so the cows have something nutritious to eat in the winter. On those rare, dry days, the grass is cut and chopped up, then placed in a vast pit in the ground, shrouded in black plastic and weighed down with old tyres to ferment. Cows love it. I've seen angry video posts by animal rights activists who think that cows being fed silage are being mistreated, but people don't always understand what they're seeing. Just because it's served into a feed trough from a machine doesn't mean it's produced by Universal Carcinogenic Foods, Ltd.

My dad was cutting the grass in more of a hurry than normal (or maybe that should be 'mower' of a hurry. Sorry, couldn't resist!). He had attached the mower to the back of the Fiat 350 Special, a small, orange, late-1970s era tractor, with a square cab, a spluttering engine, and side-mounted headlights that gave it a frog-like face. The Kiltie brothers who worked with my dad christened him 'Bertie'. Bertie was missing bits. Back then, if something happened to a door or a window, it was just added to the pile of rotting scrap metal every farm had. Something must have gone wrong and needed fixed. Dad fixed whatever was wrong with the mower, but he was in a hurry. For the sake of a few, precious saved seconds, he didn't replace the safety cover.

He continued up and down the field, desperate to get the grass cut, defiant in the face of the rain gods. On his last pass, one of the whirring blades struck a stone that was just the right (or wrong, given the circumstances) size, launched it into the air with enough centrifugal force that it flew past the place the safety cover should have been, through the gap where the rear window should have been and into the space where part of Dad's left cornea was. I can't imagine the pain he must have been in. Mum was away shopping but luckily my grandparents were around, on holiday, so Grandad drove him thirty miles to Stranraer, on twisting roads, as he held his head back trying to stem the blood flow. He was lucky not to lose the eye, but he never saw through it properly again. If you looked closely, you could see that he was missing some of the iris on the right-hand side of his left eye. One of his pupils became an oval that merged with the white of the eye.

Eye injuries are linked to increased instances of depression, and it's easy to see why. We're visual creatures. Imagine coming to terms with the fact you're now living half your life in the dark? Some people adapt quickly to sight loss, but it sent my father into a slump that triggered ups and downs from there on in. It probably didn't help that when he returned home, my grandad informed him that he'd bought a Subaru pick-up on the farm's account. He told him it was ridiculous that they only had one vehicle. I'm not sure who would have driven Dad in the second vehicle if Mum wasn't around anyway.

It was probably a few years into living at The Knock that I had a slump of my own and started seeing a child psychologist.

I must have been about twelve when it started, and Mum or Dad then took me once a month for about three years. The reason? From an early age, I often found myself in tears. It sounds strange but I didn't want to get older. I didn't want to be an adult. I couldn't handle the idea of all that entailed. I didn't understand the root of it. I just had a feeling of dread, lurking in the background, as if something bad was going to happen, as if someone was watching me. It's like walking home from the pub, slightly the worse for wear, then paranoia kicks in and you feel like someone's watching you, so you end up jogging the rest of the way home. Or maybe that's just me!

I suffered from vivid dreams that seemed so real that when I woke up, I struggled to distinguish between them and reality. The dreams could impact my memory and I'd be left with intrusive thoughts that I couldn't ignore, and false memories that felt real, even when I was fully awake. It's an unsettling thing, like your mind's rebelling against you from the inside. I've always been vigilant as a result, looking out for it in my adult self and – as it's potentially hereditary – in my kids.

Not too long ago, my son Campbell got upset. Without warning, tears streamed down his cheeks. We were confused. His brother wasn't near enough to have been the culprit, and he hadn't fallen over or anything.

'What's wrong?' Ashley asked.

'I don't want to be an adult, Mum.'

I nearly spat my breakfast across the room. I hope it was just a coincidence, as I dread passing this on to my kids.

The intrusive thoughts were disturbing for me as a child. I've never told anyone about this until recently. For years, from the age of about eight or nine onwards, I carried it with me like a sickening secret, every day. It came with the very real weight of guilt, as if I'd actually done something. My worst thoughts were that I had actually killed someone and hidden the body. I used to dream I'd done this and that everyone would find out. It seems bizarre, thinking about it now. It might even seem funny to people reading this, but looking back, I just feel sad. Sick, even. It's a bit like when you leave the house and have the nagging feeling you've forgotten something, but worse. It's a deep-rooted intuition that you've somehow done this terrible thing. You're petrified everyone will find out. When I think about my childhood now, that was a deeply traumatic experience for a young person to deal with.

From the safe distance of my early forties, I'm now confident that I didn't kill and/or bury anyone, but I wish I could uncover the deeper meaning of these intrusive thoughts, if there is one. I could be wrong about this, but it might be possible to tie this to specific events or people from my childhood. I sometimes think regressive hypnotherapy might help me find answers, but, for the most part, I find myself more focused on the future these days than reawakening nightmares. It was all such a long time ago, after all, and the person I most likely inherited this from is gone.

I can't remember the name of the psychologist I saw as a kid. What I do remember is that we met once a week, and we sat on cold, plastic chairs in a local primary school. The chairs were so small. It was a 1960s building, with pine and glass panelled doors, reinforced with chicken wire. The whole place reeked of floor polish and bleach. It could have been worse. It could have been *my* primary school. That would have been too much to handle. Tongues would have seriously wagged.

Whatever his name actually was, I called him Dr Purple Eyes. He wore lenses that flitted between purple and yellow with the movement of light. Thinking about it now, that was pretty weird for a child psychologist. I've no real memory of what we talked about, but it became this massive thing. It sounds silly but it was probably the first time I was the centre of attention. This was *my* thing; some time I could call my own, just me and Mum or Dad. I do remember that I used to do random stuff and talk shit to him. In the end, I stopped going because Dad kept redirecting the conversation towards himself. Eventually, he told Mum that he'd found a therapist. It was only later she realised that he was using my sessions with the psychologist for himself.

I'm not convinced therapy actually did me any good, in those days. In some ways, the sessions may have made things worse. They made me stand out in my immediate family for 'seeing a therapist'. If my school friends asked, I'd just say 'I'm seeing Dr Purple Eyes', and then make up the reason why. I will always encourage people to give therapy a shot if they think it will help, but in the end, it didn't really work for me for all sorts of reasons.

When I think back to that period, it's with a skewed perspective. I guess the passage of time makes you adjust the story you tell yourself, and memory can be a fickle thing. For years I wondered why my parents sent me to the psychologist and what I was supposed to do there. I initially thought I was there because I had been missing school. Mum used to have to drag me out of the house, sometimes kicking and screaming all the way to the car. But when I asked her about it, in the course of writing this book, she told me that when I was twelve or thirteen years old, I wouldn't leave her side. I wouldn't even leave her alone with my dad, and I would sleep in her bed.

Around this time, and probably not coincidentally, there was an incident that I thankfully don't remember anything about. I must have blanked it out, as some kind of survival mechanism, but it no doubt directly relates to the sense of unease I had as a child, and my desire to be near to my mother.

Mum has since told me about a thing that happened when we were living at The Knock. I've mentioned that my dad had a hell of a temper, and on this occasion, he was screaming at her. What about, I'm not sure, but there they were, standing in the small office at the front of the house, Dad going in for battle. Dad had a habit of getting up really close to whoever he was shouting at, right in their face. Thinking about it now still makes me half terrified, half sad.

Mum's office was the nerve centre of her business. I remember a huge map on the wall, with little pins that showed where all the farms were. I still go to a lot of those farms, now. There were metal shelves, piled high with files and folders. This was in the 1990s, and she was running the business she had built up out of half a converted garage. These days, it could be stored on the cloud, but then, everything was on paper – great screeds of the stuff that rolled out of a printer in one long, green and white roll. It all had to be stored somewhere.

For context, Mum had left Dad by this point and moved out of The Knock. We all had, apart from James, who, because he was James, felt he had to stay behind and look after Dad and the farm. He was sixteen years old at the time. Dad was so angry about whatever Mum had supposedly done this time. It was always a perceived slight or misdemeanour. Maybe she looked at him the wrong way or disagreed with him, or maybe she just asked a question. He was in full flow. He'd really lost it this time. He reached up, grabbed the shelves with the mountain of papers, and brought the whole lot down on top of her. He didn't realise I was standing behind him, watching. I was around twelve or thirteen and I still don't remember any of it.

If it made me overprotective, it was an unconscious reaction. That's how Mum interpreted my behaviour. She worried about it, and that's why they sent me to see a psychologist in the first place. I must have been traumatised. I was certainly aware by then that Dad had hit Mum, but I had locked away the specifics, like they were too much to deal with. Then Dad took me to Dr Purple Eyes and hijacked the sessions to drone on about what a hard time he was having.

I already felt dirty and ashamed of how we lived. The cottage at The Knock seemed to get smaller and shabbier every day. When we'd moved in, there had been plans for an extension, and for the garden. My mum planted trees and built a fence around the garden. Maybe I should say that again. *Mum* planted the trees and built a fence. Dad did nothing. The hardworking man from the days at Barmeal had disappeared. He sat at the kitchen table, surrounded by paperwork, stale dreams, and empty cigarette packets. He brooded and he stewed over God knows what. No one was allowed to move the mountain of random scribbles, or any of the chaos. It was too important to him. I think it was more important than we were.

Maybe that's why I'm always on the move today – always getting stuck into the house and the workshop, upgrading, tweaking, messing with the crush and upskilling myself. I'm afraid that if I stop for too long, I might end up the same way. These days we have mobile phones, social media, Netflix. Procrastination is easy. Back then, it must have taken some effort to waste that much time.

I'm not sure when I started joining all the dots and realised there was a lot going on behind the facade of my parents' marriage. My mum hid it all incredibly well. For the record, I don't advocate for anyone hiding anything important they're dealing with, but as a child, I was lucky to be shielded from most of the dark reality of family violence. Although it existed, I was never in the situation of having to accept it, of thinking this was normal. I'm grateful for that. But I'm sad that Mum felt she had to conceal it for so long. That should never be the case, and it may be there are more things I have blocked out and don't recall.

That said, I'm aware there was a long-established history there. Stuff that went back to before I was born, before my parents were even married. When I was thirteen, I overheard a conversation one morning. One of my brothers thought he might have broken his nose. Mum wiggled her delicate, pointed nose from side to side in response and asked, 'can you do this?' That's how we found out that Dad had broken her nose when she was sixteen, in the early days of their relationship.

After the incident with the shelves, I seemed to live with a constant sense of fear, as though I was on permanent alert – like when you're driving fast on the motorway and realise there's a speed cop behind you, blues and twos flashing, sirens wailing. Your stomach drops, and your heart feels like it's trying to break out of your ribcage. You check your speed and realise you're over the limit. You've been caught. Then the cop speeds past you, heading somewhere else, dealing with something more life and death. That feeling, and the disquiet afterwards. That's how I always seemed to feel then.

I can remember sitting on the linoleum kitchen floor on one occasion, sobbing uncontrollably, still terrified of growing up. I was upset about another recurring dream; one where I ran next to a huge fence, with lots of daisies on the ground. The earth began to churn, then opened up around me. The dream might not have been real, but the emotions it provoked were undeniably visceral. Even now, thinking about it makes me feel sick. I had the same dream for years. It was like running in a tunnel wave. It was always in the front garden at Barmeal. The place where we played with our pet lambs, the place where things had seemed better, and happier.

As if that wasn't enough, the grinding sickness came with a sense of shame I just couldn't shake. If you've never been there, you'll have to trust me that it's hard to manage, day to day. All that trauma undoubtedly left a shadow, a sense of being at fault, somehow. These days mobile phones have caller ID, but even though I can see who it is, I rarely pick up my phone. Thinking about it, even now, with no phone near me, makes my throat constrict with apprehension. As if I've done something wrong, or there's some kind of comeuppance en route. I sometimes get Ashley to listen to the messages.

I used to struggle to pick up the phone at The Knock too, as if the worst possible news was waiting, somewhere down the line. A dreaded, faceless monster, lurking somewhere in the dark, something to hurt me or my family. Probably learned behaviour. Dad used to say, 'I'm not in', whenever the phone rang. It meant whoever was close by would have to answer on his behalf, lying for him, making up excuses on the spot. Not that easy a trick when you're a child and the same person who told you to always tell the truth is demanding you do the opposite just because it suits them. Maybe he just had an irrational fear of answering the phone. Plenty of well-balanced people do. Most people don't want someone trying to sell them double glazing.

I remember Bob answering the phone with an almost practiced, 'I'm sorry, he's not in'. On one occasion, I overheard the caller yell, 'Aye, well is he in or is he not?'

You should never have to be the adult in the room when you're a teenager.

It wasn't, unsurprisingly, something my mum struggled with. In that and in a lot of other ways, my dad's sense of failure contrasted my mother's achievements, large and small. She was always spinning plates, always working hard, but she still found time for her kids, still saw her main focus as being a mother. She had studied modern languages at university, before giving it all up to marry Dad. Then she'd worked hard on the farm: rearing calves, growing vegetables, making a home for five kids. She ran a successful agricultural business. She won awards. She was viewed by everyone as reliable and hard working.

In the late 1980s, when I would have been around five, Dad had begun to struggle, and Mum had gone back to work away from the farm to support him. She got a job with the Agricultural Training Board, arranging courses on behalf of the government, then she was asked to help set up South West Machinery Ring – an agricultural cooperative. She held down one job and ran another business – all from the nerve centre Dad subsequently targeted – and she had five growing kids. She was an example of what you could achieve on initiative, tenacity and sheer hard work. She was a role model for all of us.

To Dad, she exemplified everything he hadn't achieved.

# Chapter Five

The noise is everywhere. It starts as a low, rumbling growl, builds to a howling crescendo, then drops back, with a shotgun crack, at a flick of my wrist. I change down, brake hard, turn in. Apex, power on, change up, crack. Power. Howl. Crack.

It's a visceral thing, as unsettling as it's somehow calming. I follow the undulating tarmac, through a hairpin, a chicane, a sweeping turn, green on either side, under the lead weight of a Scottish sky. White and blue rumble strips and parochial advertising hoardings bounce around my peripheral vision, framed by the edges of my helmet, but my focus is the view between the red, shark-gilled fenders.

I am thrown around in my seat. My stomach wants to empty itself. The sweat on my palms is only absorbed by thick racing gloves. I'm not thinking about my tax return, or my next dental appointment or a hundred and one other things that seem like they might swallow me up. This is my adrenalin-junkie antidote to a mid-life crisis. I am alive. I am present. I think I'm happy.

In 1965, in his Harvard paper, 'The Existential Necessity of Midlife Change', the Canadian psychoanalyst, Elliott Jaques, coined the phrase *midlife crisis*. He was, maybe unsurprisingly, forty-eight years old at the time. Obviously, it's now an established part of our social culture, with its own helpful checklist, usually for men: A red sportscar. Check. Tattoos. Check. An affair with your secretary. Er ... Who even has a secretary these days? And the feeling that you're maybe just not quite as young as you were – I'm not sure I can check that one either.

The essential argument of the paper was that people were reaching an age – usually around forty or so – when their kids were flying the nest, and they suddenly had all this life in front of them. It's not a problem I have, given that two of my kids are still in primary school. Besides, I've always liked fast cars and tattoos. There are, of course, other explanations for the crisis. Jaques wrote that, 'during this period, we come face-to-face with our limitations, our restricted possibilities, and our mortality.'

My dad, having lost his way, moved into a tiny, crumbling house with five kids and a renovation that just wasn't happening, while his wife's success eclipsed his own, and highlighted his squandered potential. Mum always said Dad could have done her job standing on his head. But he wallowed in resentment. Instead of picking himself up again, he became her biggest critic – hell bent on scrutinising the way she did things. She offered to pay for the renovation, and he wouldn't let her. Instead, he charged her rent on the tiny room she used as an office while he continued to do nothing.

I guess it was all about control. He couldn't control his own life, so he controlled her.

He seemed always seemed be sitting with a giant mug full of tea, with three sugars and milk, and a triple decker marmalade sandwich, like he was waiting for something to land in his lap.

In 1992, aged forty-three, he got what he thought he wanted.

Word had spread that Mum was good at what she did, and in the winter of 1992, she got a phone call from Arnold Kemp, the editor of *The Glasgow Herald*. He said, 'I'm looking for the

Christine Parker who runs training courses.' Kemp had been contacted by the Russian state news agency, Novosti, who were working on a project.

This was the era of Perestroika and Glasnost. Barely three years earlier, iconic images of people climbing on top of the Berlin wall, smashing at the concrete with sledgehammers, had filled our screens. It was a time of change and hope. Russia was opening up. Farming, along with everything else in the USSR, had been state owned, and operated on a different scale. We heard stories that tractor-men would plough for miles. In Scotland, a field might be half a mile long. In Russia, there were no fields in that sense, and the tractors were huge things that ran on caterpillar tracks. Guys climbed aboard at the start of their shift and begin driving in one direction, ploughing a furrow as far as they could, while sipping from bottles of vodka to ease the boredom. I think the novelty might wear a bit thin after the first day. I'm not sure how you'd even stay awake.

The Russian government were keen to modernise, and for whatever reason, they looked to Scotland, and in turn, my mum. It must have been a massive compliment and a huge buzz to be part of something like that; to be singled out, especially as a woman, in those days, as the person most qualified to run a project that could modernise the farming industry of one of the biggest countries on the planet. However she felt about it privately, Mum seemed to take it all in her stride.

So did Dad. It was his chance for an adventure.

The first step was a trip to Moscow and then to the Tchaikovsky region. We used to have an old VHS tape of the trip somewhere but that seems to have vanished, as these things do. I'm not sure what I'd play it on even if I could find it. Mum and Dad travelled with other farmers, political representatives, people in education and, I'm sure, at least one journalist. They went to the Bolshoi ballet, rode the Trans-Siberian Express and were driven all over the place in Ladas, over pot-holed roads, stopping every so often for picnics that always seemed to involve vodka.

Everyone they met seemed to be called Viktor and everyone had had their eyes lasered, which seems bizarre, considering it was over thirty years ago. Novosti made a documentary about the whole trip, part of which had Mum interviewing the head of the Russian Orthodox church. There were visiting dignitaries who stayed in our tiny house – men who arrived in outdated suits, then changed into garishly coloured shell-suits and white knock-off hi-tops. I guess they were trying to fit in.

The ultimate aim was to bring twenty Russian agricultural students, and some agronomists (there's a good word) over to Scotland, and to match them with farmers to see how we did things. As the project opened up, more students came across. Enter Tanya: an eighteen-year-old agricultural student who came to stay with us in 1993. Tanya was glamorous. That's the first thing you noticed about her. With her curls and makeup, she stuck out like a sore thumb in The Shire. It was hard to imagine her farming. She shared a room with my sisters, who were already squeezed together tightly.

From the distance of thirty-plus years, this all seems predictable, as well as being a tired cliché: forty-something guy who's made a few wrong turns in life is invited to a country that is slowly opening up and looking to trade, on the basis of who his wife is. He's depressed. He has no idea what to do with himself and now sees only opportunity. On *all* fronts.

The Russians were interested in trade. Dad took his chance, and along with Mum and a family friend, set up the Scottish and Baltic Russian Enterprise Company, known as SABRE. In the early days, Mum and Dad both went on business trips. Later, when Tanya moved back to Russia, Dad went alone, supposedly to save money. With Dad buoyed by a newfound sense of his own greatness and Tanya keen on a UK passport, you can guess what happened next. They inevitably started an affair. Keen to show off his importance, he lavished money he didn't have on Tanya. I didn't, and still don't, resent her in any way. She was young, ambitious, trying to get out of Russia, away from her alcoholic father, to a better life. I guess she didn't realise what she was walking into. She'd tried to seduce Bob first, but at fifteen years old he was too naïve, thinking he must be imagining things.

I don't know how or when it all came out. Partly, it was obvious, with the sudden interest Dad took in his appearance. At one point he became more interested in clothes and he started trying face masks. He even shaved off the moustache he'd had for twenty-odd years. If that sounds like normal behaviour, in this case it certainly wasn't. In the past Mum had cut his hair and he only brushed it if he was leaving the farm. He'd never been one for personal hygiene and grooming. My gran was once horrified when Mum told her that she expected Dad to cut his own fingernails.

He was a big, handsome guy but quite possibly the scruffiest man I'd ever met. His overalls always had burst zips, and for some reason he thought wearing a leather cowboy belt someone had brought him from America made up for this by holding it all together and reining in the belly he'd managed to accumulate. To top off the look, gold Benson & Hedges cigarette packets wore a permanent shape in his top left pocket.

Dad just always seemed to be a mess. Most people I know get changed when they've been out farming all day. Ashley sometimes makes me take off my clothes at the door. Quite right too, considering the effort she puts into our home and the smells that go along with anything agricultural; inescapable for anyone other than the person they emanate from, who is often desensitised to it.

Mum found out about the affair, eventually. They argued about it, and their relationship became more abusive as time went on. Dad shouted at her and the rest of us as his moods seesawed. He sat in his faded blue wing-backed chair, in the middle of the living room, and boomed, 'THE DOOR', making the room shake, if anyone dared to walk through without closing it.

The farm cottage at The Knock was never a happy place. The only time we didn't seem to be on edge was when Dad was in a good mood, talking about his plans for the future, the things he was going to do in Russia, the things he was going to sell, here in the UK, the fact he had been on the radio, talking about it all. I suppose he thought this was his big chance to win his father's approval. Grandad's private view was, 'Ian likes to talk big'.

Much later, during the course of their divorce, it emerged that Dad had hit Mum in front of another Scottish couple who travelled with them on the first Russian trip. Like it was no big deal. Maybe that's how well-known it had become, or how wary people were of getting involved. If that was how he acted in front of others, I can only imagine what went on behind closed doors.

Eventually, Mum couldn't take it anymore. One morning, while he was talking about his plans, she told him she was leaving. I think he must have known it was coming but that made little difference. We were meant to be going out for the day. I don't know why we carried on with our plans – maybe fear on

Mum's part and denial on Dad's. Mum had bought a car and Dad insisted on driving it. He tortured her, and us – accelerating, like he didn't care what happened. It was a rollercoaster ride. I can remember going past the bottom of the road that leads to Wigtown at Trammondford, just wishing I could get out and go to my grandparents' house. What this was supposed to achieve, I don't know. Was he trying to exercise control over Mum, with fear? If he was, he only confirmed the fact that she had made the right decision. At the end of the day, he dropped Mum and us off at my granny and grandad's house.

James moved back to the farm two days later, out of a sense of loyalty and instinct that someone had to look after the farm and the animals. God knows what he had to put up with, but I know it wasn't easy. The rest of us would never move back to The Knock.

At Granny Mo's house, in Wigtown, Susan, Kirsty, Bob and I slept on the floor each night, on cushions taken from armchairs. It must have been a real pain in the neck for my grandparents, having four kids suddenly living there with them, but they never showed it. There was the odd cross word from Grandad, who wasn't known for being particularly laid back, but he was a gentle man who was just a bit grumpy. The polar opposite of Dad.

Dad carried on drinking. He'd fill empty vodka bottles with water in a crude attempt to conceal the extent of his habit from James. He continued to try to win Mum back, and for a while it looked as though they were making progress. But then everything came to a head.

Mum eventually found a house to rent in Port William, around three miles away from Monreith and The Knock. It was a nice house and belonged to some friends of hers who were living in Spain. It was a one-and-a-half storey, stone-built cottage, like something off a postcard. It was on the small side, but I didn't feel ashamed to call it home. Things were changing. We already all went to primary school in Port William, so we had friends there. Our house became a bit of a social hub once more with people dropping in to shoot the breeze all the time; something that would have been unthinkable in the old house.

Mum found a package holiday deal to the Greek island of Kos and took Susan, Kirsty and I away for a week. That was a game changer for me. Kos is a place we have gone back to, repeatedly, over the years, but that first holiday was an eye-opener. I'd never flown before. I'd never been anywhere outside the UK. The first thing I remember is the wall of heat hitting me as I walked through the door of the plane on to the steps on the runway. That and the smell of aviation fuel. It was intense. I didn't like it at first. I'd been diagnosed with asthma when I was five and I didn't feel like it would be great for that. I was wrong.

The holiday was amazing. At the end of the week, Kirsty, Susan and I sat on the back of the bus, crying because we didn't want to go home. I wonder now how my mum could have afforded it. She'd been the breadwinner in our family for years, for sure, but she had a new roof to put over our heads now, new everything to take care of. It must have been out of season, but it felt like freedom maybe for the first time since Barmeal.

After the holiday, things appeared to be going better between Mum and Dad. They were closer again, and I think we thought they were getting back together. But it remained an abusive relationship, open to cycles of violence, presumably linked to my dad's own mood swings.

Just when it seemed as though things were going a bit *too* well, it turned out they were.

Mum went to a charity evening she'd been invited to through

work, with her friend and workmate, Linda. Bob and Kirsty were in their mid teens, so Susan and I were in the house alone with them as our designated babysitters. Dad phoned up and demanded to know where Mum was. We hung up. Then the phone rang again. The words, 'I will destroy you', hissed out of the black answerphone. We knew we were in trouble.

He turned up in person, half an hour later. People don't generally lock their doors here, so there was nothing keeping him out. He staggered down the hall, shouting, 'Where is she?' I remember hiding in the bedroom upstairs. I think Kirsty must have told him to go away. She's always had guts. She can be quaking in her boots, but you'd never know it. She knows how to stand up for herself and anyone else who needs it. Dad exploded. She ran upstairs to her room. He followed her in there and spat out words so vile I'll never forget them, and I won't dignify what he said by repeating it.

Kirsty would never see my father alive again.

Bob tried to reason with him – tried to calm him down, as he stomped down the stairs and into the night, throwing out a pile of excuses as he went. My two sisters and I huddled together on the bed, terrified. Ashamed, somehow. But that wasn't the end of it. He arrived back in the wee small hours, even drunker. My mum was back home now, horrified by what we'd put up with, but it was about to get worse. He stood in the middle of the street, shouting obscenities at the house. He accused my mum and her friend of having a lesbian affair, because why else would she have left him?

The next morning, I stumbled downstairs. There was something odd about the light in the hall. The glass front door was covered. Dad had loaded his car with bits of useless furniture from the cottage: old beds, a cot, anything heavy he could find, Then, he'd used them to barricade us in. As my mum and brother cleared the debris from the front of the house, an old woman who lived two doors down walked past and laughed. That's one of the things that stands out from those years the most: the almost routine humiliations. There was no real sense of shame in my father when he had a drink in him. You never knew who was going to show up. You could get the happy, hopeful, optimistic guy; the man with the plan, or you'd get an insecure, depressed control freak; the man who pushed everyone away and then couldn't understand why they left.

Through it all, James tried to keep things running on the farm and Mum still tried to help Dad with the family business in any way she could. When I was about thirteen, however, everything changed for good.

I don't know how it happened, or what his supposed reasons were. Mum must have 'done' something Dad disagreed with. They were very definitely separated at this point, but she was round at the house trying to help him tidy up. Bob used to help out on the farm at weekends and Mum would drop him off and try to keep things amicable.

My brothers were out working, repairing drystone dykes in a field down on the shore, and James went back to the cottage to get something – probably coffee knowing him. I've never known anyone with such a caffeine habit. He met Mum in the driveway. She was crying and didn't want to tell him what had happened but eventually admitted that Dad had kicked her. She managed to get into her car and leave. James, being who he is, was determined to find out what had gone down.

Dad came outside and James started asking questions. Dad started making excuses, then he started shouting. He moved his face closer to James's, in a way he had done before – trying to intimidate him, to make him back away. There was a struggle. Dad toppled over and hit his head on the concrete drive. He was out cold. For ten minutes, James panicked, trying to get Dad to wake up. He was about to phone for an ambulance when he opened his eyes.

Later, we found out that Dad had dragged Mum around the driveway by her hair, kicking her with his rigger boots – big, loose heavy steel toe-capped boots – as he went.

There had been other episodes of violence, Dad's affair, the separation – but that was the official end of my parents' marriage.

That night, Mum tried to speak to Dad's parents, to tell them that he needed help. Bob tried to tell them the same thing but was told Dad had been 'driven to it'. I picked up the extension, during a phone call, and told them exactly what I thought of them.

I would pay for that later on.

Mum eventually met a new man – Davie McGarvie. He would become my stepfather and introduce me to the world of hoof trimming. He was around five six in heels, considerably shorter than my dad, but what struck most people about Davie was his build. He had forearms thicker than most people's calves. They were definitely thicker than my calves. That's not an exaggeration, although I'll admit I don't have the best pair. There's a reason you never see me in a kilt.

You know those acts of inhuman strength you hear about? The ones where people lift cars off their loved ones because they have no choice? Davie was *that* guy. His brother once got stuck under a slurry tanker – a tonne and a half of tank, on wheels. Without really thinking about it, Davie lifted it clear and freed him.

He seemed to be good for Mum. Nothing was ever too much trouble for him where she was concerned, and I was happy about that. We all were. It was the normal relationship that everyone thought she deserved.

Everyone, except for my dad.

He began stalking Mum. She'd be driving around in her red Nissan Sunny – which we used to call 'the wee red shed' – and one of us would see Dad's car, a silver Volvo. I still remember the number plate: C575 AOS. I'll never be able to forget it. It's etched into my memory. Every time I saw it, I expected something bad to happen. It usually did.

Dad pulled various and increasingly elaborate tricks to try to work out where Mum was, so that he could follow her or harass her. He might wait until James had phoned Mum and then quiz him on her whereabouts, or he might just figure out where she was likely to be, based on her work, but somehow, he'd always turn up, freaking everyone out in the process.

One night in early March, the year after the driveway incident involving Mum, Dad and James, it snowed heavily and unexpectedly. Mum, Bob and I had been visiting Granny, after school. We were driving home in the wee red shed, with Mum taking things steadily. Snow isn't uncommon in The Shire, but it rarely lies. We're on a peninsula, surrounded by warm, salty air from the gulf stream, which quickly melts the snow.

We were close to home when the car lifted into the air, then came to a gentle thudding stop. We were confused, but when we got out, we realised what had happened. We had hit a hidden snowdrift. That had acted like a ramp, propelling us upwards, and then we'd landed in about a foot and a half of snow. I'd never even seen a foot and a half of snow before.

Davie came along a back road to get us. He had a 4x4 truck,

much more suitable for that sort of weather, and was about to drive up behind us to pull us out. What we didn't know was that Dad had got James to phone Granny's house, to find out where Mum was. He wanted to make sure she was okay, he said. As Davie arrived behind us, the snowplough emerged through the drift ahead, clearing the way. Through the lights, my dad walked towards us, with his loping stride, filthy Aran jumper and glowing cigarette end. He drove Bob and I back to the house in Port William and left quietly. I can't recall if we expected some kind of awkward confrontation or if we were apprehensive about what might happen next. All I remember is a slightly uncomfortable drive back to the house.

I'm not sure at what point Dad had noticed Davie's truck. Much later that night, Mum was putting out some rubbish and heard some kind of commotion outside – the sound of breaking glass and snapping plastic. She turned to see where the noise was coming from. Crouched down low, next to Davie's truck, was Dad. She couldn't see his face, or what he was doing.

'You come here; I'll sort you out,' he said.

Mum turned away and walked inside.

As she walked in the door, Davie walked out. Dad was climbing back into his Volvo. He fired up the engine and swung the car round, hard. Davie managed, somehow, and only just, to avoid being run over. My dad was now blocked in and about to learn what it was like to take a beating.

Later that night, my father was arrested for drink driving, breach of the peace and criminal damage. He had been slashing Davie's tyres when Mum discovered him. When he'd told her to come closer, he'd been holding a box cutter. I shudder to think what else he might have done if she hadn't gone back inside the house when she did.

James moved out of The Knock after that. Dad, undeterred, continued to stalk us. He'd turn up in random places when we least expected it, and that bastard silver Volvo scared us to death every time it appeared. Back then, attitudes to stalking and harassment were different. The police refused to get involved. They said it was a 'domestic matter', despite the numerous instances of violence, the threats, and the fact they didn't actually live together. They had been living separately for a year.

Despite all this, we made the best of it. We were generally happy, even though we were properly skint when we lived in Port William. Mum was holding down the fort as a single, working parent, so money was scarce. We bought tins of chicken soup and Kirsty would make tuna pasta, chicken and broccoli bake and a whole load of other cheap but filling and nutritious foods. It's only now, looking back from a very different perspective, that I can appreciate how hard it must have been for Mum, looking after five children. I didn't fully realise at the time what a mess everything was. It was all normal to me. And, as weird as it seems, I still had a great time. We all mucked in together. She was an amazing mother to us, and still is, but all of that must have been incredibly hard on her.

Over the following year, Dad's behaviour grew steadily worse, forming a pattern that would eventually lead to the most bizarre and frightening episode in my life – an incident that involved the police and a court case. As time went on, I had the sickening dread that the mostly private events of our dysfunctional family were becoming too public, and turning us into the talk of our small, close-knit community.

I would be proved right.

# Chapter Six

The Knock sits high above the shoreline on the Irish Sea. From there, it's a sheer three-hundred-foot drop down to the beach in places, and a sharp descent to lower lying outcrops in others. One of those plateaus is heavily manicured and landscaped, despite its windswept location. Since 1905, it's been the home of St Medan Golf Club. It might just be my favourite place in the world. Although, saying that, it holds some seriously mixed emotions. I've seen some of the best and worst times of my life there.

St Medans, as the locals call it, is the most southerly golf course in Scotland, in one of the country's wildest and most idyllic corners. If you go into the clubhouse – a brown wooden shack of a place with an awesome view, a decent line in comfort food and a cheap bar – and you check out the names on the captain's boards, you'll see my great grandmother's name as well as that of my great uncle, Robert Glen Parker (we're not too original with names). The place is entwined with my family's history. It's in our bones. It's bordered on all sides by The Knock, and the sea.

When we were kids, we'd make the trip there most days in the summer holidays; down through the fields, scraping past jagged gorse bushes, avoiding the green and black striped adders that basked in the long grass on the warm days, waiting to bite someone. Adders are the UK's only venomous snake. I've never heard of anyone getting bitten by an adder locally, and they aren't particularly dangerous to humans, but I don't fancy testing that theory.

It's a strange place full of myth and history. The name comes from Saint Medan. Local legend has it that she travelled there on a rock that sits on the beach below the course. I remember my gran telling me that Saint Medan, a princess, was forced into a marriage she didn't want, with a man she didn't love, that she plucked out her own eyes, and boarded the rock and floated across the bay to Kirkmaiden. When she arrived, she washed her eyes – or presumably, her empty, no doubt bloody, sockets – and her vision was restored. It's exactly the sort of miracle that has guaranteed the passing down of these legends, and why they're still told today. The spring down there used to be known as the chincough well. Chincough is an old-fashioned name for whooping cough. It was thought you could cure it by drinking from the well – again, the facts on this are sketchy, but generations of local people would have tried it in the days before vaccinations.

Above the beach sits Kirkmaiden old church – a small, ruin of a church with strange gravestones; some have pictures, some have skulls, wings or symbols instead of an inscription, or accompanying the carved text. One of the graves belongs to Francois Thurot, a French Privateer (a pirate sanctioned by Louis XV of France to raid British ships), merchant navy captain and smuggler who died in battle, off the Isle of Man on the 28th of February 1760, and was washed ashore in Monreith Bay. William Maxwell, the local laird, had him buried in the cemetery with full military honours.

We used to walk all the way down to the course with our golf clubs in bags on our backs. It never really crossed our minds to use trolleys and buggies. They just wouldn't work down there on those hills. It would have been amusing to try, though. I was never well enough off to afford golf shoes, but James did whatever he had to, to scrape together the funds and have all the gear. He loved golf. He could have turned professional when he was sixteen. He was offered a pro job but turned it down when he saw the low starting salary. He spent every spare minute he had on that course, although in his eyes, I don't think they were spare minutes. Nothing came before golf.

He once spent an entire day playing golf, with all of us taking turns caddying for him. He got members of the club to sponsor him per hole and raised a decent amount of money for charity, although I now can't recall which one. He covered a hundred holes. There's a picture of him and my dad somewhere, on the last hole, with the sun going down. James is in shorts, standing half the height he is now and showing off a decidedly knobbly set of knees.

There was some interesting, er, science behind his golf training. He once welded a lump of steel to the head of one of his clubs to build up his 'swing' muscles. I guess it worked. He could out-drive most people I know, and he regularly smashed the course record, just not in competitions.

If we weren't on the course, we'd still be down there, crawling through the long grass, pricking ourselves with thorns and hitting the ground with a seven iron, trying to dig out buried treasure – golf balls that overshot the mark on the 8th hole. We'd gather what we could, pool our resources and climb the wall into the field next to the farm cottage. We'd hit ball after ball, regardless of the consequences of where they might end up. Losing balls was a badge of honour, when it meant you'd blasted them out of sight. On the course we'd make up our own holes. It was a small course, and the first was a normal hole, but all the other holes crossed over each other, so there would be balls flying everywhere. When you play as many rounds as we did you can get a bit bored. We invented new courses, challenging ourselves to hit further. We'd hit our drives from the tee of one hole towards the hole of another, criss-crossing the course in new and interesting ways.

Some of our challenges might have gotten a bit over the top. There's a single-track road that runs across the course, cutting through the six and seventh fairways. If we spotted a Transit van trying to make a delivery, James and I would wait on the 6th hole and try to hit the side of the van. I never managed to hit any moving vans, but I'm pretty sure James did. I don't think I would have liked to have been on the receiving end of that one. Although there should never have been any delivery vans in that area anyway – the road led to the sea.

I think the most unorthodox shot James ever played was one he hit from the rough at St Medan. The rough sits on the side of the hills there – basically where no one can mow the grass. James hit his drive, and the ball landed in there. It must have been well in there and he must have taken a good swipe at it on his next shot. He hit his ball so hard, he managed to take a sleeping adder with it. The snake swirled through the air as the ball flew higher. I'm pretty sure that woke both of them up!

When we weren't hitting golf balls in the field next to the house, we'd use it for other games. We'd jump the electric fence, usually without getting any shocks, but there was always an outside chance of a livening jolt. It was called the pump field, named after the old well on the farm. It was the lowest lying ground and fairly flat, so good for most ball sports. We used to play rounders there for hours. For American readers, rounders is a sort of simpler, gentler mixed-sex version of baseball. There are way less rules, and we tend to play it in parks, fields or on beaches. I'm proud to say I've ticked off all these venues.

We gave cricket a good go, too, because of Dad. He was as proud of his Yorkshire roots in Scotland as he was of his Scottish roots when he was in Yorkshire. I don't think you'll get anyone more patriotic than a tipsy Scotsman, watching Braveheart, in the country they've emigrated to. The Yorkshireness and Dad's public-school education meant cricket had a hallowed status, and he thought he was a solid player. He had a musty old brown bag (the kind of thing you might take to Hogwarts) with the entire cricket set inside: willow stumps and wickets, a bat you could disarm a burglar with, and an old leather ball that would probably do the housebreaker nearly as much damage again. We had a good stab at cricket whenever someone found Dad's quidditch bag and we took the notion to play, but after golf, rounders was our favourite. All three sports basically meant smashing a ball with as much power as possible. I guess that was about our level. I never said we were sophisticated.

We always walked down to the golf course, but my parents drove. That presented the odd challenge. One morning we looked out the window of the cottage to see the family car seriously banged up. There had obviously been an accident, but we're not talking about a normal everyday prang. This was Dad, after all. He didn't like to do things by halves when he could demonstrate a higher level of commitment. The car was mangled and twisted in about three different ways, and the roof on the back end of the estate (or station wagon) seemed to have taken the worst of the hit. What could have hit a car that high up, none of us knew. Had he reversed into a fleet of flying pigs?

It took a few years before I found out what had actually happened. There was – and still is – a big drinking culture in Southwest Scotland, and the problem seemed to be particularly rife in the golf club in those days. People would arrive for an afternoon's golfing, leave their cars in the car park and walk the rest of the distance up the track to the club house. They'd play a round or two of golf and then retire to the clubhouse, and the bar. An out-of-the-way location, competitive camaraderie and cheap booze created a perfect drinking storm. It wasn't unusual for someone to get trashed and then decide to drive home.

We lived about a mile away from the clubhouse. Dad had decided it was worth the risk. Ever keen to impress, he'd decided to reverse up to the clubhouse to collect his drinking buddy. What he hadn't reckoned on was the difficulty of reversing up the embankment at the start of the access track in the dark. He managed a few yards from the carpark, then drove off the side of the road. His left rear wheel hit the downward slope and gravity took over. He slid, sideways, down the hill. His rear wheel hit the bottom first, then caught, and flipped the car into a roll. Once again, he was lucky to escape unhurt. He didn't have a mark on him.

In yet another example of the kind of luck he had, the friend he was with was a mechanic. They walked back to the farm to decide what to do, stopping at the cottage to think it over while they ate marmalade sandwiches. They eventually went to get the tractor with the loader from the farm, drove back to the club and carried the car back up the road. Their solution for securing the car was to impale it on the fork of the loader. That was the end of that particular vehicle. When my mum woke up the next day, there were marmalade sandwiches everywhere and a family car that Picasso would have been proud of was parked outside our house. Dad became known as the only person who could roll a car at five miles an hour. The wheel marks, where he'd struggled to gain traction, stayed on that slope for years, like a constant reminder every time I went there.

During the golf season, from April to September, there were weekly competitions that James and Dad sometimes entered. Dad had a set of Swilken golf clubs. I used to think they were the business, but now I realise they were probably a bit cheap and nasty. After googling the company, I discovered they went out of business in 1995!

After a game, the whole family would go to the clubhouse for dinner. I seem to remember it was always scampi. There were purple faux leather armchairs, everything was pine panelled and there were arcade games in the changing rooms. I very definitely grew up in the eighties. To me, that was about as posh as it got: dinner out, scampi, fizzy drinks.

Looking back, there are a lot of happy memories there – but things were about to turn in a way none of us would ever have imagined.

As the months dragged on, we continued living in the rented house in Port William, and Dad kept up his stalking. I remember Mum, stuck in a layby once, ear pinned to her new mobile phone, wondering what to do because he'd followed her all day. It started to seem inevitable that it was going to end badly.

In the meantime, my parents' separation became permanent when they finally got divorced. It felt like a turning point for everyone. Maybe now that everything was official and there was no way back, we could all move on in some way. Dad had managed to avoid much liability, in financial terms, and provided minimal child support. My mum even wrote off £25,000 she'd put into the farm from her income when he said he was struggling. An entry from Dad's diary around this time even shows that he thought he'd gotten off lightly. His lucky outcome should have encouraged him to count his blessings and get on with his life, but he chose to head in a very different direction.

After the tyre slashing incident, James had been living with us all again for a while. He'd been away from The Knock and his beloved golf, but he decided he was going to compete in one of the weekly competitions. The Lagganharrie Competition was named after the hill the course was built around. It's the biggest competition on the yearly fixture list at St Medan, and Mum and James had decided to play as a pair. Keen to get in on the action, I offered to caddie. We all jumped in the car and drove the three miles from Port William to St Medan to get started. It's a big event in a small area, and teeing-off times for each entrant were published in the local newspaper, *The Galloway Gazette*. Dad knew the precise time we'd be there.

We were a quarter of a mile away, on the single-track road that crosses The Knock, when we spotted him up ahead, standing in the road. Experience had taught all of us that he was unpredictable. Mum locked the doors, wary of what he might do. As we drove on, he just stood there, staring at us, saying nothing. Mum slowed down to walking pace, two wheels on the verge, and steered around him. I tried not to look at him. I was really fucking scared. He moved only slightly, as we passed.

We were all scared then, I think. But then we got to St Medan, where sixty other people were, unaware of anything we'd just seen. This was normality. This was reality, surely. We all knew each other. There was safety in numbers. Everyone knew Mum and Dad had just got divorced, but no one really knew how dark things had become. Surely Dad wouldn't turn up and make a fool of himself in front of the whole club, in front of most of the people he knew?

We headed out to the first tee, accompanied by a couple Mum and James had been paired with. I looked up at the rock face and the farm above. It's hard not to do that when you're down there, to drink in the view, especially when it's home and you don't live there anymore. I spotted Kim, our cocker spaniel, darting in and out of whin bushes, playing. It was a strange place for her to be. She normally hung around the house all the time. She wasn't where Dad had been when we met him. I felt as though the ground was opening up again.

We reached the second green, next to the farm wall. We heard the revving engine first, then Dad appeared, on the track above the course, riding the farm quad bike, swigging from a can of lager. Kim, the friendliest, most loyal dog in the world, trailed him, her ears flapping around in the breeze. Dad sort of fell off the bike, then stumbled down the hill towards us. He was wasted.

When we got to the second green, he was there. He said nothing. We tried to ignore him, like some twisted, human version of the elephant in the room. The maniac on the golf course – only he's your own father. He might go away if you ignore him even if the sting of the humiliation never does. Mum and James carried on playing.

When we were done with the second hole, we walked to the third tee. Dad was there, watching.

'James, you're gonna fuck up that shot,' he shouted. 'You're gonna pull it into the rough.'

James took his shot, and the other golfers – a couple Mum and James were matched against, just to add a more-up-close-and-personal audience into the mix and dial up the tension for dramatic effect – did the same. We all started walking, down the slanting dip of the third fairway, away from the farm and the maniac's domain. When I dared to look round, he was clambering back up the hill, towards the track.

When we got to the third green I saw him again, a hundred yards up the hill, lying on his front, facing us. It didn't make sense at first. And then, all too clearly, it did. He lay still, in the long grass, lining his family up in the telescopic sights of his .22 rifle. At least, that's what I thought I was seeing. But could I be wrong? Could this be real? How could I be sure?

Social pressure is an incredible thing. Deep down, I knew what I was seeing, but I didn't want to make a fuss. I didn't want to falsely accuse him of something that seemed so inconceivable. Of something I could see plainly but just couldn't accept. *I can't say that out loud,* I thought. *Imagine how embarrassing it's going to be telling people my dad's got a gun.* My head was screaming it must be true, but somehow, my body resisted.

'Dad's got a gun!' I hissed.

Shit got real, quickly. We all crouched as low as we could. Dad jumped up. He climbed onto his quad bike and rode it along the cliff to a spot above the fourth green. Now he had a clear line of sight. We couldn't move anywhere without being a target. How was this happening?

I don't know how they did it, but I'll always be grateful to them. At what was undoubtedly great risk to themselves, the two golfers Mum and James were playing with made their way back to the clubhouse and phoned the police. It took an unbearable amount of time for them to get there, though I suppose it must have seemed much longer than it actually was. Crouching down in the grass with a gun-toting psycho on the loose gets old pretty quickly, but eventually the police turned up. They escorted me,

Mum and my brother back to the clubhouse. I don't know where the hell Dad had disappeared to by then. And when I told the police about the gun, they didn't believe me.

Things had escalated beyond all perspective now. Here was my father, rifle loaded, sights lined up, aiming to ... what? Kill my mother? Kill me and my brother? We all went to the local police station and made statements. Mum begged the police officers to listen, to just go back to the spot where I had seen my dad lying down and check the scene. They assured us they would, but they never did.

It fell to James to do it instead, and sure enough, when he walked up along the cliffs, he found the gun, lying there on the grass.

I hadn't imagined any of it. Dad had aimed his gun at us.

# Chapter Seven

The gun incident was both terrifying for us, and the peak of Dad's very public display of mental health deterioration. The police eventually got their collective asses in gear and did their jobs. He was arrested soon afterwards and charged with 'misbehaviour with a firearm.' He went to jail, on remand, while he waited for his trial. It seems wild, looking back on that period of our lives as a family. He made it into *The Sun*, a national newspaper in the UK. The headline reported the story of a suspected shooting incident on the golf course, like it was a comical aside – 'farmer goes rogue on golf course'. If anyone in the local area *hadn't* known about what was going on before, they certainly did now.

The sense of shame I'd been nurturing all those years had really come into its own.

Dad was unrepentant. He told my brother stories about prison like it was just another of his adventures. His two cell mates had been smoking skunk one night and offered him some. He'd said no. For all his alcohol abuse he was never into drugs. The cell mates had gone to sleep, and Dad had been struggling to nod off, so he smoked the rest. The next day the two cell mates were arguing about who had smoked the rest of the joint, and it looked like they were about to come to blows. Then the cell was raided for drugs, and nothing was found, meaning they'd all had a lucky escape. He probably thought it was like public school. He was happy as long as it gave him a good story.

Who the hell was this guy?

Dad eventually had his day in court. The sheriff was a local farmer. Dad pled guilty to misbehaviour with a firearm, and because he'd spent time in jail waiting for his trial, his actual punishment was only a few hundred hours of community service. We all felt as though we were paying far more for what he'd done than he was. We were still dealing with the aftereffects, the sense of disgust and, in some ways, the guilt by association that went along with everything Dad had done, somehow. None of it felt real. Nothing felt safe anymore. If your dad, the person who is supposed to look out for you, to protect you from the worst excesses of the world, can aim a rifle at you on the golf course – the place you feel most at ease – is anywhere safe anymore?

Dad had, by this point, neglected the farm for years – by paying other people to do the work and then later relying on James to do it, while he sat and devised his latest masterplan, or whatever it was he did when he was supposed to be working. His laziness had now moved into the realm of abandonment.

The farm buildings hadn't been in good shape since the bank had refused to spend any money on them after my great grandfather's death. Now they were even worse. The ancient mortar had crumbled, with time and the elements, leaving piles of stone where there had once been walls. There were holes in the slate roofs so large you could see between the wooden rafters, and they were rotting quickly. It was worse in the corners where the roof was hipped and blasted from both sides by the wind and the rain.

But the buildings were nothing, really. The sheep and cows were suffering. Eventually the animal welfare officers were called in, and they had to shoot some of the cows. Dad went to court, yet again, this time on a charge of animal cruelty. It was a long way to fall; from being the man with the reputation for breeding good cattle, the man who regularly topped the market, to being unable to look after his animals' basic needs.

I feel embarrassed and ashamed, even writing this. I nearly didn't include it in the book, as I feel somehow responsible. I grew up wanting to be a farmer, and it genuinely affects me to see farms neglected. I work on some amazing farms, and I have a lot of respect for farmers around the world, so this feels like the ultimate failure on my behalf. Even though, rationally, I know there's nothing I can do about it. It was my dad's own personal humiliation, but it still feels dirty to me.

It was hard to imagine at that point how things could get much worse for Dad, but somehow, they did, and in a way that led to fifteen years of shame, doubt and unanswered questions for the rest of us.

Part of the reason the farm had fallen into such a state was that Dad had begun spending an increasing amount of time in North Yorkshire, after the divorce. His parents still lived down there, and, following on from his time in jail and his trial, he seemed to be living in their house. We also heard stories about an old girlfriend of his who lived there, someone he had dated when he was a teenager. All we knew was her name: Sarah.

We assumed that they were together again in some way. I hadn't spoken to him in months. It was a confusing situation for me. I think most things are confusing when you're fourteen years old. The inside of my head was a war zone. I would have told anyone who listened then how much I hated that man. But deep down, I missed him.

I know from talking to Bob while writing this book that he phoned my grandparents in Yorkshire one night, back then, and accidentally got Dad on the phone. He was so thrown by the whole thing that they carried on talking for a while as if everything was normal. That's how we know about the prison incident. Bob didn't know what to do. Talking to someone you've built up as the devil in your head, who is, in fact, pretty affable in person, is enough to confuse anyone. But when it's your parent and you're a teenager, you automatically assume you're in the wrong, even when you know you're not.

As part of his court case for animal cruelty, Dad had agreed to sell all his livestock. He rented out the fields at The Knock to his friend, Norman. Without a farm to run he'd decided to go back to university. At the age of forty-eight, he enrolled to study Business in Scarborough. That took him back to Yorkshire on a more permanent basis, and, we heard, gave him a relatively new lease of life. Ever compensating for his insecurity, he regularly boasted to family friends about how much the younger students looked up to him, and how much he was helping them. It was a strange time and an unexpected turn of events, but somehow, he seemed to have got back on his feet. If only he'd done it all ten years earlier. My mum remembers having conversations with him about going off and doing something else, *anything* else, if it made him happy. He could have sold his stock and started again at any time, but I guess he was always frightened of what his father thought. As it turned out, none of us would get to have the same problem.

One lazy Sunday in June 1998, the phone rang, and I answered it. It was my auntie Lindsay, Dad's older sister. There was no small talk; she got straight to the point.

Dad had been found dead, floating in a river, that morning.

I laughed, a lot. Hysterical, uncontrollable, laughter. That might sound odd, or cold, or disrespectful. I still don't really understand my reaction now, over twenty-five years later. It just seemed so out of the blue, as though I'd been winded when I least expected it. The only thing to do was laugh. Laugh at the shock of it. Laugh at the sheer unlikeliness of what I was hearing and how utterly unprepared I was for the news. I suppose normally when a parent dies, you get a chance to prepare yourself in some way. They might be ill or elderly, but Dad was forty-nine and fit, despite his best efforts to trash his body and mind.

There was a bizarre sense of conclusion to his death, as if it had only ever been headed that way. My gran openly admitted that her son's death was a strange relief to her. I can't ever imagine saying that about one of my own children, but I understood what she meant. How bad must things have to be? How far gone do you have to think your son is before you write him off, before deciding that a quick, early death is the best option? She was blunt about it in the way her generation were.

'He was terribly tortured,' she said. It was for the best.

I'll never really understand my reaction, and I'm not sure I want to. I can look back now and categorise it as a combination of shock and maybe the idea that some sort of karma or comeuppance had got him in the end. There was definitely a sense of fatalism. I tend to think things happen in the way they were always meant to. If you knew everything, I'm pretty sure you could predict the future – the synapses in your brain fire a certain way based on the neurological pathways you've set up over time. You're always going to do what you were fated to do. You just make the best decisions you can at any given time, with the facts you have available to you. Maybe you think that's a load of old codswallop. I'm comfortable with that. I've no real urge to convince anyone one way or the other.

When I told James, he started laughing too. There we stood, in the long, low-ceilinged kitchen, in Port William, both of us laughing at the news of our father's untimely demise. Weird, eh? When Kirsty found out, she screamed and crumpled into floods of tears. I guess everyone handles grief in different ways.

Things then seemed to happen very quickly. There was a funeral to arrange and a body to get back north of the border. Dad was to be cremated in Yorkshire, and there were a few ideas about what to do with his ashes. Some of us thought he would have liked to have been scattered on The Knock, on top of the cliffs overlooking the Irish Sea. Mum felt that we needed somewhere we could visit, to know where he was in some way, somewhere removed from the location of his death.

He had died in a place called Forge Valley, near Scarborough on the North Yorkshire coast, in the early hours of that fateful Sunday morning. He'd then been found, floating, face down in the water, by an unsuspecting dog walker.

We all travelled down to Malton – some of us stayed with Granny and Grandad again, like we had as children in the summer holidays, minus the usual sense of joy. Transporting a body from England to Scotland involved a lot of red tape, so the Yorkshire cremation made sense. There's no limit on where you can take a box of ashes.

James decided not to go. He's never liked funerals, and, I think, wanted to say goodbye in his own way. When he was a teenager, someone told him he should go out and buy nicer clothes if he wanted to get himself a girlfriend. He replied, 'Why would I want someone who was only interested in me for what I look like?' He doesn't do peer pressure, and I respect his decision for not going to the funeral. Like a lot of what he has done in his life, it took guts. Mind you, it also took guts to wear some of the stuff he did, back in the day.

The crematorium was a busy place. Yorkshire is far more densely populated than Wigtownshire. The population of Yorkshire is, in fact, roughly the same as the whole of Scotland, so we had to wait two weeks before the funeral took place. In Scotland, the tradition is that the sons, or male representatives of the deceased, gather at the door to the church, shaking the hands of mourners as they arrive. It's a tradition that has more recently changed to include any relatives or representatives of the deceased. It adds a personal touch, and frankly it gives you something to do, rather than sit there, waiting. Speaking to people gets some of the nerves and the awkwardness out of the way. Usually they're people you know, people you're related to. In my family, funerals are pretty much the only occasions we all catch up.

If we had been expecting to greet people at the door, it wasn't happening. And we didn't know most of the people there anyway. I don't know if the traditions are different in England, or if that was just the way my grandparents wanted things, but we simply stood near the door as the priest arrived, in full frock-like garb, at the head of the undertakers who were carrying the coffin. He started his address to those gathered in the crematorium, as he walked slowly down the aisle. We followed him in at the head of the crowd and found our seats at the front.

The service was short and to the point. I don't remember a lot about it. I spent most of the time staring at the coffin, wanting to cry, to react in some way that got the emotions out – anything to release the tension. I kept thinking I *should* be crying. I just couldn't. I put up a wall and stood watching the scene from a safe distance behind it. Who was in that coffin? I didn't feel like I knew him, or anything much about him. The priest spoke about someone I didn't recognise, reciting a vague description of someone he didn't know, written by parents and a sister who barely knew him any better.

When we emerged into the daylight again, two Royal Air Force Tornados, out on a coincidentally timed training exercise, flew low over the crematorium, splitting, and banking off in different directions. Someone remarked that it seemed to have been set up, and wasn't it appropriate that Ian loved flying so much?

What would have been more appropriate was if he had tried to stay alive, made an effort with his kids, and not attempted to murder his wife and sons.

The wake was at my grandparents' house. We all stood around on the flagstone patio, next to the grand lawn, eating nibbles and talking. There were a lot of people I didn't recognise. Some of them were young and tearful, seemingly more upset than his own kids were. These were his fellow students from Scarborough. Like the priest, they described a stranger. They told us what an amazing man he was, how they felt privileged to have known him. A couple of them broke down, the worse for wear from alcohol. I saw my mum comforting one of his lecturers, who was overcome with emotion. This was the effect he'd had on them.

They knew nothing about his life back home, the mess he'd made, the trail of screw ups and misery he'd left behind him. All they knew was this amazing, talented guy who had gone back to study in his late forties. He was an inspiration. Another one of his lecturers said he was on course to graduate with a first-class degree and that they were considering creating an award in his name. Without exception they told us how lucky we were to have him as a father. But he'd edited his life. He'd cut the bits of his past that didn't fit the narrative. He'd embellished his business background and SABRE and everything else that had been a pipedream. The whole thing felt like a nightmare.

I sometimes think he would have done well in the social media age. People on social media edit their own lives in the same way these days as he did then, in person. Their timelines are carefully curated. It can lead to bystanders, like the students and lecturers from Scarborough, misunderstanding. I suppose people could say, 'that's a bit rich, coming from you. Don't you do the same thing?' It's part of the reason I've written this book, to make sure people understand that what you see is a highlights reel. Only the best bits. On social media it's all about positivity for me, but there is another side hiding just behind the face I'm prepared to show the world. Instagram can't properly show what's missing in my life.

We didn't belong there, at my grandparents' house. Dad was posh and we had Scottish accents. He was privately educated, and we went to the local high school. There was a sense that some of the family were *more* family than others. It was in the way they spoke, their attitudes to certain things, how they dressed. None of them, for example, felt the need to be properly suited and booted, even for the funeral of one of their own.

We drove home the next day and Dad's remains followed in another car, with Bob, and Paul, a friend of the family, who took him back to his own house. Mum was determined our last memory of Dad wouldn't be a box of ashes sitting on the kitchen table.

A day or two later we gathered at the church in Glasserton – the parish The Knock sits in. The church is old and wearing badly these days. It's split level, with pews on an upper tier, from the days when it was well attended. When we were younger, Mum had made us all go there every Sunday, in an effort to help keep the place open. The six of us bulked up the numbers significantly. A few of my relatives are buried there: my great uncle Billy, a man who swam to the Isle of Man, and my great auntie Lexie, a woman with more letters after her name than anyone else I've ever heard of. Dad was about to enter familiar ground.

According to *The Statistical Accounts of Scotland,* Glasserton kirkyard 'is romantically embosomed in wood, which sheds around it a venerable gloom, as if it were a druidical temple, or the sacred grove of some Syrian idol.' They put it a lot better than I could. The sun always seems to split the trees there, as if someone has booked the weather in advance. But on the day of Dad's funeral, the 'venerable gloom' was out in force. We arrived under a slate grey sky to meet a handful of people waiting in cars. Then, as a group, we crunched across the gravel and into the church. Beyond the immediate family – me, Mum, Kirsty, Susan and Bob – there were a few old friends, all of whom were there for Mum. It was another service to get through – this time with a much smaller box to stare at. Dad's ashes were in a sort of mini coffin. A small, square wooden box with a brass plaque giving his name, his date of birth – April 22nd, 1949 – and the date of his death: 7th June 1998. If the service and the spectacle in Yorkshire seemed somehow bigger than it should have been, this was an anti-climax. No one huddled round the door greeting mourners here because no one needed to. There just wasn't enough of a turnout.

I can't remember much about the service, other than that it was run by the local minister, Alec Currie. Alec knew us and knew my father. I would say I've sat through plenty of his sermons over the years, counting down the number of hymns we still had to sing on a numbered wooden board. It has probably all merged into one, for me, but my most striking memory of Alec isn't as a minister at all.

My friend, Neil, was sleeping over at ours one night. In the middle of the night, we all woke up. There was some kind of commotion going on outside; a heavy, diesel engine, flashing lights, silhouettes. We opened the curtains to see Alec Currie, staring back at us in full firefighting gear, in front of a fire engine, in our driveway. The local fire service is voluntary. Even the local minister gets to fight fires. It turned out our chimney was on fire, but it hadn't been serious enough to wake us all up until help arrived.

Two funerals in a week is a lot for a fifteen-year-old to properly take in, never mind hold in his memory and regurgitate a quarter of a century later. I do remember that we gathered around the grave, and Bob placed Dad's ashes in a small hole in the ground. Later, a black granite stone was added, and, as my mum intended, we now have somewhere to visit. I'm pretty sure we all do whenever we're in the area.

I recently went to Glasserton with Keir. He wanted to know where his ancestors were buried. The sun was beating down as usual when we rounded the back of the church. Three older hikers sat on a wall, drinking tea from a thermos. One of them stood up as I approached. 'Are you the Hoof GP?' I couldn't help but laugh. 'Most people call me Graeme.'

I find myself missing my dad more and more as time goes on. Now that I have kids of my own, I wonder what he'd think. But, back then, my preoccupations were different.

My father was dead and buried and there were still questions to be answered.

# Chapter Eight

Whatever sense of relief or closure we might have felt from Dad's death, based on our acceptance of its inevitability, was short-lived. Any temptation we may have felt to get on with our lives was stalled by the obvious violence of his death, and the endless questions it raised.

He had been found floating, face-down in a river. We knew some of the facts of his death, but we didn't know why or how it had occurred. From Port William, some two hundred and forty miles away, it seemed inconceivable. Dad was a strong swimmer. It ran in his family. His uncle Billy had trained with the UK swimming team ahead of the Olympics. The only reason he hadn't competed was that he'd had rheumatic fever, and his father banned him from competing, believing it could kill him. Dad didn't train like Uncle Billy, but he was a keen and capable water baby. One of the more famous stories about Dad in our family relates to his swimming escapades at my christening. I was christened at Glasserton church in 1983, along with Robert, James and Kirsty. I think my parents thought they'd just get us all done at the same time. That must have been before Mum was pregnant with Susan. In typical fashion, Dad got slightly drunk at the christening, and decided he would visit his friends down on the shore, at Monreith. He reckoned he would swim there. He was wearing a suit at the time but kept that on, and emerged from the sea after about a mile, with a bottle of whisky.

He managed that, and yet he drowned in three or four feet of water.

He had been found in a river less than half a mile away from where Sarah lived. His shoes were on one side of the river, and he was on the other. His car window had been smashed. His face had a sizeable gash on it. His wallet had been found in Sarah's garden. They found letters to her in his car, apologising for going to the pub next door to her house and for upsetting her daughter. Far from being in a new relationship with her, it looked like he had been stalking her instead. And then we found out she had a partner who definitely wasn't my dad. Things were shifting again. Nothing was as it seemed. Dad's supposed life turnaround was unravelling before our eyes.

Hardly any of these details were mentioned by our Yorkshire family. One thing the English upper middle classes are effective at doing is closing ranks around the slightest whiff of scandal. Everyone there knew each other, and there was no mention of these facts to us at the time. We only found them out at the inquest into his death.

In our heads something sinister must have happened. Dad had been out in the woods walking. He had been stalking Sarah. There had been a confrontation. He was dead. They – his parents, everyone he knew there – were covering it up.

His best friend, Chris Inman, turned up at my grandparents house, drunk, saying Dad had been murdered, that it was something to do with drugs and someone he had confronted at university. Chris hadn't been at the funeral. Like Sarah, my grandfather had told him to stay away. Toxicology reports on Dad's blood showed he had the equivalent of a bottle of vodka in his system and a significant quantity of barbiturates, so Chris's claims didn't sound too wide of the mark. When questioned by the coroner, however, on what he thought had caused my dad's death, Grandad simply said, 'Drink'.

I wasn't allowed to attend the inquest. I realise now that I was too young, but that didn't help at the time. There were differing opinions about his state of mind, some of which came from policemen who had stopped him travelling at thirty miles per hour on the motorway and taken him to hospital. They said he'd 'looked like he had no one in the world.'

My aunt decided it was suicide, based on a note he'd written and never sent her.

The coroner recorded an open verdict. It would be fifteen years before we worked out the truth.

He left an incredible mess behind – emotionally and psychologically, but also legally and financially. Years beforehand he had written a simple will and left it in the care of his solicitor – a distant relation – in Newton Stewart, near Wigtown. Mum and Bob collected it from his office, after Dad's death. Everything was as expected – his estate had been left to his children, in trust, for seven years. This is common in Scotland. The seven-year gap protects you from having to pay large death duties.

Then another will turned up. It was with my grandparents' solicitors in Yorkshire, written on what looked like fax paper, in scrawled handwriting, even scruffier than my dad's usual scribble. It left the bulk of his estate to five people, a couple of whom he hadn't seen in twenty years. I distinctly remember Mum breaking the news. It was like a knife in the heart, a final act of spite. It wasn't about the money. It was the fact he didn't want his kids to have anything that got to me, after everything he'd put us through. I can't think of any word, other than hurt.

As with everything in Dad's life, his death was complicated.

The argument over the two wills hinged on where he'd been living when he died. My grandad argued that he was technically domiciled at The Knock, and that was his home address, even if he was away studying. Most students don't count their term time address as home, and Dad supposedly did have a term time address. He had been renting a room from one of his lecturers, but I think there had been some kind of falling out, which sounded par for the course. Among the witnesses at his inquest, one of his fellow students and a security guard said that they'd seen him sitting in his car on campus at odd hours, sometimes drinking. His car was full of unsent letters and clothes. It looked like he'd been living out of a Ford Mondeo.

After an extended legal back and forth, none of which we were really part of, they decided to accept the English will. The will made 'gifts' totalling £65,000 in cash to his friends and left the rest of his estate to his children. There was, of course, no sixty-five grand in cash. In fact, there was no cash at all. Everything was tied up in the farm. My grandmother still owned a thirty percent share in the business as part of the deal my dad and grandad made when they fell out and went their separate ways. The partnership agreement had been drawn up with the future in mind. If and when Granny died, Dad could buy her thirty percent share out for a nominal sum. Nobody could have foreseen it would be the other way round

The English will might have been the one that stood, but there was still room for manoeuvre. It was agreed Granny would buy Dad's share for a nominal sum. They'd write off as many of the bad debts to Dad as they could. She'd sell the farm and make sure we were all protected and get whatever inheritance we were due down the line. It seemed simple. It would prove to be anything but when it came down to it.

James was nineteen years old, capable, and he desperately wanted to take on the farm. Mum asked my grandparents if they would consider letting him carry it on, or at least get it into decent shape before they sold it. Their answer was a flat no. The farm sale went ahead some time in 1999. The Knock and the few fields Dad had kept from Barmeal went under the hammer.

We would never get our intended inheritance.

We would never get to live our farming dreams.

The sale of the farm was the end of a future both James and I had probably held in our heads since birth. Barmeal, The Knock, the herd of pure-bred Charolais – all of these things were embedded deep in the fabric of our family and what we stood for. And now what were we?

A couple of years later, when Dad's will was finally, fully resolved, we got a letter with a cheque from Sarah. She had been one of the executors of Dad's will, along with my aunt. There hadn't been much left from Dad's estate, so the £65,000 in legacy had wound up being only a couple of thousand pounds. The beneficiaries all had to agree to either take the money, or not. That was how it worked, according to the law. But they couldn't agree. Most of them wanted to decline the cash, but a couple of people believed that if my dad had willed it to them, they should have it. The solution the others reached was to agree to take the money and then to send us each a cheque. It was decent of them to do that and I'm grateful for their gesture. I just wonder what the ones who kept the money were thinking.

We received a few hundred pounds each and now I'd say

I'm grateful for that. I didn't receive any handouts in life and that's probably a good thing. I've had to make my own way in the world. Where would I have been if I'd been given a big cheque in my early twenties? I might not have made it to my thirties.

Farming was my life as a child. It was all I'd ever known. It could well have been all I ever got to know if we'd kept on the farm, but I had to take the path less travelled. Everything from that point on was about rebuilding. I had my family, and I had my health, but I'd lost what I thought was my vocation in life.

'He who wanders is not always lost' – it's an inscription I have tattooed on the underside of my right arm. It's a corruption of the line from J. R. R. Tolkien's *Lord of the Rings*, though I didn't know that when I got inked. If I'm asked, I usually tell people it's because I've lived in thirty-seven different houses, which is true, but that's not the real reason behind it.

I've tried a lot of different things in life. I explored anything I was interested in, anything I thought I might be good at. My problem was that I had no clue, no sense of what I really wanted, no preconceived plan, other than the one I'd been forced to abandon. And yet, maybe my big advantage in life was the *lack* of an agenda. My mind was always open going in, and in some ways that's priceless. I like the notion that you have to go walkabout, get out there, experience the big, wide world, let it wash over you, smooth your rough edges, make you stronger.

There's another saying I like to rattle off whenever I get the chance: 'Some of the best places I've found are when I've been lost'. Like the happy accidents you have, I think there's a lot to be said for chance, opportunity and good old-fashioned luck. But it's what you do with it that matters.

Dad's death and the events around it cast a long shadow. I've read that you don't get over grief, you just get better at managing it, and I think that's true. It becomes part of who and what you are, the backdrop to your life – which in my case, at this point, was going a bit off the rails.

# Chapter Nine

Perhaps unsurprisingly, my school attendance dropped off a cliff during this period of my teens. When they finally calculated the days that I'd actually gone to school, it came in at twenty-one percent. Quite an achievement. My brothers and Kirsty seemed to hold everything together at the time. Bob was at university in Edinburgh, James and Kirsty were at college and I was clearly in drift mode. I didn't know then that both Bob and James would drop out in the end. Nothing happens in a vacuum, and Susan had her own attendance problems that she dealt with in different ways.

I was trapped inside my own head, paralysed by anxiety, grief, and an undiagnosed mental health condition I'd never heard of. Sometimes I forget this stage of my life was pre-internet. You couldn't just google what was wrong with you then. Maybe that was a good thing.

There was no breakdown, no one big moment I can point to, where I lost it and walked out. It was just a slow descent in my attendance figures. I felt like I had no control over it, as if I were destined to keep repeating the same compulsive behaviours. It can't have helped that I didn't mix properly at school, and I didn't have many friends. I was fifteen years old, and I wasn't showing up where I should have been. I had zero focus, and at this stage, I had no one pushing me to do better. I suppose I'd dropped out by default, by simply not turning up when I was expected to. I was quietly quitting, before that was a thing. As the pressure from the school's management team eventually began to pile up in the weeks after my dad's death, I decided to leave while it was still my own idea.

It wasn't a tough decision for me. I think it was toughest on Mum. She didn't know what to think. Officially, you had to be sixteen to leave school. But I wasn't turning up anyway so I think they made some kind of exception; on the condition I remained in – or maybe that should be *got back into* – education. That left me with only a couple of viable options: the local college in Stranraer and a bus journey every day; or a move, to Dumfries, the largest town in the region and more than sixty miles away from where I'd been living in Port William with my mum. That meant leaving home, leaving behind everything and everyone I knew, and heading out into the big wide world. I chose the go-for-broke option, and a course in Information Technology at Dumfries and Galloway College of Technology.

I packed up my stuff and off I went. I would be living in halls of residence. I would be among new people, but I'd be away from the scrutiny and judgemental eyes. Here, I could reinvent myself. Here I could be me, whoever *he* was. I had one, solid link to my roots, however: Kirsty. She was studying at the college and staying in the same halls. We've always been close, as I've said. My auntie Loreen[2] always fondly remembers that when I was a

2. In The Shire, and in our family, an aunt or uncle isn't necessarily your literal aunt or uncle. They could be your cousin or a parent's cousin or no one's cousin at all and completely unrelated to you. Auntie Loreen is actually my mum's cousin. My uncle Chris, on the other hand, was my dad's best friend. Confused? Welcome to my world. Regardless of the genetic relationship, if they have the title bestowed upon them, they're your aunt or uncle.

kid, aged around maybe four or five years of age, she made me ... well, not sing for my supper exactly, but definitely *ask* for it.

'What do you want for dinner, Graeme?'

Kirsty replied instead. 'Chips!'

Auntie Loreen tried again. Kirsty spoke up again, this time with more gusto, as if she were an old-school British tourist who thinks that you can make a Spanish-speaking local understand you better just by saying something to them in English, even more loudly than the first time you said it.

'CHIPS!'

Auntie Loreen was having none of it. 'If you want chips, Graeme, you have to ask for them.'

That got me talking. Up till that point, I think Kirsty did most of my communicating when she was around. Now she was there in the background – like a safety valve, if the pressure at college got too much. Kirsty and I stayed in the same halls, on separate floors. Being there with my big sister was always going to give me a leg up in the social stakes. We were popular. We both stood out, because of our shared sense of humour, even if we mostly directed the gags at each other. Kirsty would go into my room and rub toothpaste all over the bed or maybe throw things round a bit, so I'd get revenge by emptying the ashtray all over the inside of her car.

Some of the jokes got a bit out of hand. I remember a bunch of us used to try to rob the local bakery – not my proudest memory. We'd sneak round the back when the night shift were at work and try to pinch a meringue. A group of us went there one night, singing 'I don't know but I've been told ...' from *Full Metal Jacket*. I nearly got caught and had to run from a man in white overalls with flour on his face. It was like being chased by Casper the Friendly Ghost.

Kirsty and I went shopping and on nights out together. She was on the girls' floor, so I'd come up with any excuse I could to visit. I'd be up there, trying to show off and get a bit of female attention, but I was younger, so I felt a bit like the hall pet. They were a bit of a gang up there. They'd be awake in the middle of the night talking and then decide they needed to go to the twenty-four-hour garage for supplies, in their pyjamas.

On one of those midnight runs, Kirsty was driving. She took a wrong turn and got lost somehow. The next day, Mum got a knock at the door from the police. Two officers told her that her car had been seen hanging around the local prison. The local constabulary suspected it was part of a drug smuggling plot, so they'd set up roadblocks. Unfortunately, they'd based the location of the roadblocks on Mum's home address. Meanwhile, Kirsty had driven back to college, in the other direction, evading justice. It was all sorted out pretty quickly when they realised what had happened.

None of my own antics made me popular with the senior residents – the adults put there to babysit us. I was in Kirsty's common room one day, demonstrating a trick I'd worked out. It was fairly simple. I swung from the doorway, making sure an audience was watching. Then, I threw my legs back between my arms, ready to flip over, land upright and welcome my applause. Somewhere in the middle I got stuck. I panicked and let go. I slammed into the door and a pain shot through my hand. I looked down at my fingers. I was pretty sure they weren't meant to go that far back.

In a bit of a state, I asked Ena, the senior resident, to help me. She shook her head. She'd seen enough of my pranks before. She wasn't about to be taken in. She told me she knew I was double-jointed, and not to be so stupid. Eventually, I went to

Accident and Emergency in the local hospital. The doctor there was Indian and couldn't quite understand me – the Scottish accent is known for being difficult at the best of times, and I wasn't making much sense. Every time he tried to touch my fingers I flinched and pulled my hand away. Eventually, we agreed on a solution, and he watched as I bent my own fingers back into place. It was excruciating. They still don't look quite right.

Although we messed about a fair bit, Kirsty did all her course work. I did none of mine. I had her there to support me, if I needed it, but I might as well have been on my own, with the freedom I suddenly had. I could come and go as I pleased. I could eat what I wanted, when I wanted, and as long as I could get in the door of my establishment of choice, I could live the life of a proper student; one over the drinking age – eighteen in Scotland – even though I wasn't old enough yet.

My old limitations, the things that had held me down, the guilt about my house and the farm and the state of everything, the cage I'd built for myself, all fell away. Yes, I lived in a one-size-fits-all box that could almost have been a cell, but so did everyone else staying in the halls. I had nothing to feel embarrassed about. We were all skint students. There was no material difference. It was all about personality. Everyone was busy trying things out, pushing their own boundaries, trying to figure out who they were.

Stripped of all the excess baggage, a new version of me began to emerge. I walked taller. I was more engaging. The new me had an answer for everything, and weirdly, people wanted to listen. I started hitting pubs and clubs. I met girls. And, for the first time, they were almost as interested in me as I was in them. Almost.

I was in one pub one night, talking to the landlord about joining the pool team. I must have been talented enough to be asked and maybe the compliment threw me a bit. That, and the alcopops I'd been throwing down my neck all night. I almost outed myself as being underage by asking if you had to be eighteen to join the team. The owner looked at me, considering this for a beat or two.

'That's a strange question for someone who comes in here all the time.'

I'd been a directionless mess only a few weeks earlier. Now here I was, with some kind of path in front of me. In some ways I had to embrace the mess. I was just about to turn sixteen. Everything felt shiny and new. I felt as though the less self-conscious I was, and the less I tried to keep the people around me happy, the more they seemed to like me. I lived in those halls for two and a half years and I can honestly say they were some of the happiest times of my life.

Dumfries is part of the bigger region of Dumfries and Galloway. D&G is a big area. Not in American terms, of course, but for the UK, it's a fair size. It's one of the largest regions in Scotland, but also one of the most underpopulated, unspoiled areas in the UK. Dumfries is really a small town in the countryside, built in distinctively red local sandstone. In many ways the culture is the same as my wee corner of Wigtownshire in the far west of the region. It's steeped in history, for one thing. It was home to Roberts Burns for the last years of his life, and, much earlier, it was a key location in the Wars of Scottish Independence. Robert the Bruce famously murdered John Comyn the Red in the town's Greyfriars Kirk, setting him on a collision course with Edward the Longshanks. Remember the formidable and unforgiving beardy English king in *Braveheart*? Yup, that's him.

It's kind of close in culture to The Shire, even if they are all townies. People start drinking at a fairly young age. Or they did in my day. The main reason seemed to be a lack of things to do, and we didn't have anything nearly as interesting as YouTube in those days.

When we went out in Dumfries, we sometimes got asked for ID, but there were plenty of places where the landlords happily looked the other way. On my eighteenth birthday I was finally legal. The world was – I felt – very much my lobster. I decided to celebrate by going on a pub crawl, armed with my provisional driving licence. No one could stop me now. And no one asked for my ID.

I think that must have been some kind of anti-climax. I decided not being ID'd was a bad thing and got myself thrown out of a pub, after starting a bit of an argument. I resolved to make my escape by jumping over a railing at the edge of the car park. The railing was about three feet high. If I'd thought about it for a second or two, I might have worked out the obvious: the railing was there for a reason. One second, I was at the top of a well-executed arc, like a leaping gazelle. The next, I was still dropping, further, then further ... I hit the ground hard, with my arm. It looked pretty bad, but luckily I'd landed in some generic, local council bushes, albeit in a heap. My night out was over.

The halls were three miles away and it was snowing. But I was incredibly drunk, and that meant I was bullet-proof. I began the walk to Heathhall, on the outskirts of town, fantasising about fluffy, white pillows. The halls were always roasting. All I really wanted was my warm bed. Common sense told me snow was cold, but I was tired and starting to have my doubts. My last memory is the blanket of snow beneath my feet and the comfort it seemed to offer.

I opened my eyes, stiffly, to a familiar room. My college cell. It was the morning after. The thickness of my head told me that. But how the hell had I got there? It took a bit of asking around, but I tracked down the culprits later in the day. Two of my college mates, Stuart and Martin, had been walking home, through the snow. I'm guessing they were better dressed for it, and maybe slightly less wasted than I was. They saw someone lying in the white stuff but kept on walking. That probably says more about Dumfries and Scottish drinking culture than I should probably dwell on. They were laughing because the guy lying in the snow looked a bit like me. A quarter of a mile further on, they were still talking about it. They decided it probably *was* me, and that they should probably turn back and rescue me from the warm, welcoming kiss of hypothermia.

Their decision *probably* saved my life.

The college tutors were all very supportive towards me. The head of the IT faculty was called Venus Caru. A pretty cool name. Venus was a tiny, driven, Indian woman with a lot of patience. She needed it. She made me feel welcome and comfortable in college. Not like school. But my attendance record was still grim.

The reasons were different, now. I was happier. I'd found my feet in Dumfries, but my world beyond the college had started to get in the way. I partied all the time. I wasn't studying hard enough. I wasn't studying at all, in fact. There were probably deeper reasons. At this point it had been less than a year since Dad died, so I was certainly processing everything that had happened, but I knew I couldn't use that as an excuse all my life. By the time I got to the end of my last term, I'd properly flunked my IT course.

I liked where I was, though, and student life suited me. I decided I was just on the wrong course and moved over to an HND (Higher National Diploma), the first two years of a Scottish degree in Photographic Science, at the George Street

School of Arts. I still lived in the same halls but now I was kept on a much shorter chain. The manager was called John Scott. He was probably in his mid-forties at the time – a real grown up. He was a nice guy, but very direct and he didn't put up with any nonsense. He probably needed to be that way. My new room, A1, was about four metres from his office. Probably just as well!

I think I might only have taken the photography course because my dad had what I thought was a really decent camera – a Minolta SLR. It's a random reason, but as good as any, really. I soon realised I loved photography. And I was pretty good at it, too. I had a feel for it. It felt like something of a vocation. The lecturers really lived their subject, and that was contagious. My attendance went up. I was proud of what I was doing. The only bad part was that a lot of our lessons were in the pub.

Around the same time, I got a job in Dumfries's most notorious nightclub: The Junction. Now there's a claim to fame. I still wasn't quite old enough to work behind the bar at this stage, so that was out, but I was a pretty good fit for PR work. My job was to get people in the door, by any means necessary. And I do mean *any* means. That usually meant approaching randoms in the street. So, to fill the place up, to get it buzzing, I concluded that the best strategy was to fill myself up, with anything I could find to get *me* buzzing. Not a long-term career strategy, but at the time, it seemed to have legs.

We'd get hammered at the start of each shift and take things we really shouldn't have. We'd drink cheap wine called Charmaine, which we lovingly christened Chateau Le Shit; Buckfast was yet to become a big thing. If you don't know what Buckfast is and you live in America, it's basically the Scottish equivalent of Four Loko – a fortified wine, with caffeine. Delicious.

Once we were sufficiently tanked up, we'd head into town. When we got there, we'd begin approaching anyone who looked like they were out for the night, or anyone who looked like they could be persuaded to stay out for the night. If we kept up the energy and the fun factor, it didn't feel like a chore. And one of the main perks of having to speak to people you don't know is that you get to speak to people you don't know – especially the ones you might want to get to know.

After we'd persuaded enough people to fill the place up, we'd finish for the night and then head out ourselves, hitting whatever club the collective mood demanded. We'd all be in a real state by then. For a while there was a trend for snake-eyed contact lenses. They disguised the state of everyone's pupils. We felt like we were living the dream in a lot of ways, with our fifty pence bottles of rocket-fuel wine. I must have lived like that for a good eighteen months. Not something I could do for the rest of my days, but formative. It taught me a lot, most of which I've probably forgotten, for obvious reasons. Some of the people I met then are still my best friends.

In the meantime, I'd moved out of my halls and into a small flat, with my then girlfriend, Karen. She was my first serious girlfriend. Karen was the receptionist in the club. She had dot tattoos on her knuckles. Each one represented something dodgy that had happened when she was younger.

I really thought I was in love.

# Chapter Ten

Karen and I split up on Christmas Eve, 2001. I reacted by getting drunk on blue WKD – a nasty artificially coloured alcopop that was hugely popular at the time. I didn't really sober up until the following March, and by that time I was well on my way to flunking my photography course. Surprise!

Being solidly inebriated for that amount of time takes work, not to mention money, but it can be done. First of all, you need either a group of friends who are actual alcoholics, or – and this is the approach I went with – three groups of friends. I had the friends from college. I had the friends from work at the club. And then I had another sort of miscellaneous group of friends, who really weren't a group at all. I just batched them together, to make sense of them in my own head.

A month or two into this period I'd moved into a house with a guy called Andy. Andy was an odd character. He was a short guy with a high-pitched voice, but he had a real way with girls. He just seemed to know what to say to get talking to anyone, and most of the time *anyone* seemed to be models. Our house was a party zone. Something happened every night of the week and everything seemed to be going at a hundred and ten miles an hour. Drinking does that. I remember sitting in a bar, down by the river one afternoon. The sun was out. I was hammered. I hadn't a single care in the world.

'Are you not supposed to be at work in half an hour?' someone asked.

Home was on the other side of the river. The nearest bridge was a good half hour walk away. The next thing I remember is being in the water, fully clothed, fighting the cold current, to the sound of whoops and cheering from the beer garden I'd just left. I was in the Dock Park, in the centre of Dumfries. Down there, the River Nith is a hundred yards across. I was terrified. Was I mimicking the folly of my dad? More than once, I thought I'd made my last, stupid mistake. Entertaining my audience might have been the only thing that got me through.

My run came to an end for a couple of reasons, and James Devlin was one of them. He's a sound guy, James, but very self-disciplined. He loved a laugh and a drink, but he was a bouncer on the doors of Chancers – Dumfries's other notorious nightclub. He once threw a guy out for being too drunk. The guy came back with five friends. A one-sided fight ensued. James was charged with five counts of Grievous Bodily Harm.

We were out and about one warm spring day. I was telling him about whatever had happened the night before, which I'm pretty sure would have involved some drunken heroics on my part.

'When was the last time you were sober?' James asked.

'I honestly don't know,' I said.

'Look, Graeme. You're going to stop drinking or I'll kick the shit out of you.'

It seemed a fair deal. I think I must have realised at that point that he was genuinely worried about me. Maybe the fact I registered that someone else was alarmed about my drinking was a reality check, with my dad's history with the bottle. I never wanted to be that guy.

The other reason was my flatmate, Andy. I'd never really thought too hard about how he managed to do what he did, money wise. He was a chef, and not particularly well paid, but he always had money for booze and drugs. Andy was the registered tenant, so it was his name on the lease. I paid him my rent money and he was supposed to pay it on to the landlord.

Yup. You can see it coming. Can't you? I wish I had. I realised something was wrong only when we were about to be evicted. He'd spent all my rent money on drink and drugs and now we were about to be out to the street. That was pretty bad on its own. Then he decided the best way to deflect any blame was to turn it all around. In his version of events, I stole all his money and that was why he was now homeless. What hurt the most wasn't that he turned out to be a liar. That I could have handled. What really got to me was that my so-called friends believed him. I never protested my innocence, and I regret that now. A couple of them told me how 'out of order' I had been. There was no showdown. I was hurt that they thought I was a dickhead who had stolen money, or hadn't paid money, or whatever. I wouldn't even have minded so much if they had been *his* friends, but I'd introduced them to each other, and now they'd all turned on me.

I'm not proud of what I did next. But I was nineteen and cornered, so I thought *fuck them all*, got on a bus and went home to Wigtown. I'm not sure what happened to my clothes or anything else I owned at the time. As it turned out, I'd be travelling light soon afterwards anyway.

Back in Wigtown, I worked hard to save some cash. That wasn't without its own hazards though. I was working behind the bar in The Ploughman, a local hotel named after a scandalous book titled *Wigtown Ploughman: Part of His Life*, by controversial local author, John McNeillie. I was the only person working at the hotel most evenings, so you'd think I'd be safe enough in that situation. One night, there were only three couples in the bar. It was dead. I was 'busy' polishing a wine glass. What could possibly go wrong? It's not like I was trying to do some kind of Tom Cruise-style *Cocktail* routine. I can do that stuff, by the way, but these days I like to do it in the kitchen, for the kids. As I turned the glass in my hand, the stem snapped. Blood spurted out of my arm. I remember screaming, 'My arm!'

The couples sat there, just looking at me. No one moved. Then a woman threw up in her hand. I managed to cover the wound with a towel. I needed someone sensible. I walked, as calmly as I could, to the Co-op, the local supermarket just over the road. Looking for someone sensible. I was lucky. Davie was there. He ran me to the local hospital in Newton Stewart, while I held my arm tight.

When we got to the hospital, the nurse asked me to uncover the damage. 'I don't think I can do that,' I told her. 'We need to take a look,' she said, in the way only someone who deals with nervous customers can.

I uncovered my arm. Blood arced into the air.

'Cover it up!' she shouted.

I'd originally told them I'd accidentally slashed my arm. 'Filleted it, more like,' was the nurse's final analysis, once she'd managed to stem the blood flow enough to actually get a look.

I decided then that I needed to get away, somewhere sunny, somewhere I could party, away from everything I'd left in Dumfries. I was going with my friend Gary. Gary's the best presented heterosexual man I've ever met. He's unbelievably well organised – the kind of person who has a file on everything, with poly pockets, and an indexing system. It's no surprise that he works in a desk job for the police these days. He's the soundest, most buttoned-up guy I know. Back then, he had very good-looking girlfriends.

Ayia Napa, in Cyprus, was the place to be. It had its own music scene, its own club culture – nothing like the small-town rip-off in Dumfries. It was the new Ibiza.

By now, you might have worked out that organisational skills are not my superpower. I had booked the holiday on a wave of optimism. Minor details weren't going to faze me. What did it matter if I didn't have a passport yet? I soon realised I wasn't going to get my passport on time. The booking couldn't be cancelled, so I gave it to another friend. The day after my flight left, with someone else in my place, my passport arrived in the post.

After all that, I was even more determined to go. I booked and paid for the next flight I found. We were in Ayia Napa for a week, and it was all the holiday I'd ever dreamed about. I'd been to Greece a few times by that point. Mum had started going every year, and had always taken us along, but this was different. Ayia Napa felt like the centre of the universe at that specific point in time. We drank a lot, slept on the beach hungover and met girls. It was all I really wanted to do at that age.

Three of the girls we met were called Kelly, Laura and Allison. They had all come on holiday together. None of us had any idea how much of an impact two of them would later have on my life, in very different ways.

Allison and I really clicked, but nothing happened between us. Don't get me wrong. I really wanted it to, but she just seemed to be in a different league. At the end of the holiday, we exchanged numbers, and a month later she invited me to stay with her. I was keen, thinking it might be a date.

It wasn't.

Allison lived in Preston, a city in Lancashire, in the Northwest of England. It looked nothing like anywhere in Scotland – all red brick houses and tight-knit streets. It was built on industry; textile mills, the kind of thing that drove the industrial revolution. I didn't know it, but I was very near the place where my great, great grandad, Robert Parker had been, more or less, when he was sold to the mill. Preston seemed like a sprawling metropolis compared with anywhere else I'd spent any time. It was full of bars, clubs and coffee shops; everything I was pretty sure I needed in my life. Like Ayia Napa, it was everything Dumfries wasn't, everything home wasn't. I belonged there. Allison took me to a sleek club called Mood in the city centre. She knew the manager, Kenny, and we got talking. By the end of the night, he had offered me a job.

I had only gone to Preston for the weekend, after meeting someone on holiday, and now I had a job offer in a busy bar in a happening city. Kenny only needed to make the offer once. I pretty much ripped his arm off in saying yes to it. Kenny was the general manager, and I would be the bar manager. By this time, I had progressed through PR work to running a few bars in Dumfries, so job-wise it was more of a natural progression than a leap into the unknown. But it was big. In terms of life changes, it was *massive*.

I moved down pretty much immediately. I booked myself into a hotel for the first three weeks, just to get settled in Preston. In the short time I worked there I got to know Kenny well. He was Scottish, a sort of older version of me, who smoked. By the end of it, he was more like an older brother. Mood was busy; packed out five nights a week, with a queue that stretched around the block and back again. In my head it might as well have been Studio 54 in New York or China White in London. I was on another planet, but I was home.

We took £50,000 a week. The hardest part was keeping the drinks coming quickly enough. We were out of our depth, and I loved it. I made friends with the bar team quickly. Disco Dave and Chris really stand out from that time. At the end of the busy nights, we'd gather up our tips and head to a local curry house. We'd already be well lit behind the bar. Chris and I would have a pint of orange juice handy, mixed with any white spirit we could find. 'How's your orange juice?' we'd ask each other. We'd secrete our drinks in the glass wash, on top of the ice machine. We did what we had to, to maintain our energy levels.

Preston has a big Asian population. That means you can get some seriously decent Asian food, and that meant curries for us. We'd stuff our faces on the hottest we could find, washing it all down with Kingfisher lager. The restaurants always seemed to be dark, with a ruby-coloured backdrop. The chefs passed plates between them, like a band of pirates. In my head they have missing teeth and dirty chef whites. I know for a fact they were off their heads on speed.

I can feel my stomach start to rumble just thinking about the sweet spice, the cold beer and the satisfaction of a job well done. I remember it feeling like the place I most belonged in the world, then. Fifteen of us would go there every night. There were no cliques, and there never seemed to be any in-fighting. It sounds cheesy but it really was a sort of extended family.

Mood is also where I met Beth. She would change my life too, in the best and worst ways.

# Chapter Eleven

Beth worked in Mood. Everyone called her 'the Ice Bitch'. It would have been massively misogynistic, were it not for the fact that the women there called her that too. She was bad tempered, spiky, and never had a nice word to say to anyone – especially me.

Of course, I chased her. There was more than a hint of masochism there. Maybe I thought she was right to diss me, but if I could win her round, it would prove something. Who knew? I threw caution to the wind, and the chase led to a nine-year, on–off relationship, and the birth of my beautiful daughter, Maddie. That's something I can only ever be grateful for. But Beth was a mess. She was mixed-up. She was trouble. She was a lot like me.

Our relationship was destructive from day one. There was me, not knowing I had bipolar disorder, trying (and often failing) to get my life under control, trying to figure myself out. When I told her about losing my dad, she told me the same thing had happened to her. I felt like I had found someone I could talk to. Someone who could understand me and what I was going through. A soulmate.

A few weeks after that conversation, we were out in the car, on a road I'd never been on before. Beth turned to me and said, 'My dad lives down that road. Would you like to meet him?' She asked as if it were the most normal question in the world, but it felt like a trap door had just opened beneath me. Maybe I'd heard her wrong. Maybe the person who'd died was another relative. Maybe I'd been drunk and imagined the whole conversation. I can still remember the name of the street her dad lived in. It's funny, the details that stay with you decades later.

We seemed to live in a perpetual red mist. Nothing ever felt clear or certain. Beth was nineteen. She had lost her brother, four years before we got together. She described him as her best friend. I know how close I was to my siblings growing up. Being one of two must create a special bond. She told me he had been run over by a bus. It had been a freak accident. Much later I heard another version of the story; he had deliberately jumped in front of the bus. It's no wonder she was mixed up. She was nursing a lot of anger. And, I suppose, if the person you trusted the most in the world can just abandon you like that, how do you ever trust anyone again?

We'd been together for a year when she fell pregnant, but she had a miscarriage soon afterwards. Rather than bring us closer together, it seemed to make things worse. We were both sad, and I wanted to be supportive. I wanted to help. If I could have taken the pain away, I would. I just don't think I stood a chance. Beth was so determined to push anyone who cared about her away then. We were already prone to conflict, but if our arguments were surreal before, we'd have given Salvador Dali pause for thought now. Conversations routinely descended into blistering rows, that in the end, I couldn't untangle. We eventually agreed to end things. I needed to go home, and I needed to get my head together. I had no idea I was both bipolar *and* depressed. Looking back, my own behaviour must have been strange. I was probably hard to deal with. Now, I can think clearly, but then I never seemed to be able to.

So, at least part of the blame fell on me.

It's important to say there were good parts – of course there were. I'm not a complete masochist. It was as exciting as it was fiery. We were both as wild as each other at times and we had lots of laughs. We shared a reckless streak and egged each other on to do daft things – like the time we stole her stepdad's jeep and went out for the day, feeling like proper adults.

When I got back to Scotland after the split, one of Bob's best friends, Dave Old, took me under his wing. I'd never spent that much time with Dave, being a bit younger than him, but he was just coming out of a marriage, and I was newly single. People tend either to settle down young in Wigtownshire, or they go off to study. There isn't much of an in-between. It was natural that as a couple of single guys, Dave and I became partners in crime. We were on a bit of a mission to cause as much mayhem as possible. We got into all sorts of scrapes over the course of the next nine months, and Dave is now my best friend in the world.

One dull Tuesday night, we went to The Pub, in Stranraer (yes, it's actually called 'The Pub'). We arrived sober and should have had our sensible heads on. I ran my eyes along the gantry at the back of the bar we were in and spotted the radioactive green absinthe bottle. If you haven't encountered it, absinthe is lethal. It's the stuff Van Gogh was drinking when he cut off his left ear. A challenge formed in the space between my ears. I decided to see how many shots I could drink.

In most bars, for reasons of common sense, there's a one shot maximum on absinthe. I managed to down twelve of them. My main memory is what happened to my mouth. Full sentences were the first thing to go. I'd start lucidly, then I'd get stuck.

My tongue melted and my speech slowed to a slur as the night progressed. Dave told me I threw up twice on the way home. I stayed in his spare room, but he wasn't daft. He left the door ajar so he could keep an eye on me. I think that was because he was genuinely worried that I might die, and not because he wanted to watch me sleeping.

Dave was only four years older than me, but he was a proper adult. He lived in a nineteenth century, stone cottage he'd bought and renovated himself. He'd managed to fall asleep, during his vigil, but woke to a noise in the night and shot out of bed. He was greeted by the sight of me, standing in the middle of his spare room, peeing on the floor. Worried that I might permanently stain the oak floorboards, and that there was a danger of everything running down through the gaps to the ceiling underneath, he ran for a bucket. He still likes to remind me how he had to chase me round the room, while I did an impression of a wonky sprinkler system. He finally caught me as I was finishing my stream and claims he only had a couple of drops to show for his trouble.

'You bastard.' That was all he said, from the other end of the hallway, when he heard me stirring the next morning. I don't remember any of it, and I hope it stays that way.

I got my old job back at The Ploughman and worked hard, when I wasn't partying with Dave. We talked about going away travelling. Being in Wigtownshire, it just seemed like the thing to do. Eventually, we decided on Canada. Dave had always fancied it, and I was happy to tag along. More wandering. More self-discovery. We'd managed to save some cash and had booked the flights to get us out there. It was going to be big. Canada wasn't going to know what had hit it. We were all set.

Then Beth got back in touch.

Dave ended up flying to Canada by himself. We'd made a deal that if things didn't work out with Beth, I would head out and join him there. Dave ended up staying in Canada for three and a half months of what turned out to be awesomeness, for him. I sometimes wonder what might have happened if I'd made it out there myself. The pair of us might still be there. But it didn't work out that way. I went to Lancaster, where Beth was living by then, to see if we had any sort of relationship to salvage. I ended up living there, with Beth and her mum and stepdad. I also got a new job. I was running The Royal Hotel, a six-hundred-year-old, white-washed inn, with stone walls and exposed brick and beams. It was in the equally olde-worlde village of Heysham, with its chocolate-box stone cottages and picturesque coastal scenery. Things were going fairly smoothly, in one sense. I was doing well at work, but everything else was getting more complicated in my personal life.

Beth fell pregnant again. Our daughter, Maddison, was born in the Royal Lancaster Infirmary at 2:57 a.m. on the 5th of December 2004. She was six weeks premature and weighed in at four pounds and two ounces, but she was okay. In fact, she was the most perfect little thing I had ever seen in my life. I remember the pink hat she wore in the hospital, her face all squashed up. She was very suddenly everything in my life. I get that all parents say that, but it was, and is, true. The day after Maddie was born, Dave drove all the way to Lancaster to see her. I was amazed that anyone would go that far out of their way, but Dave has always been that kind of presence in my life.

I was twenty-two years old, and Beth and I should never have been together. Our relationship was still a disaster, but we had produced this one, tiny, beautiful thing. I counted all her fingers and toes. They were so small, I wanted to make sure none of them had been forgotten. She had dark, dark hair, loads of it, and olive brown skin. She had to stay in hospital for two weeks. We had a room in the neonatal unit, and we lived there until she was able to go home.

I couldn't be there to take her home from the hospital because I had to work to support us. I felt like such a failure because I couldn't do just this one thing. And then, by coincidence, I found myself outside a Waterstones a few minutes' walk from my place of work, while on a quick break, at just the right time to see Beth – driving home from the hospital. I had somehow made it to be part of this moment in my life, and more importantly, in Maddie's.

She wasn't a great sleeper. I used to run the tip of my finger down her nose, slowly, so that her eyes closed in time with the movement, and then she'd drift off. If that didn't work, I'd lie on the couch and put her on my chest. She'd curl up into a ball and I'd stare at the ceiling. That worked every time.

She laughed at a really young age. I remember her first steps in her granny and grandad's living room, wobbling on the wooden floor from the TV to the couch, with all four of us watching intently. Her first words weren't what we expected. She did start off with the standard 'Mama' and 'Dada' to begin with, so maybe I should count that, but the next thing she said was a bit fruitier, and that was our fault. Beth was driving one day when we were out, and she had to hit the brakes to avoid something.

'Ah!' she exclaimed.

'Shit,' Maddie responded.

It was a word Beth had apparently tried to stop using for a while.

We had some laughs and some good times, but nothing was ever consistent in our relationship. We'd be getting along well and then the most extreme fights would come seemingly out of nowhere. It was difficult. I wasn't perfect, but Beth was hard work and sometimes I think she wanted it that way. It felt as though she'd change her opinion just to keep me guessing. Or she'd base her opinions on the opposite of what she thought I wanted. I never knew where I stood, or how she was going to react to anything. I walked on eggshells, constantly.

I'm sure I was no angel. I was up and down a lot. I worked tiring, split shifts, mornings and nights. Beth was studying at university, so practically, it made sense in a lot of ways. It meant I could look after Maddie during the day, while she was out. But Beth decided it wasn't fair for me to be in her parents' house while she was elsewhere. That meant when she was out, *I* had to be out, even though I was looking after our daughter. I tramped the streets for hours, in all weathers, to fill the time until Beth returned from classes. Even worse, so did Maddie. I killed time hanging around Lancaster and Morcombe.

Morecombe is a seaside town that opens out onto a bay; it's an old-school English resort, with a promenade. It had seen better days then (and is not much improved today). It could be the calmest day everywhere else, but the wind would howl round us there. I'd have Maddie all cosied up in a sort of sleeping bag in the pram while I spent hours and hours just walking up and down, aimlessly.

Various family members came down to see Maddie (and me, of course) after she was born, but I have very few memories of those visits now, other than feelings of intense discomfort. There was nowhere for anyone to stay, and they were probably worried about my circumstances, so it was all a bit awkward. I do remember Mum coming down to see us once, and I had to meet her in some forgotten 1960s hotel, rather than in Beth's parents' house. The place had clearly been a nice house once, before someone had shoved a cheap conservatory on the back of it. The chairs were bright red and gold. It was naff but it was off the streets. God knows what Mum thought.

We kept up this bizarre routine for two years. I don't know why I put up with it, but I did. If I ever saw anyone in that position now, I'd demand to know why they were tolerating it, but it's often hard to see how unhealthy a situation is when you're the one living it.

During the day, I felt as though I was on my own all the time; like I was a single parent. A homeless, single parent. I can remember walking up and down the same streets, taking longer strides, doing anything to make the walk slower and the time pass more quickly. I felt like the lowest of the low, unable even to provide a warm space for my baby daughter.

The one person I got on really well with was Beth's stepfather, Alan. Alan was an interesting character. Like me, he managed hotels. He had given up drinking years before because, by his own account, drinking turned him into 'an arsehole'. Alan was no match for Beth and her mum though, and he was probably scared to take my side in front of them. Beth's manipulation meant that I couldn't talk openly to anyone else, either. Even if I phoned home, or talked to Kirsty, Beth kicked off and we'd argue. The story about her dad should have been a giveaway, but I was desperate to believe her. I wanted her to be genuine. I knew she was a mess because of the death of her brother, so I felt as though she was owed a chance. As time went on, however, I began to see she had her own version of reality. Before I knew where I was, the toxicity in our relationship had seeped out into my wider world; a world that was now shrinking rapidly as a result of my enforced withdrawal from it.

I appreciate that Beth doesn't have the space here to reply, and that everything's subjective. We all have our own version of events, and I really didn't help matters at times – especially when I used my frustration to justify lashing out at others.

A year after Maddie was born, I was out in Preston city centre. I had properly hit the hard stuff. (Yes, I know. Here we go again.) I was in full-on, happy, goofy, potentially annoying, drunk Graeme mode. I've never been a violent drunk. That's not what I'm about. I'm not someone who goes looking for fights, but if someone attacks me, I'll defend myself, and I'm a stubborn, overconfident drunk, instead. I've climbed lampposts. I've played stupid drinking games that involved seeing what you could steal from a pub and then leave on their doorstep. I am, essentially, a benign nuisance.

On this occasion, in Preston, I was thrown out of a club.

My first mistake was in consuming too much alcohol, with so much going on in my head. I was a mess. That's why they threw me out. But I was now in full-on, pedantic asshole mode. I stood in the doorway, refusing to move.

'This is private property,' one of the bouncers said. Poor guy. How could he have known he was dealing with an idiot like me?

'It isn't. It's a public thoroughfare,' I said. Then I backed up my point by demonstrating. I put my foot in the doorway and then removed it. Then I did it again, and again, back and forth, like some demented version of the hokey cokey. Eventually the bouncers realised there was no reasoning with me and called the police. They turned up, took one look at me, and decided that the best thing they could do was put me in a cell until I was sober enough to function, without getting my head kicked in by a bunch of gorillas in black puffa-jackets. The next thing I can remember is gulping a huge intake of breath and peering up at four nervous looking policemen. One of them had a packet of bourbon creams (a sort of chocolate sandwich of a biscuit, or cookie, depending on where you live). He was waving them in my face, as if I were a toddler he was trying to coax out from under a table.

There was blood everywhere, and judging by the look of the cops, it was mine. They took some time to calm me down and explain. They had been walking me from my cell to a finger printing area when I collapsed in a heap. On the way down, I had bounced off a tiled corner, face first. Blood oozed from the point where my eye socket joined my nose. The biscuits were to try to get my blood sugar up.

Once they were happy that I was calm and they'd bandaged me up, they drove me to the hospital, where I found out I'd fractured my eye socket. Then they gave me a lift home. I was lucky not to be charged with a crime. I still have the scar. It runs up the bridge of nose and over my eyebrow and looks more like a wrinkle these days. It glows red when I'm too hot.

And it's certainly not my only war wound.

I've hurt myself A LOT over the years. To paraphrase Edward Norton's character in *Fight Club*, I never wanted to die without any scars. They're evidence of a life lived. The fractured eye socket in Preston is one of several injuries I've inflicted on my face.

I don't know how many times I've broken my nose, but it's a lot. A few years ago, I was hoof trimming on my own, before Craig came on board to help. My cattle crush was set up in a pen and there was a lot of straw on the floor. Farmers traditionally use it as bedding for cows, although these days, a lot of cows have actual mattresses. Some of them even have waterbeds. On this occasion the straw helped break my fall. A waterbed might have been nicer.

I had been gluing a block on to a back hoof, and, as I always do, I left it to set. Suddenly I was on the ground. I thought I had tripped over a bucket. You have to laugh in that situation. Or at least I do, because it happens so regularly. No point overthinking the fact that you're lying injured on the cold, concrete floor of a darkened cow shed – that never helps. I struggled to my feet and looked around, trying to get my bearings. There was blood. A *lot* of blood. My face felt hot. There was no pain. I did the self-conscious thing and checked for an audience to my folly. There wasn't one. That was good but I could smell and taste blood. I realised I must have blacked out. Then I felt the pain in my nose. I checked it in the mirror on the pick-up. I was bleeding heavily from both nostrils. My nose had changed shape. It was badly swollen, and worse than that, pointing in the wrong direction.

This wasn't good.

It took a week for the memory of what actually happened to return. I'd wandered round to the front of the cow, and she'd swung her head up into my face. It was like putting my head in front of a train. There was no give. I can remember the hot feel of her hair, even now.

I still finished the hoof trimming that day. That probably sounds stupid, but my main concern was not having to come back to finish her feet. Once I was done, I washed up, packed up for the day, hitched on the crush and headed to Accident and Emergency at the nearest hospital, in Dumfries. After a bit of a wait and some seriously bad coffee, the doctors checked me over.

I looked a real state, with a busted nose and two black eyes slowly beginning to emerge. The A&E docs decided they didn't have the expertise to reset my nose, so they sent me home, with a plan to come back later in the week and get everything straightened back up. I was in Dumfries, looking like I'd been badly banged up. This was an opportunity I couldn't miss.

Kirsty lives near to Dumfries, in a town called Dalbeattie. I had to pass there on my way home anyway. Once I'd been discharged, I got back in the pickup and made my way over to her house. She'd had a falling out with a family member, so I used this knowledge to my advantage, because why wouldn't I?

I arrived at Kirsty's door and let myself in, with my phone camera switched on. I shouted to her, and she greeted me by calling me a name. When she finally saw me, her eyes widened. She'd never make a good poker player. I said the family member's name, along with a couple of expletives, and I let Kirsty's brain fill in the blanks. She covered her face and screamed. In her head, I'd met this guy, had words with him and then received an absolute kicking for my troubles. I'd stood up for her and taken a panelling. I watched as her reaction turned to horror, then rage-filled tears, and finally, laughter when I fessed up. Then she started to hit me. Then she realised she really shouldn't do that because of the state I was in! I filmed it all and put it in a very early YouTube video. You can still find it if you go back far enough in the archives.

I had to walk around with my comically wonky nose for a week, before returning to hospital to get it reset. They put me to sleep. I was grateful for the rest. It's still the best sleep I've ever had, so much so that when I later booked myself in privately for a vasectomy, I paid extra to get put under general anaesthetic. They told me that when the swelling went down, my nose would be straight. It wasn't. It *was* much straighter, but it wasn't the fine example it had been. There are things in life you never appreciate, until they're gone. Nose straightness is definitely one of those things, along with good teeth and a hairline that stays still over the years. I missed my straight nose, but I didn't have a lot of time to worry about it. I was too busy injuring myself again.

A month or so after my nose was reset, I went mountain-biking. It's something I did pretty seriously for a while, and still like to do when I can. I love the thrill of the downhill, the speeds you can reach, the different obstacles each course throws at you. I was getting fitter. I was starting to grow in confidence. I was taking greater risks as time went on. I picked up a few bruises along the way, usually by flying down a hill and colliding with a tree trunk. I'd seen other people pick up worse. It seemed a fair price to pay.

On this particular Sunday I was out with my brother-in-law. We had hit the trails on the edge of the Galloway hills. We were on the black run – a stretch that dishes out some punishing technical climbs over rocks, with the dangling carrot of some epically fast downhills. I love that run to this day. The sun was shining, we were up high, surrounded by greenery, sweeping our way down curving tracks that cling to the side of the hills, past tree trunks and the ever-present possibility of a rapid, crunching halt.

It was a good run. Thirty-three kilometres in, half a kilometre from base, I cycled ahead into the fast section at the end of the trail. I felt good. I was pleased with my performance. I cut a corner between two trees, over a three-foot drop. From there the trail goes into a tighter corner. I was riding a hard tail. I had suspension on the front of the bike but nothing on the back. I was mechanically attached to the pedals, with pegs. That means you can go faster, but freeing your feet from the pedals is more difficult. I turned, expecting the bike to absorb the blow of the drop. My hands never left their grips and the whole bike came with me. I remember gravel and grit, and earth pushing up into my face and along my teeth, as if it was trying to rub my features out.

'Your face is fucked,' was the first thing I heard from my brother-in-law. I couldn't see anything because of all the blood.

The laceration ran from the original police station scar above my eyebrow, down one side of my nose, over my top lip, and down my bottom lip to my chin. One side of my face was disconnected along that line. There was nothing they could do in Dumfries. The damage I had done was too severe. They tried to flush the wound out, but they couldn't let the skin dry out, so they stapled my face together. There were student doctors there, looking on. I was quite the case.

'That's the right side of the jaw you can see exposed,' the teaching consultant said.

They wouldn't let me see myself in a mirror. I kept asking, and they kept pretending to forget. When Ashley arrived, I got her to take a photo. They wouldn't let me see it in case I went into shock. I was taken to Glasgow, and straight to a plastic surgeon. Ashley said she was amazed I still had teeth. She could see them through the holes in my face.

In Glasgow, there were at least six people around the bed, taking my details.

'You've broken your nose,' one of the surgeons said.

'Yeah,' I replied, 'that was a few weeks ago.'

They looked at each other. An awkward silence passed.

'Well, you've broken your nose again.'

The photos are still frightening. They show a man with life-changing injuries. And yet today, you'd hardly know it happened. I still have a loss of feeling round my nose. Sometimes, when I drink, it pours out of my mouth. That's not just when I'm drunk either. But the scars are conveniently placed. The lines more or less blend in with the ones that were already there. It helps that I have a beard most of the time and I was lucky. So lucky, in fact, that one of the first things they did in the hospital was restraighten my nose. It now looks as straight as it ever has.

I've been fortunate that the scars on the outside have always healed well, but the emotional wounds have always taken a lot longer to mend. There would be plenty more to come.

# Chapter Twelve

Unsurprisingly, Beth was far from impressed with my overnight accommodation in Preston, and the state of my face when I returned. But we moved past the incident, and the issues caused by living with her parents, when we eventually got our own house.

I quit my job at The Royal Hotel and went for a total change of career. I got a job as a welder, making cattle floats and trailers. It was a change of hours. It meant that I would have more time to spend with Maddie. Being a dad was priority number one. My own dad did nothing but work when I was very young. He was always there, but even when his mental health declined, and he sat around the house for hours on end, he was distant, unavailable. Always thinking about the next big plan, always trying to talk to Mum about whatever *he* wanted to do.

He never ever really spent any quality time with us kids. He never took a holiday or took us anywhere if it wasn't linked to work. The one time I remember him doing anything we wanted to do, he took us to a leisure centre, to go swimming. But we only went because a bunch of Russian students were going, and when we got there the pool had shut for the day, because of a fire alarm. He spent half an hour doing his best 'don't you know who I am' act, trying to impress the Russians. It certainly didn't impress the leisure centre staff. I enjoyed spending time with him working but he was never really present. He always seemed to be in his own head.

I was determined I would be a different kind of father.

Beth and I talked through my job change and agreed it was worth trying. I'd give it two years, and if it didn't work out, or if I wasn't happy, I'd go back to running pubs. There was a lot I enjoyed about welding. I loved the process. There's a real art to a good weld. I was MIG welding and laser profiling – using a plasma laser to cut through metal. The gas and the electric current flowing through the metal you're working on heats the welding wire and allows you to stitch everything together. It's consuming. You can get lost in that, and in the process of making concise, clean welds.

The best thing about the place was the people. Working in a factory atmosphere meant a real sense of camaraderie. Some of the guys I worked with were real characters. There was Mal, an Asian guy who always had a smile on his face and shuffled about like a short-sighted wombat; Jim, the guy who took me under his wing, a gruff, seasoned factory worker, but a lovely guy who made you feel like a friend from the very beginning; and Glen, who seemed like he was seven feet tall. Glen was obsessed with hygiene and always had a comb for his hair, ready to restrain any wayward locks. He worked with metal, and that's an oily, filthy job. Any time he picked something up, he lifted some paper and wiped his hands afterwards. He was so big he could have been a WWE wrestler, but he was a big softie when he worked with me.

I bought a motorbike to get back and forth to work. There was a real culture around that, in my job. There were older guys with bigger bikes that could really move, and I gained a new respect for welding, something I'd seen Davie do but had never really appreciated. I would use those skills later on, but back then I grew bored.

Two years to the day I started working in the factory, I left. I enjoyed my time there, but working in metal fabrication all the time, for someone else, wasn't for me. I went back to work for my old employers, Mitchells of Lancaster. They were a fairly big hospitality group and owned The Royal Hotel, along with lots of other pubs. They knew something about what I was capable of and how dedicated I had been to my former role at The Royal, so they put me in charge of ... a windmill.

The Windmill Tavern was a gastropub, new to the company, and a new start for me. It was a place that would give me a lot of memories and teach me a great deal about myself. As the name suggests, it was an old windmill – a white tower, capped with the black wooden box that would have turned with the sails when they were still there. It's thought to have been the second tallest of its kind in England and reputedly dates back to 1778. The buildings that surround it are typical of the traditional villages you find in the north of England, with ramshackle brick walls and black painted windows, but on the inside, there was a nice touch of modernity.

It was also our home. The restaurant was in the base of the windmill and the surrounding corn stores. We lived on the upper five floors. It was quirky. That's always been a good thing for me. The only slightly annoying thing was that none of the furniture fitted. The walls were round, but nothing else was. I made the most of the opportunity and started to mould the place into what I thought it could be.

I turned into a bit of a foodie in the time I was there. I've always had an obsessive streak, but now I could turn it to my full advantage. I went after awards. I wanted the best of everything for the place: good food, quality cask ales and an atmosphere that tied it all together. My team were all young, enthusiastic and hungry to be the best at what they did.

The head chef was a guy called Danny Brannan. He was and still is a seriously good chef. We're still good friends today. We had a similar drive and work ethic. We were both very serious about what we wanted to achieve with The Windmill, but that didn't mean we couldn't have some good laughs along the way.

The days were long but that didn't matter. The restaurant didn't open until noon but there was always a lot of prep to do. I'd start with the chefs at 8 a.m. I'd bring Maddie downstairs with me, and she'd sit on the stainless-steel kitchen counters, watching the commotion. We'd try out the food for the day and she'd get involved. She'd try anything the chefs gave her. It maybe sounds odd, but I remember being proud of how adventurous she was, trying all these new things.

Danny and I would work until midnight, cooking hundreds of meals in the thick heat and tight timeline of the kitchen. At the end of service, we'd sit in front of the old log fire, with a glass of red wine, and snack on freshly baked rolls, dipping them in olive oil, balsamic vinegar and pesto. I knew it was a special time, even as it was happening. When I think back, there is a definite rose tint in my mind's eye. We were in this old, rustic building, at the foot of the Bowland hills, in an area called The Fylde – a coastal plain that sticks out into the Irish Sea. I was at home there. I was acutely aware how special it was, even then. I remember thinking how strange it was that I was so aware of it.

We were what's known as a 'managed house'. That meant we had guidelines on the brand the company liked to stick to; the food and drinks we served, and how we served it, should all adhere to company policy. Not a phrase I like to hear. We weren't great at following the rules. We spent time coming up with the most out-there combinations we could. We figured it was better to take inspiration from Michelin-starred restaurants, rather than a rule book.

Sea urchin was a particular highlight, along with bacon and egg ice cream and the duck we used to smoke in our home-made smokery. We'd use a cheap barbecue, with a chimney we'd stuck on top, and some wood chips. The whole place would fill up with smoke out of hours. The results tasted amazing. I was proud of what we were doing. When I think back, I still am. But some of the bosses who checked in on us were not amused. They wanted us to stick to their branding. There was a boss called Harvey and he and I wound each other up constantly. He was a rugby-playing man-mountain in a bromance with himself. We argued all the time, always over stupid details, like how we served mince pies or ginger chicken. He resented the fact we were doing well without sticking to his rigid formula. But the more we did what we did, and the more we deviated from the norm, the more packed out the restaurant became. In the end, the bosses had to leave us alone. The operations manager was called Eddie. He was a lovely guy. He absolutely loved what we were doing and fought our corner. He used to come there with his wife, which kind of speaks for itself. He told us to keep what we were doing under the radar. It wasn't easy.

We had a strong team. Nikki worked during the day. She had an evil sense of humour, so I probably don't need to tell you that we got on well. But there were times when I took things a bit too far. I remember her having a boyfriend, a guy she'd been chasing for months. She was like a dog with two tails, now that she'd got him hog-tied. They'd been together for just two months when he had to fly to America on business. The day after he left, he sent a sizable bunch of flowers to The Windmill, with a note telling her, in detail, how much he loved her, how much he was going to miss her and that he was desperate to get back so he could see her.

Intercepting them was difficult. It was pure luck. I saw them coming through the door, put two and two together, and graciously accepted them. Then I replaced the message with one of my own. She'd only just stopped crying by the time I summoned up the courage to tell her it was a joke.

With all the hard work we were doing, we needed to let off a lot of steam. Pranks were a part of everyday life in The Windmill. Some of the kitchen porters were easy marks, and quite often wound up being on the wrong end of the joke. One of them, Paul, was pretty gullible. I walked into the kitchen one day and found him looking pale and a bit shaky. Some of the chefs had decided to wrap Danny in cling-film, spray him with water and then put him in the blast freezer. The water froze quickly. When Paul was sent to fetch something from the freezer, he thought he'd found a carefully hidden body. Another time, I walked into the kitchen to find Danny in a rage and the kitchen porters looking decidedly sheepish. In the background, a faraway voice shouted for help. 'Come on, what's happening?' I asked, trying to calm Danny down. Someone had bet Paul that he couldn't fit his massive head in a microwave. He'd accepted the challenge. He'd completed it. Now he couldn't get his head back out. He was stuck, behind the line of one of the busiest kitchens in the area. The kitchen was small, and that meant everyone had to squeeze past him at speed.

I think my favourite prank happened after I took part in a health and safety session with the whole team. I don't think H&S training is anyone's favourite anything, but what came afterwards was worth it. I concluded the training with words along the lines of, 'It's not your responsibility, it's not my responsibility, it's *everyone's* responsibility. If something needs fixing, then use your initiative and fix it.' Inspiring stuff, eh?

At the end of service that day, we were all knackered. It had been busy. It started to pour with rain. I walked into the kitchen holding a mop and bucket and presented them to Paul. 'It's pouring with rain outside. Someone is going to slip on the front steps. I shouldn't have to say this. Get out there and start mopping those steps!' Following what he thought were serious orders, Paul dutifully headed out to the steps and into a futile battle with an angry sky. I couldn't stop laughing. I eventually had to send the assistant manager outside to bring him back in. We didn't even tell him it was a prank in the end. We didn't want to upset him. Later, I took him aside and thanked him for his efforts. Maybe the jokes were another part of what made me feel at home. Growing up we were merciless with each other as a family. We still are. Every event that requires us to sit round a table together is punctuated with the sounds of outrage and laughter. It's part of what home means to me.

Life was busy. There was a constant buzz around the place and there was always something to do. I can admit that I was addicted to work back then. At the ends of those long days, when I walked back upstairs to our living quarters, Beth was there, and she wasn't happy. Maybe that's part of the reason I spent more time working and maybe it became a self-perpetuating cycle. She hated the place and resented my relentless schedule. To try to make her happier and to have a better work–life balance, we decided that I should leave The Windmill.

I got a job selling websites. Why not? It was a different sort of career shift but had the advantage of something more like normal office hours. Selling was addictive, and I threw myself into it, even if I secretly hated it. We moved to a brand-new penthouse, right in the middle of Preston. It was everything I thought I wanted then. It had crisp, freshly plastered walls, new fixtures and fittings. It even came with a massive roof terrace.

Then our new neighbours moved in. Francival Suarez da Silva – known to everyone as Francis – was my Brazilian assistant manager in The Windmill. He and his partner, Pedro, and their dog, Madonna (yes, really), moved into the penthouse in the block across from us. They also had a massive roof terrace. We could talk to each other across the street. We even joked about fitting a zip wire. This was too much for Beth. She thought she'd escaped everything about The Windmill, and now, here was another connection. We had the mother of all rows, during which she says I smashed a TV. I have no recollection of doing that, but even the idea of engaging in the destructive behaviour that my dad was prone to was sobering.

'Fuck off back to Scotland for a few days then,' she said, finally. It was more of a command than a suggestion. 'We'll talk when you get back.'

*Okay*, I thought. *This is an opportunity to go camping.*

I thought I was supposed to be giving her some space, while taking some 'me' time to regroup. It turned out I was supposed to be regretting my actions, then returning home a broken and repentant man. This is why communication is important in a relationship.

I went camping anyway. I took the craziest man you will ever meet in your life. His name's Jamie Diable and he's the most dyspraxic person I know. We went up into the Galloway Forest. I had a great time and, of course, I told Beth that when I phoned her.

It was just one mistake in a whole series of mistakes, as I would later discover.

On the way back down to Preston I was excited. I was really looking forward to seeing Beth and Maddie. I'd enjoyed my time away in nature, but that didn't mean I wasn't homesick. My life was there now, with them. I phoned Beth, pleased with myself for what I was about to do.

'I'm a couple of hours away,' I said.

She told me she was sitting on the couch in our apartment. That she couldn't wait to see me.

I was actually only two miles away, visualising myself walking in, surprising both of them. A few minutes later I opened the front door, trying to summon up my best 'surprise' face. Beth was gone. All her belongings were gone. All Maddie's things were gone. Looking around, I realised everything seemed to be gone. The TV I'd supposedly wrecked and any evidence proving that, was gone, as was the couch, everything really – all except for a heap of my clothes, in a corner.

I phoned her straight away. I didn't tell her I was home. Everything she said was the same. She was still sitting on the couch, still desperate to see me. There I was, standing in our apartment, listening to my partner, the mother of my child, lie to me as if it were the easiest thing in the world. All I wanted then was see my daughter. Nothing else mattered. I knew where they must have gone. I drove forty miles into the Pennine Hills, to where Beth's parents ran a pub and lived in the apartment above. They had to be there. It was eleven o'clock at night by the time I arrived. The rain was hammering down and the pub was closed but I could see the staff inside, silhouetted against the lights in the bar, enjoying an afterhours drink. I could see Alan, Beth's stepfather. He was a reasonable man. He was my only chance of getting any sense out of this situation, so I kept it simple.

'I know Maddie and Beth are both in there, so either send Beth down to speak to me, or I'm coming in.'

'I don't know what you're talking about,' Gordon said.

'I'm here now and I'm coming in in three seconds.'

I'm not proud of what I did next. There were two big terracotta plant pots in front of me. I remember my fingers digging into the dirt, thinking they were too big to lift. I picked them up, somehow, and threw each one, in turn, through the conservatory windows.

The glass shattered. The staff ran. I climbed inside, over the brick wall at the base of the conservatory. I wasn't there to cause trouble. I only wanted to see Maddie. I accept, now, of course, that I wasn't acting rationally, and that I may even have frightened her. I just wanted to see her for myself. It was like I was on some kind of drug, that there was a critical sense of urgency. I needed to see her there and then. I stomped up the stairs. Alan came to the door with Beth first, then her mum appeared. We all started shouting at each other. They threatened to phone the police. The whole scene was nasty, shameful and surreal.

I was so angry. She'd lied to me. Of course she had! But she'd done it in the cruellest possible way, weaponising my own daughter against me, hiding her from me. That was what had pushed me over the edge. They'd lied to me for years, Beth and her mother, but I'd never come close to acting this way before.

Then Beth's mum pushed me – a short, sharp angry push at the top of the stairs. Things were getting physical. I didn't want this. I didn't want to be the guy who smashed things up and I definitely didn't want to be the guy who got into a physical stand-off with a woman half his size. I wasn't my dad. My brain was scrambled.

*How the hell did I get here? What the hell have I done?*

The shove brought me to my senses. It was like someone slapping me across the face. Instant reality. I ran downstairs and climbed back through the broken window, out into the darkness. The wind blew the rain into the gaping holes where the windows had been, slapping me, hard, in the face. It was no less than I deserved. The sky was red – lit up by the light pollution of the nearby industrial towns – and I could see the reflections of blue flashing lights bouncing off the clouds. I could hear sirens. The police were on their way.

It was time to go.

I jumped back into my Vauxhall Corsa and floored the accelerator. The window was down. The wind and rain howled into the car. The interior was caked in blood. I must have cut myself on the broken glass. I started to cry; hysterical, uncontrollable sobs, the tears warm against my cheeks. I kept on driving. I switched the lights off. It was reckless, but I didn't want them to see me. I drove further into the Pennines and turned them back on when I reached the next village. I didn't want to draw any attention to myself, but I had no idea where I was going.

Eventually I calmed down enough to stop and make the necessary phone call.

'Hi, I'm Graeme Parker. I'm responsible for damaging the pub. I know what I've done is completely wrong, and I know you want to speak to me right now. I've hurt myself somehow, but not seriously, so I'm going to spend the night at a friend's house and then I will hand myself in tomorrow.'

They kept asking me where I was.

'I'm not telling you where I am,' I said, 'but I'm phoning to say I'll come in in the morning.'

I felt like I was talking about someone else. None of it seemed part of me. Who was I? What had I become? How the hell was I going to get out of this mess?

I handed myself in at the nearest police station the next morning. I was arrested. They took my shoelaces. I spent a few hours in a cell thinking about what I'd done and wondering why they'd taken my shoelaces. Eventually, unbelievably, I was released. I'm still filled with shame by the whole incident, but I now at least understand my behaviour in the context of being mentally unwell and experiencing the manic part of bipolar disorder.

Mitchells of Lancaster – the chain I'd worked for – owned the pub. They certainly weren't happy about the situation, but they had decided to give me a break, knowing who I was. I'd only broken a couple of windows, and I gladly paid for the repairs. Beth and her family couldn't press charges. It wasn't their property, and I hadn't threatened or hurt anyone apart from myself.

When I got back to the apartment, I realised Beth had completely stripped the place. She'd taken furniture, cutlery. She'd even emptied the fridge. Not only that, but our bank accounts were empty. I had nothing to eat and no way of getting anything.

Francis took me to Morrisons (a UK supermarket) 'for a coffee'. It was a flimsy pretext. He bought so much food while we were there, I thought he was grocery shopping for him and Pedro as well. He started picking up random things that I thought he surely had. It wasn't until we were back in the car that he told me it was all for me. I got pretty emotional then. He didn't have that much himself. It was such a kind gesture, and

I'll never forget it. I remember that the bill came to £121.47. I swore one day I'd pay him back, and eventually I did.

My relationship with Beth was over. When I think back to that night now, it feels more like a hallucinogenic experience – another one of my recurring dreams, the perfect, terrible night – than an actual memory. She wouldn't let me see Maddie anymore – things were just too strained between us – and there was nothing else keeping me in Preston.

So, I moved back to Wigtown, into a depression that came close to killing me.

# Chapter Thirteen

It was 2009. I was twenty-six-years-old and living back in Wigtown with my mum. I was also suicidal. One of my favourite quotes is, 'I bear the scars of unseen wounds'. I thought it might belong to Shakespeare, but I can't find it anywhere. That was me, though. I couldn't stop thinking about my own death, and the thoughts seemed frighteningly logical. Did it make sense for me to be around anymore? Who was I here for? How did my life impact people and how would my death affect them?

I decided – rationally, I believed – that I wasn't part of anyone's life, then. I wasn't in contact with my daughter and couldn't see a way back from that. Being dead would surely only impact me, and only in a positive way. My pain, the suffocation and the grinding, meaningless day-to-day would stop. It was that simple. I wasn't upset. I wasn't even sad. I just remember the logic. I knew deep down it would affect other people, but I thought only about the greater effect it would have on me, about my feelings being greater than the weight of the suffering it might cause other people. I *knew* there would be a massive release, and I looked forward to that. I wanted to let the pressure out. I wanted to be free of it all.

Even now, looking back, I can understand my thought process, only because it made sense at the time. I didn't know what my future was. I didn't know I'd meet Ashley and have the boys. I didn't know then the amazing life I would one day have.

I went to a few supermarkets. I bought as many paracetamol tablets as I could, but there was a two-box limit in every shop. There's only one supermarket in Wigtown and only three in Newton Stewart, so it took some thought and a bit of time to get what I needed. Then, one afternoon, when I thought I had enough, I crushed all the pills together and dissolved them in a pint of orange fanta. I remember saying goodbye to everyone in my head and trying to resolve the things I needed to make peace with. Strangely, I didn't write a note.

I sat in my bedroom, staring at the cocktail of death I'd just mixed. I was just about to drink it when the phone rang. I answered. I still have no idea why. On the other end of the line was Kelly, one of the girls I'd met in Ayia Napa, all those years ago. I hadn't heard from her in ages, so we spent the next quarter of an hour just catching up.

The room I was staying in at my mum's was at the back of the house, and dimly lit. It was a beige room. A place I never liked being. As I spoke to Kelly on the phone, I walked out of my room, downstairs and out the back door. In the garden, the sun was shining. I sat on the wooden bench next to the fishpond, in amongst Davie's prized flowers. It was good to hear from someone with no agenda; someone who wasn't angry with me in any way. Someone who had only phoned to talk to me for the sake of it, because they wanted to. As we ended the call, I looked around me. I felt better about the world.

It seems strange to say it now, but I was calm about my impending death. I'd made peace with it. I thought it meant the pain would be over. In reality, if I'd taken a paracetamol overdose, the pain would have been far from over. It's supposedly one of the most excruciating ways to kill yourself, by destroying your liver in the process. I'll always be grateful for Kelly's phone call. Even if I've never told her she accidentally saved my life.

I didn't speak to her again until 2019. I was on a stag weekend with some friends in Edinburgh. We were sitting in the sun, on a sandstone wall, in a Victorian crescent, somewhere in the west end of the city. Three women walked past our group, and I thought I recognised one of them. I was sure it was Kelly. I watched as they shrank into the distance. What were the odds? She lived in Lancashire. Why would she be here, in Scotland's capital? I was fixated on her. My friend was trying to get my attention. I let her wonder further on so that I'd know if it was her when I shouted, so that I didn't look silly.

When she was far enough away, I stood up and just shouted. 'Kelly!'

One of the three girls turned round. I ran after them. It was her. I gave her a massive hug. I was shouting, 'I can't believe it's you. You're here.' I think she might have been a wee bit overwhelmed with my enthusiasm. I'm not usually a hugger, and she wasn't to know the impact she'd had on my life ten years earlier. She looked at me like I was nuts. She knew who I was but that was about it. We hadn't spoken since that call. I wanted to tell her everything, to thank her for what she'd done, but I decided talking about suicide in front of a bunch of her friends on a city break was a bit heavy.

It felt like the closing of a chapter. We chatted and then headed off in different directions. She never did find out the truth, unless she's reading this now.

I wish I could say I had the presence of mind to get rid of the evidence of that day, but my mum found the whole lot later on: empty paracetamol boxes, glass of fanta, but luckily, no note. Later, I found her crying. It didn't matter what I said, she just wouldn't accept that there was no danger anymore. Why would I just change my mind and abandon the idea when I had been so prepared?

Mental illness is like that, and at this stage I was still undiagnosed and unmedicated. If I couldn't understand my rapidly changing mood cycles, how could Mum?

I'll always feel sad about the years of worry it caused her after that.

I'd snapped out of my desire to end my life, but I still needed to get away. I needed to put some distance between me and the familiar thought processes and triggers that had put me in that headspace. I needed to start again and rebuild. My easiest route out of Wigtown then was to take another job in hospitality. So, I moved two hundred and sixty-nine miles north, to Glen Affric, near Drumnadrochit in the Scottish Highlands. I'm not sure if I can prove this, technically, but Drumnadrochit sounds to me like it could be the most Scottish place in the world. Or maybe that's Auchtermuchty. Answers on a post card, please.

It definitely has the things most people think of as Scottish. It sits on the banks of Loch Ness, near Urquhart Castle. I took a job running a restaurant, part of the Loch Ness Inn, a small hotel in the nearby village called Lewiston. I rented a cottage in Glen Affric. It's a place where JM Barrie, the author of *Peter Pan*, stayed when on retreats to Scotland – in a bothy, perched on the hillside. It's a good place to dream up stories.

The Highlands were a revelation. It's easy to get complacent about your own country, and the beauty that lies just outside your front door. You take it for granted. After life in Preston, and the familiarity of Wigtownshire, I was somewhere new, with time on my hands. I got into exploring. I was a tourist in my own land and spent every bit of my spare time driving through the countryside, walking through the vastness of those green Highland landscapes, all hills, mountains, glens and lochs, like something out of a Runrig song. It was everything I needed, right at that point in time.

The one thing I missed, constantly, was Maddie. As far as the rest of the world went though, I was happily out of it, decompressing, and, I suppose, recovering.

Loch Ness is a crazy place. It sits on a geographic fault line, the same one that formed An Gleann Mòr – The Great Glen. It's two hundred and forty metres deep, twenty-three miles long, and could easily hold the water volume of all the lochs, rivers and streams in the rest of the UK. It's also pitch-black, because of all the peat particles floating around in there. The view from Urquhart Castle on the shores of Loch Ness is iconic. It's the one you see on postcards and films. You feel a huge swell of patriotism when you're up there, like you're more Scottish, somehow. It's almost as patriotic as the feeling I get watching *Braveheart*, after a few fruit ciders, or when the Proclaimers crank it up.

Now, I know what you're thinking here. You want to know about Nessie, don't you?

The Loch Ness Monster is actually a pretty controversial subject in the area. It's like discussing politics or football: best avoided in pubs. The legend goes back to Saint Columba in 565 CE – sort of. He supposedly encountered a monster, but that was in the River Ness (and he used his servant as bait ... allegedly). The more recent sightings began in the 1930s when they built a new road. Then there was the infamous surgeon's photo taken in 1934. It was later proved to be a hoax, set up with a toy submarine and a model dinosaur, but it stood for a long time because the photographer was a respected London doctor, Robert Kenneth Wilson, and was therefore presumed to be above suspicion. Take it from me though. Doctors are as warped as the rest of us. It might have been a hoax, but it helped set the tourist industry alight.

Some of the locals refuse to talk about Nessie. Some really believe they have seen the monster, but they're sick of people taking the piss out of them. In my experience, the younger generation take a much more cynical, or maybe a more pragmatic view of the whole thing, believing it's all hype for gullible tourists. There are very strong feelings on the subject, so much so that if you walk into a pub in the area and try to talk about it with one of the old boys in there, they might just send you on your way, with a fat lip for your trouble.

For the record, I don't believe in the Loch Ness Monster, but I have seen one or two strange things. One warm summer day when I was eleven, and we were still at The Knock, I was down by the new sheds at the bottom of the farm. The 'new' sheds were probably about twenty years old at the time but it's all relative. That field was littered with implements and contraptions, some new and being stored there, and some old, rusting hulks. There were different types of trailers. There was a muck spreader, a big, yellow Massey Ferguson digger, and some unusual machinery I couldn't name. I was playing down there one day when I looked up to see a big, green vintage car driving down the track towards the sheds, at speed. I was confused. The driver had flaming red hair and wore a cream dress. She was about to drive off the end of the road. And then she, and her car, disappeared. I ran to find her, but she had vanished. At the time it wasn't a scary thing at all. I just thought, *Why's that person up at the farm? I'll need to find out who they are and tell Mum or Dad.* I still remember it clearly.

I was confused. I went to find Mum. She said it sounded as though I had just seen my great aunt, Alexandrina, the doctor with all those letters on her headstone at Glasserton kirkyard. She'd been dead for forty years. I saw her photo a few years ago. The resemblance sent a chill right through me.

Working in a gastropub style restaurant in a hotel environment was comfortably familiar. I knew what I was doing, and I felt at home, but I didn't have the same level of commitment. Mentally, I wasn't where I had been in The Windmill, or at The Royal Hotel. I just didn't feel the same drive. The restaurant itself was a good one, and I got on well with the people working there, but I never clicked with anyone there, or with the job itself.

I had been told they wanted to win awards. That was what I was used to, what I expected to get stuck into, but there were a lot of staffing issues. Work felt like swimming through treacle with my hands tied behind my back. For me, just for once, it was all about my leisure time and the location.

Then I got phone call from Beth.

It came completely out of the blue, given the dramatic events in the Pennines, and the months we'd spent apart, estranged. I was wary, but she needed to get away from her mum's house and I was desperate to reconnect with Maddie. I told her she could come north to stay with me. Maddie came with her, and we toured around, seeing the sites and hunting monsters. It all clicked back into place, and everything felt nice for a couple of days. Out of nowhere, against the odds, it looked like we were going to get back together. Luckily, we started arguing.

Then, I got another phone call – one that would change my life, for good.

My stepdad, Davie, had fallen ill, and urgently needed my help running his business. Davie had been in business for over twenty years as a hoof trimmer. He also did freeze branding – stamping numbers on bums. Cow's bums, to be precise. It was and is a very physical job. Davie didn't have the famous Appleton Steel crush either. I've said it before, but he was an absolute beast of a man. He had the strength and demeanour of an ox.

He had developed an abscess on his spine. The abscess had led to blood poisoning and a six-week stay in hospital. His line of work was so precarious that those six weeks of no income were all it took to put his business in jeopardy. I remind myself of that all the time. It only takes six weeks. It's part of my mantra, now. I got the call only four months into my time in the Highlands, newly reacquainted with my daughter, but I felt I had no choice: I had to go home and help him. I agreed to look after the business, and keep things ticking over, until he recovered.

I told myself this would be a temporary thing. I didn't want to make any sort of ongoing commitment and certainly not one that would leave me forever stuck – as I saw it – in The Shire. There were so many bad memories there, with the death of my father, and then my suicide attempt. On the other hand, I wasn't really enjoying my life in Drumnadrochit, so leaving there didn't seem like any sort of sacrifice, but if I was able to see Maddie, I felt my life should be wherever she was.

Now I was heading home to deal with more ghosts. I wasn't

sure about anything, but I was needed, and that was all that mattered. I thought I was making yet another impulsive career change, but I also believe family comes first, so I went home and got stuck in.

I had no idea exactly how much was about to change.

# Chapter Fourteen

To be clear, I didn't just pick up Davie's knives and start hacking away at cow's hooves. It's not something you can just decide to do on a whim, although there's technically nothing stopping you from doing that. In fact, there are absolutely no legal training requirements at all. I really wish there were. If you want to be good, you have to put the hours in, and there really should be some kind of minimum standard required to do the job. The stakes are high. You can cure an animal, or kill it, depending on what you do or don't remove from a hoof.

I'd seen the toll that hoof trimming had taken on Davie. He might have been strong, but he had a bunch of health problems other than the spinal abscess, most of which were linked to a combination of overwork, not taking proper care of himself, and the type two diabetes that left him with. Davie was an expert. He'd run training courses, teaching others how to trim hooves. Like me, he'd been around cattle his entire life, and like me, he knew how to work with them on a deeper level; the places to stand or not to stand, the directions to walk in, depending on whether you want to move the cow this way or that. We used to joke that Davie saw himself as some kind of cow whisperer, but, looking back, he probably was.

Although his cattle experience was vast, Davie's own entire

hoof trimming training had been about forty minutes' worth on a farm. He was shown what to do and then immediately told to get on with it. A lot of what he learned was the result of his own trial and error. He later went on to teach people at the Scottish Agricultural College, now known as Scotland's Rural College. He was around at the dawn of hoof trimming. No one had done any of this before.

Cows are herd animals. That makes them behave in certain way. Some of them, hill cattle for example – the kind that you'd find on a place like The Knock – are easily spooked. In contrast, dairy cows are pretty placid and used to humans, day to day, so they're easier to work with. There are also certain types of behaviours specific to humans who're not used to cattle, who haven't grown up around them. I've seen truck drivers turn up to load cattle on their wagons, brandishing lengths of hose. This isn't remotely necessary if you know what you're doing. I will use one as an extension of my arm, and wave it about, but I never hit cows. Most people who have experience with cows will talk to them as they go, encouraging them along, with a 'come on, lass.' You don't need to lash out with a hosepipe. That's what scared people do. Simply standing still and waving your arms is usually enough to turn even a rampaging herd around.

Cows have what we call a 'flight zone'. Every cow's flight zone is different. It's like their version of the beeping on a parking sensor. If you approach a cow, she starts to register it. Eventually, she'll give you a warning to tell you you're too close, but you can manipulate the flight zone. Cows are more responsive on their left. You can move them much more easily using their left-hand side. I've worked with people who will stand alongside the cattle crush, not knowing that this is guaranteed to freak the cows out. The American animal behaviourist, Temple Grandin, has written extensively about this. She's designed pens, cattle races and chutes to keep the animals in as little stress as possible. I think that's the very least we should aim for.

The lack of learning opportunities around hoof trimming were irrelevant, though; I simply didn't want to be a hoof trimmer. I could see how *hard* it was. I could see it had left Davie in a bad way, physically and financially. I started out freeze branding, instead. That was something I could do, to keep things going and get the cash flowing while Davie recuperated. Numbers on bums time.

Most people my age and older will have seen the old-school hot branding used on cattle. It's the kind of thing you see in cowboy films where numbers are singed onto the rear ends of cows. Freeze branding is the clean, less stressful, modern equivalent. The main difference is that you're using extreme cold, instead of extreme heat. Freeze branding uses carbon dioxide, chilled to minus eighty degrees centigrade to kill the pigmentation in the cow's hair follicles. The hair then grows back colourless, and the number becomes visible in white. Although, interestingly, if you freeze brand a Suffolk sheep, the number comes up black. Hot branding just burns off the hair, so that it never grows back. That's illegal here in the UK, for obvious reasons. Would you like having a red-hot poker jammed onto your left butt cheek? Nope. Didn't think so. That's why we do freeze branding.

I worked away at it steadily. I've always got on well with customers and I was enjoying being in different places, different parts of Galloway, even different parts of Wigtownshire I'd never seen before. I really started, for perhaps the first time, to properly appreciate the beauty of the area I'd always taken for granted. I'd taken some of the appreciation I'd learned in the

Highlands home with me. My life was on a different timescale now. I loved the way my daily travels took me to weird and wonderful locations, like all the small back roads you drive past when you're in a pointless hurry.

I didn't feel like I was on the run either. That was a big change. I was back where I'd come from, facing up to a challenge and coming out on top. I was happy to be helping my stepdad out. Word started to get around, and I was in demand. Davie's business had always had a good reputation, all over mainland Scotland, and even as far as the Hebrides. I was proud to be able to back that up with the quality of work I was putting in. I had a sense of purpose and responsibility. We all need a bit of that. I know I did, anyway. As time went on, my opinion of myself started to reflect what everyone else was telling me, and my confidence grew.

Davie and I had battled a lot in the past. I respected him as my mum's partner, but we were very different characters and both of us had short tempers where the other was concerned. We still fought a lot. That part hadn't changed, but I think we each started to gain a new appreciation for what the other was doing and what they were capable of. I was doing things on my own terms, and I was there through choice and that meant a lot to him.

If I was sparring with Davie, though, I finally *wasn't* fighting with Beth. Our relationship was now strictly platonic and centred entirely around taking care of Maddie. Beth went back to Preston with Maddie when I left the Highlands to return to The Shire, so I drove the four hours down there every Friday after work to pick Maddie up from school and bring her back home with me for the weekend. It was an eight-hour round-trip, but I couldn't have cared less. She was everything to me. Maddie and I were very close, in a way I never could have been with my own father. I'd been apart from her for too long, and this meant we got to spend the whole weekend together. It reminded me of when we spent all that time together when she was young, just the two of us, and I was tramping the streets with her in Morecambe, or she was sitting in the kitchen with me at The Windmill. It also meant my family got to see a whole lot more of her and include her in their important occasions.

Maddie actually went on Bob's stag do, where she put at least one of the stags to shame. She was with me for the weekend, and I wasn't going to miss our time together, but I couldn't really miss my brother's stag party, either. The first part of the day was at Xsite, just outside Glasgow – a big leisure centre with indoor skiing, bowling and climbing. I decided I would take her with me.

We went on the climbing wall first, just to warm up. Maddie loved it. She was fitter than a few of the twenty- and thirty-something men there on the day. Then we took things up a level, literally. The Skypark is an obstacle circuit with a difference. Starting with a zipline, you progress along climbing walls and dangling ladders. You're harnessed in, and that's a good thing, because you're hanging fifty feet above the ground. The zip-line ended on a small platform. That's where Bob remembered his fear of heights. When he landed there, he turned to the instructor, pale-faced and shaking, and said, 'You need to get me off this thing.' The instructor shook his head and tried to suppress a laugh. 'The only way off the course is round the course'.

I'd like to say James and I were helpful, that the gentle kicks to the back of our older brother's legs were for encouragement, but I'd be lying. Maddie, on the other hand, took the whole thing in her stride, then went off to stay with her soon-to-be-auntie Caroline, while things got stag-night messy.

Over the years, I grew really proud of how far I'd driven to pick her up. I do like a random statistic, and my running total stands at just under 150,000 miles of driving to get her. That's six times around the planet. I used to joke that I had the longest school run in the world, but I was delighted to do it.

Freeze branding began to take me well beyond my own corner of Southwest Scotland, as Davie had built a loyal client list that extended the length and breadth of the country. The locations depended on the landscapes and what sort of farming they were suitable for. If it was cattle country, I went there. That could mean Galloway, or it could mean the Northeast, around Aberdeen, or the west coast, down to the Mull of Kintyre peninsula, or even the islands, like Islay and Gigha.

I remember feeling the romance of it. As if I were an intrepid wanderer, some kind of frozen iron-brandishing vagabond. The countryside was stunning everywhere, from the rugged beauty of the Highlands to the rolling hills and glens of the Northeast to the storm ravaged openness of the Atlantic coast. The farms brought back good memories. The people were colourful. On the island of Islay, the locals told me stories I sometimes hoped were true and sometimes didn't. They had a different spin on life. One I found very enticing.

There was always something missing, however, no matter where I went.

I would soon discover what that was.

In February 2010, I was in a pub in Wigtown – The Galloway. It's an old-fashioned pub. The kind you probably don't find in many places now, all dark wood and sport. It's had a new lick of paint since then, but the sport remains a firm fixture.

My favourite ever story about The Galloway is one my friend James McGill told me. McGill is a one-off. I think he might be the funniest person I know. We once drove to Glasgow to see a stand-up comedy gig and the promoter was determined to get him on stage. McGill's response to that was an exasperated 'I can't be bothered with that shit'. The promoter replied that McGill's attitude was exactly why he should be a stand-up comedian. Along with Dave Old, he's one of my best friends. I've known him since primary school, and, like Dave, he started out as a friend of my older brothers. He's six feet five, with a monster of a black beard, and proudly refers to himself as a hillbilly. If you can imagine a sort of non-ginger, non-bald Groundskeeper Willie from *The Simpsons*, that's McGill. Don't let that fool you though. He's the kind of guy who knows everything. The type of person who just educates themselves in a way you can't with a university degree.

McGill maybe doesn't realise this, but he's a big part of my headspace. He's someone I've always respected, and he's helped me out of trouble more than once. I was once on the train home and fell asleep. Trains are a bit useless around here. Most of the stations were shut in the 1960s, and that means you have only one local option: Barrhill. It's a tiny station in the middle of the hills, about forty minutes' drive from Wigtown. If you're carless, or a masochist, you can take a rattler of a bus for a vomit-inducing hour and a half. Unfortunately, on this occasion I didn't make it as far as Barrhill. I woke up on a darkened train, in Ayr station. I phoned McGill and he drove over fifty miles to pick me up, along a goat track of a road through the hills, with no questions asked.

One time he asked for a hand to help replace some joists in a house he was renovating. I helped him out, but I probably spent quite a lot of time pranking him. He had a habit of wearing AirPods while he worked. That was a total gift. I'd arrive, unannounced, then stand behind him until he 'noticed' me. That usually resulted in a massive fright for him, which, now I think about it, could have been dangerous for me if he'd been holding a nail gun at the time. When we'd finished the work and replaced the joists, McGill presented me with a handful of cash. I really didn't want to take it. I just wanted to help him out, but he must have known I needed the money, and he wouldn't take no for an answer. That's the kind of guy he is.

Obviously, I wouldn't be friends with him just for his decency towards me. He's one of the farmers I admire most. He also happens to be a notorious legend for random, stand-out moments. After we all got horribly drunk at Bob's twenty-first birthday party, and then even drunker at an after-party in the house in Port William, McGill walked home in odd shoes, with what turned out to be a slightly broken leg. Back on the farm, he limped into the kitchen just as his parents were having breakfast. Dairy farmers start the day early, but not usually to the sight of a man in a suit, carrying an inflatable seal called Elspeth under one arm, and a bottle of orange liqueur under the other.

McGill once woke up with a crazy thirst he couldn't understand. He went downstairs for some water. In the kitchen, he met his mum who asked, 'What happened to the lime cordial?' It turned out he'd glugged the whole lot, straight from the bottle.

On the night of the legendary Galloway story, McGill was standing in the street in Wigtown, talking to someone he knew, when a firework went off along the street. Undeterred, McGill and his friend carried on talking. More fireworks went off, and then one went a bit too far. Someone set off a rocket that flew past them, across the main street and towards The Galloway. The timing was unintentionally perfect; the door swung open, and the rocket flew straight into the pub, setting off a commotion inside. Talk about rough trade. No one was hurt though, which is the main thing.

My cousin, Alix, was in The Galloway one February night, and I fell in with her group. I sort of knew some of them. One of them had a really nice car. An Audi TT, the original version, a small, silver German coupé that back in the day looked like nothing else on the road but seemed to be everywhere. Nowadays it's a modern classic, but then it was just a cool car.

The driver was blonde, and I liked the look of her, too. 'I like your car,' I said, as casually as I could. She was my cousin's best friend. I'd seen her around – usually behind the wheel of her TT. Her name was Ashley, and after talking to her for a while, I realised she was the most easy-going person I'd ever met.

We met again, this time on purpose. I took her for a walk at St Medan, the scene of our Parker family drama all those years before. That might seem like an odd choice for a date, but, like I said, it's in my bones. It's still my favourite place in the world, so it seemed like the logical choice. We just clicked. As first dates go, it was effortless. We walked across the golf course and sat on the fourth fairway. It was one of those crisp, clear nights you only seem to get in Galloway. We could see the stars, but it wasn't cold. We sat there talking into the night, totally at ease in each other's company. It was very chilled. Although, I couldn't help being vaguely aware that the place below was where Dad had fallen off the quad bike trying to find another shooting spot.

Ashley had just come out of a relationship, and after nine tumultuous years on and off with Beth, I felt pretty damaged, so we took things very slowly. It was very casual for a while. I think, at first, that was what we both needed. We liked each other a lot but neither of us wanted to overthink it. We weren't an official couple for a while, which I suppose meant we really got to know each other properly first.

Looking back, I don't think I knew which way was up. I had no idea what I wanted. I was still trying to get my head straight over everything that had happened. I didn't know what was going on with my mental health. I was still years away from being diagnosed, even then. But I was also officially single, so I still wanted to talk to other women. My head was up my own ass.

I still don't know how or why Ashley put up with me during that time. All I do know is that I'm glad she did. I was anything but a safe bet.

# Chapter Fifteen

It was around this time that I managed to acquire another scar. My friend David and I decided to go on a road trip round Scotland and on to the north of England. I knew him pretty well, or I thought I did. Everyone locally knows David as 'Fousse' and they have done since primary school, but I'm not sure anyone knows why anymore. Much like Dave Old when I'd arrived back in The Shire after separating from Beth, Fousse had just split up with his wife and needed a break. I was enjoying my life a lot more, but I was young, and I felt like I needed to get out and see as much as possible. I enjoyed the work I was doing but felt the weight of the responsibility. I was due an escape once in a while.

We headed up north and spent a few days there first. We went canyoning in Aberfeldy. Canyoning is a fairly straightforward sport. The rules and the equipment required are minimal. You just have to be able to jump off eighty-foot cliff faces into water, preferably avoiding death. Simple! I was good at it – although no one was there to award me any points for skill. They gave you a hard hat. Clearly just to tick a health and safety box. I'm not sure what that would have done, if you misjudged it and face-planted on the rocks. We kayaked down the river Tay, and went to Go Ape, a tree-top adventure experience set up with an array of zip lines. Perfect for the adult on first name terms with his inner child. In this case, me.

A few people had warned me about Fousse. He was unpredictable, they said. He'd been known locally for getting heavily into drugs a few years earlier and didn't have a great reputation. But old reputations follow you around Wigtown and, as I feel sure there are more than a few odd stories about me in circulation, I've never taken these things too seriously. I'd worked in his Dad's hotel years earlier and Fousse had been the manager, so he'd been my boss. We'd always got on well. I'd never seen any bad side to him, apart from the time he tried to superman-jump through a first-floor window to get downstairs to hit his dad. I didn't know what they'd been fighting about, but he'd lost his temper so badly that he managed to get halfway through the window frame before they dragged him back in. Despite what people said, I'd much rather take people as I find them. And I knew how fractured relationships could be when it came to fathers and sons.

After the adrenaline-fuelled madness of Aberfeldy, we stopped off at Fousse's mum's, in Edinburgh, for the best paella I've ever had. Then we went back to my old stomping ground in the Northwest of England. We were out on The Golden Mile, in Blackpool, drinking and gambling. It was supposed to be the last night of what had been a great getaway. It should have been fun. We headed into Preston afterwards, and after a week away from anything I knew, it felt a bit like coming back home.

We went to a pub I knew in the city centre. It was a Saturday night, and the place was jumping. We got talking to a couple of women – of course we did. Having just got out of a marriage, I think Fousse was out to prove something to himself. One of the women took a bit of a liking to me. She made it crystal clear, and

I did my best to make it equally clear that I was now happily involved with Ashley. I felt like I had to keep talking to both of the women, because it was obvious Fousse was keen. I wanted to be a good wingman. I wanted to convince anyone who would listen that he was a good guy, because as far as I knew, he was.

We spent most of the evening with these two women, winding our way along a sort of memory-lane style pub-crawl for me, and a trip round the sights for Fousse. He was both my old boss and six years older than me, so I suppose I wanted to impress him a bit. I wanted to show him the best bits of somewhere I still sort of considered a second home. I tried everything I could to draw attention back to him and to big him up in the eyes of these women.

Everything seemed fine until I went to the toilet. I was in there, obviously doing whatever I needed to, when Fousse barged his way through the door. He looked like he was in a hurry. He started shouting at me. I was getting in his way, he said. Why was I cock-blocking him? Why was I trying to make him look like a dickhead? Somewhere in his version of events, I was chatting up the woman he liked, just to annoy him. Just because I could.

I told him I wasn't interested. That I had been building him up for all he was worth, but he didn't want to hear it. He was a long way past reasoning with and had lost all sense of perspective. I'd never seen him like this. It was as if someone else was pulling his strings. Then he absolutely lost it and ran at me from the other side of the room. He lunged at me, arms flailing. He was a big guy, but I took a swing that caught him on the chin, trying to halt what was coming. He fell, but that wasn't enough to stop him in his tracks. He went for my legs. We were on the floor, wrestling, in a stinking toilet cubicle. I had to end this, now. He was face down. I jammed my knee into the back of his neck and pressed his face into the place where the base of the toilet met the floor. It was covered in brown gunge. I needed something decisive to stop him.

I had him pinned and yelled for the bouncers. After a painful wait for both of us – while Fousse struggled, cursed and issued threats – two doormen arrived. They lifted him to his feet and sent him back out into the street. They were good about what had happened. They knew this wasn't my fight and they let me stay in the pub until, I hoped, Fousse had calmed down. I don't know how long I stayed in there, but I know it was long enough for any reasonable person to have sobered up and seen sense. Any *reasonable* person.

He was leaning against a wall when I left the bar. He was on the phone. I realised he was talking to Ashley. What the hell was he saying? I hadn't done anything wrong, so I grabbed the phone. He turned and walked away, still shouting, snarling insults like he was deranged, hell bent on finding the worst possible things he could say. Something inside me broke. I still had his phone in my hand. I threw it at the ground and heard a satisfying crack. It was reckless, impulsive. I knew that even before I saw Fousse's reaction.

I'd really done it now.

He ran at me again, gouging his head into mine. We fell to the ground. I hit him, hard, again and again. I had to get him off me. We were in the city centre, on a busy Saturday night, rolling around in the gutter. There was an audience, but no one was doing anything.

The police eventually arrived. They took him away and I was left there, in a kind of disconnected calm, with two paramedics determined to examine me in the cold clinical light of their ambulance. I thought it was overkill. I didn't need an ambulance, surely. I didn't really know what I needed, but I definitely didn't want to be fussed over by a couple of guys in green uniforms who could be helping people worse off than me. They were manhandling me now, frustrated. I was confused. They frogmarched me over to the front of their ambulance. To the wing mirror. The face staring back didn't look like my own. There was a red, sickly gouge down one side of what had been my jawline.

When Fousse's head had struck me, he hadn't been going for a headbutt. Nothing that simple, nothing so benign. He'd bitten me. I had a mouth-sized wound on the right-hand side of my face. It was horrific. I could see where his top and bottom teeth had penetrated my skin. He had almost managed to extract the bit in between.

So, he was arrested, and I went to A&E. When I got out, I had to call my mum and ask her to come and pick me up. It had taken stitches, tetanus shots and antibiotics to get me out the door and there was still the very real risk of sepsis or tissue necrosis. A human bite is a filthy, germ-ridden thing, way worse, even, than a dog bite. I'd also broken my hand, for good measure. I had a splinter fracture along my little finger.

I didn't want to press charges, but the English Crown Prosecution Service put together a case on their own. By the time I got home, Fousse's version of events had overtaken me. I'm still not sure what that version was, exactly, but the gist of it was that it was my own fault he'd tried to bite off part of my face. He was eventually convicted of Grievous Bodily Harm and given a suspended prison sentence. He moved to Edinburgh, and we haven't seen each other since. I still have the outline of a bite mark on my jaw line. It's the reason I always have some kind of 'designer' stubble.

Well, that, and the fact Ashley says you can see too much of my face without it.

Back in The Shire, with my newly acquired wounds healing, Davie was making his own, gradual recovery, but he wasn't the man he had been. He had begun hoof trimming again and I kept on going with the freeze branding side of the business to help share the load. Ashley had a full-time job, working as a hairdresser, but she started coming with me on freeze branding trips whenever she could. We travelled the country together and I loved showing her the bits of Scotland I'd found. She was perfectly happy reading a book in the van while I worked during the day. In the evenings we'd go out for dinner and then back to a hotel. I miss getting to spend as much time with her these days, but we have bigger responsibilities now – even if they are technically still little ones.

Cattle are only branded once in their lives, but farms buy and sell stock, and that meant I had recurring visits – places I went to several times a year. I got to know the farmers and farm workers well. Farm life isn't like freeze branding, or hoof trimming. I get to come and go, but these guys are stuck in the same place. And even though some of the places are amazing, it must be refreshing seeing a new face. I always got a warm welcome, especially in the islands and over in Campbeltown.

I met some really amazing people on my travels. When I went to Campbeltown it was like being in another country. It's not that far from Wigtownshire, as the crow flies, but I'm not a crow, and that meant an extended drive north, through Glasgow, up past Loch Lomond and then a U-turn, down the peninsula parallel to the way you just came. A ferry ride would be quicker, but then you wouldn't get to drive all that way, past some of the most stunning scenery in the country, down the wild Atlantic coast and into another world.

They have one of the biggest runways in Western Europe there, at Machrihanish, built to take US bombers during the Cold War and then upgraded as a back-up landing for the space shuttle. They used to have thirty distilleries. Now there are only three, but they punch well above their weight. I loved arriving there and passing the sign for Campbeltown Airport that someone had artfully changed, to say 'Camel toe airport'. I think that might be my third favourite thing about the area, behind the scenery, and, above all, the people. To say the community in Campbeltown is tight knit is a bit like saying my hair has a slight kink to it, or that I like the odd coffee. There's a proper community there, like all agricultural areas would've had in the past. There are big farming families. Everyone knew everyone and they all had the same surnames. McSporran is a personal favourite of mine. It's awesome.

The farms in the area were pretty small, so I'd maybe have ten cows to do at one farm and then the farmer would say, 'I'll phone John and let him know you're running half an hour late,' and I'd wonder how he knew where I was off to next. Or I'd say I was off to the next farm, and they'd tell me, 'No, no. I've arranged for you to drop in at Donald's farm, before you go to see Angus.' It got to the point that they were arranging my days for me. Because the work was scattered, I'd do as many farms as I could get through in a day. I'd be invited in for lunch in different places and I'd be told stories, some of which I'd heard before, but always with a slightly different slant.

Freeze branding is physically hard, and I took real pride in seeing my numbers come out clearly every time. There's a real knack to it. You have to balance things just the right way. The branding irons have individual numbers or letters on them. You chill them in methylated spirits that is in turn cooled by dry ice – frozen CO2 – to minus 82 degrees centigrade. You need to take the cold iron, place it on the cow's rear end, and keep it in place for just the right amount of time. The trick is to keep applying a firm, even pressure and time everything.

Every Monday morning, I drove to Bellshill outside Glasgow and picked up the dry ice. I had to be there for 8 a.m., so I left at 6. Thankfully I was able to drive in daylight hours, as it was a summertime job. That's when most branding is done, and I remember the camaraderie of the work.

I was working with heifers – year-old cows that haven't yet had a calf. They were wilder, jumpier, and they had more room to move around. I wasn't using a fancy crush back then. I only had a plank of wood to keep the cow forward and a tyre to bolster the skinnier cows by keeping them snugly in place. Unsurprisingly, my primitive attempts to position the cows weren't foolproof. One heifer managed to kick me when I was only wearing a sleeveless T-shirt. To add insult to injury, the number nine freeze branding iron hit me on the arm. I had that number imprinted on me for weeks. I was convinced it would be there forever.

I often get asked if I ever get kicked while hoof trimming. That's actually very rare. I got kicked all the time when I was freeze branding though. Every. Single. Day. That shouldn't be surprising. You're applying a cold iron to their rear end, and they don't like it. The trick with freeze branding is to learn to take the kicks. If you do that you can deal with them. You become almost immune. It's the people that try to avoid them that do themselves the most damage.

I enjoyed working with the employed farm workers. We took

our lunch breaks sitting in the dust, around hundred-and-fifty-year-old barns, with their slate roofs and white-washed walls, basking in the sunlight. I'd eat Feast ice creams straight from my ice box. It was nice to have the opportunity to eat lunch. I don't really get that chance now. These days, we just keep going. It's better for us and for the cows.

We do need to stop for coffees though. That gets us through the day.

When I was out freeze branding, I began to hear the same thing on a regular basis. I remember being at a farm I knew well. The farmer, Martin McCormick, who lives just up the road from where I am now, said to me, 'Graeme, you really should be hoof trimming.'

I laughed at him. 'I can tell you right now, I will never trim a hoof.'

A few years later I was, of course, back on his farm, eating my words and trimming thirty of Martin's pedigree Aberdeen Angus herd, while he gloated about his prediction. But, back then, knowing how hard freeze branding was, I could only see hoof trimming as an even harder and dirtier alternative. I wanted absolutely no part of it. Life was going well enough for me. I was enjoying my job when I wasn't fighting with Davie, and I was happy in my shiny new relationship with Ashley.

But then we had another death in the family, and that led to the final unravelling of the fifteen-year mystery surrounding my father's own, untimely demise.

# Chapter Sixteen

My paternal grandmother suffered a massive stroke in the spring of 2012. She was left bedridden and paralysed down one side of her body, unable to open her eyes or speak properly. I drove the two hundred-odd miles to see her in hospital, in York.

She had always been bit of a character. A force of nature. I remember visiting her and she told me about a run-in she'd had with a delivery driver. The driver had dropped off her grocery shopping and left, at which point my granny, who was already a wheelchair user at this stage, ran through the list of shopping and realised some of her groceries were missing. She immediately phoned the supermarket and demanded to speak to the driver. After some resistance, the driver came on the phone and Granny demanded to know where her bag of shopping was. The driver stood firm.

'Mrs Parker, I told you. I hung the last bag on the back of your wheelchair.'

She had been wheeling round the house like an angry wasp all morning, and all the while the missing shopping had been swinging along behind her.

Now, in a hospital ward in York, she looked small and uncharacteristically weak. Her face had sunk, and her teeth were missing. I held the hand that wasn't bandaged and attached to tubes, and I told her I loved her. I felt her squeeze my hand. 'I'm sorry, Graeme,' was all she managed to say. The voice was high-pitched, grating. It didn't sound like hers. I wasn't sure what she was sorry about, exactly. Was it the fact my grandfather hadn't spoken to me for years, because he thought I'd been insolent to him on the phone after the incident that finally ended my parent's marriage? Or was it something else? I would never get my answer. She died a few days later, back in her local hospital, in Malton.

The funeral was in her church – the sort of bucolic, English rural church that appears in *Four Weddings and a Funeral*. Ashley, my mother, my two sisters and I travelled down together. It was strange seeing so many people I hadn't seen in years: cousins, second cousins, my aunt and uncle.

There were a lot of mixed feelings, and the heat was relentless that week. The kind of heat we never seem to get in Scotland. We were two hundred and fifty miles away from home and in a totally different climate. A totally different community. After the service, people gathered on the lawn at the nearby Old Lodge Hotel. It was quite something, all Jacobean limestone with battlements, fake towers and huge, multi-paned windows. This place was almost as posh as Granny. A year earlier we'd all been there celebrating her ninetieth birthday.

The next day we drove to the crematorium my dad had been cremated in. It was a weird sensation, being back there, but I suppose you could say this time the occasion was much more the natural order of things. Granny was ninety-one when she died, not in her late forties. You can rationalise it more easily when someone that age dies. It's part of the normal ebb and flow of life and the passage of time. Grandparents die. No one should go at forty-nine, a stranger to their own family.

Inevitably our minds were on Dad. Kirsty, Susan, Mum and I had spoken. We'd decided that now Granny was gone, the time was right to do a little investigating. We'd all had so many questions over the years, most of which remained unanswered. After the cremation we went to Scarborough for fish and chips. Granny had loved the Victorian seaside resort, with its seen-better-days vibe, and its views out to the pale, blue expanse of the North Sea. We sat there in the sun, knowing we had all just agreed to do something rash.

We figured that Sarah, my dad's ex-girlfriend, surely knew more than any of us did. Now that Granny was gone, we wanted to see the place where Dad was found. We would never have felt able to do that when Granny was alive, out of respect, more than anything else. We agreed now that we would go there on the way home.

We knew the rough area, near a local village, but we couldn't find the exact spot. We just didn't have the local knowledge. We knew that he had been found in the River Derwent, near a weir. We knew roughly where we were but wanted to be completely sure. There was only one way we could find out. We would need to visit Sarah.

We went back over the things we had learned from the inquest or otherwise knew – that Dad could easily swim for miles, but had drowned in shallow water; that he had been found dead close to where Sarah lived; that he had been stalking her; that his car window was smashed and there had been letters to her inside; that his wallet had been found in her driveway; that she had a new romantic partner. We churned this information over again, between us, shaping it into the likeliest scenario.

With so much being hushed up by my grandparents and everyone around them, at the inquest, anything seemed possible.

Maybe there had been some kind of altercation between Dad and Sarah, and maybe her boyfriend, too. Maybe one or both of them had finally confronted him. According to his autopsy, Dad had been drinking and had taken barbiturates. He was probably out of it. I felt pretty certain he would have been in the wrong, somehow. Maybe there had been an accident. Maybe that was why the cover up had been needed.

The coroner had recorded an open verdict, but my grandmother and my aunt were convinced his death had been a suicide, because of a specific letter they had found in his car. To us, it looked like more of an apology, or a list of apologies for all the things he'd done, than a suicide note. None of us believed he would have done that. But, of course, you can never really know what's in anyone's head. I know that more than most.

We didn't tell Sarah we were coming. We asked a mutual friend where she lived and just turned up on her doorstep. She lived in a limestone cottage, in a village near Scarborough. This was more like somewhere a fairytale granny would live than the residence of our imagined wicked witch of the West. I can still feel the tension as we watched Kirsty and Susan waiting for that door to open, wondering just who was on the other side – this woman we were convinced had been lying to us all these years.

Sarah opened the door, and my sisters introduced themselves. Understandably, she looked shocked to see us. I don't know why, but it hadn't occurred to me that she might be. The sight of five strangers with questions would be enough to put anyone on the back foot.

In spite of her shock, she quickly caught up. I don't know who I'd been expecting, but Sarah wasn't it. She couldn't have been nicer. She told us about Dad trying to get back into her life, and that she had a partner and had made it as clear as she could that she wasn't interested. She told us how she'd seen him in her garden, looking through her windows. She painted a picture that matched the drunk, menacing figure we all recognised. My stomach twisted with disgust, with the thought that this was my father, and this was what he'd done to yet another innocent woman.

None of it was my fault. I know that now, and I knew it then, in that moment.

She took us to the spot where he'd been found. We stood there, in a quiet, leafy clearing, on the banks of the River Derwent. I started to laugh again, but this time I knew why. I was looking at some hand-hewn steppingstones. Sarah explained that at the time Dad died, the river's water level would have been higher. The stones would have been under water – slippery, and barely visible. They'd found him in the water, close to the stones. His shoes were on the other side of the river.

I knew then what had happened. It was painfully obvious. Dad's car was on one side of the river. Sarah's house was on the other. Dad wanted to cross the river but didn't want to get his shoes wet. He had thrown them to the other side. I would have done exactly the same thing. Then he'd tried to cross the river and slipped on one of those greasy, hidden stones and hit his head on another. He'd knocked himself unconscious and drowned. It was a characteristically stupid accident in a long and distinguished career of them. He'd written off cars, run over the back of an angry bull, fallen in the mill race and blown himself up with petrol. Eventually, his nine lives had run out. I couldn't believe that no one had considered this at the inquest. How had they missed it? I suppose, in the rush to cover up any hint of a scandal, no one wanted to dwell on the details, and my grandparents were comfortable with an open verdict being recorded.

We'd spent fifteen years thinking about the possibilities, and now, from just one conversation, we knew the truth. Thanks to a very patient woman, and a short drive to the place he was found, we had our answer. It was instant closure. I felt a palpable sense of relief, as if not knowing had weighed me down all these years without my realising.

I'd spent all that time thinking something violent had happened, and I'd been wrong.

Ashley loves fortune tellers, palm readers and mediums; anyone who is, as I usually like to call them, 'at it'. A few months before we went on this voyage of discovery to Yorkshire, she'd gone to see a medium in Stranraer. I don't know why I went with her on this occasion; I was probably curious to see what kind of nonsense they came out with. We sat there, in the smallest shop in the world opposite a plump woman in her sixties, with massive, hooped earrings and conspicuous rosary beads.

She told me, in no uncertain terms, that my dad was around me, all the time, and that he was looking out for me. I can see how people fall for this kind of thing. It's seductive. It gives you a sense of comfort, buying into that notion. She told me to look for white feathers. Okay, I know I'm a cynic, but if someone tells you to look for white feathers, because they signify a coming lottery win, or meeting the love of your life, or the end of days, you're going to be on the lookout for them everywhere, consciously or otherwise. It's all just confirmation bias. Right?

When we arrived there, on that riverbank, Ashley shouted. 'Look Graeme. Look!'

In front of us, a white feather fell from a tree, and just for a second, I wondered.

# Chapter Seventeen

Back in the reality of the day job I was fairly content, but it wouldn't be long before I got restless again. This time, the change would be closer to home.

I was freeze branding flat-out, full time, for four solid years. On average, I branded fourteen thousand cows a year. I was branding more than anyone else working in Scotland, and I'm pretty sure I was doing more than anyone else in the UK, mainly because I don't think anyone else would be that daft.

The longest day I ever had, freeze branding, was for a guy called Andrew Innes, a tenth-generation dairy farmer on the Cawdor estate, up near Nairn. For nine of those generations, his family had rented the farm, right up until very recently, when Andrew had bought it. Those farming ancestors of his had all been born in the same house, so it must have been quite a moment for him, finally owning the land.

He kept phoning and asking me to do his cattle, but he was over two hundred miles away, in the very north of Scotland. I didn't have any other clients in the area so I couldn't justify such a long trip. He wasn't giving up and I eventually found an opening in my rammed diary. If I worked the Tuesday in Galloway, and then drove the seven hours to his farm, I could just about squeeze him in and make it home for the following morning's work. The result was that I branded one hundred and sixty-three of his cows in a single day, then drove seven hours back so I could start work closer to home on the Thursday. It was the hardest day I've ever worked. I still don't know how I did it.

I charged the farmers £5 per branding. I got to keep £2, and Davie got the rest. Freeze branding comes with heavy overheads. Every Monday morning, I had to drive for two hours to Bellshill, just outside Glasgow, to pick up the dry ice, then drive back to wherever I was going that day. Dry ice evaporates in the heat of a vehicle, slowly filling it to a lethal level of carbon dioxide gas. I had to drive the whole way back with the windows open, so I didn't suffocate. It was a delicate balancing act; keeping the windows closed enough to avoid wind burn, and open enough to fend off certain asphyxiation.

Because dry ice is so expensive, you need to make sure you use it as efficiently as possible, by getting through as many cows as you can before your supply runs out. It's a logistical tightrope. Part of the skill of the job is in organising your route. On top of the dry ice there are other costs: methylated spirits, diesel, vehicle maintenance. It all adds up. The first day of my working week earned me nothing. I was glad if it covered the costs of the rest of the week. If I managed to brand two hundred cows in a week, I'd only be breaking even. In financial terms, hoof trimming is an entirely different proposition. You can trim ten cows' hooves in a day and still walk away with a wage you could survive on.

Freeze branding is risky. You're working at the dangerous end of the cow. Those year-old heifers are young, skinny and restless – much like me, once upon a time. Yes, they're restrained in a crush, which holds their heads in place. Or you find your own creative (or in my case, unreliable) methods of restraint. But there's nothing to stop those back legs when they lash out

I've mentioned that I got kicked, hard, every day, for four years. I expected it. I conditioned myself to the pain and got somewhat used to it, as long as the kicks landed roughly where I intended them to. I remember freeze branding at a local farm one day. It was tight in the race – the narrow corridor separating the cattle from the rest of the herd – which had high, wooden sides. Great for keeping the cattle in, but not so great for getting away if it all went wrong. I was pushing hard against a heifer's bum, doing my best to get a clear number on there. Without warning, she flipped up, driving both back legs into the air. The branding irons shot upwards and smashed into my mouth. I could feel the warm blood in my nose, and I could taste the familiar metallic tang telling me there was a bit of damage. The guys I was working with, known locally as Bhuda and Skeeda, were determined to get the cow out of the crush. But I kept her there, got the irons straight back onto her bum and got the number out clearly, before the irons warmed up. That was the hard side of the job, but you just had to accept it.

Before branding, I quickly shaved the area with a set of cattle clippers. If I didn't shave the site, the hair would get in the way, insulating it from the cold. I've heard of the odd farm worker, and at least one cocker spaniel, getting an impromptu haircut courtesy of a set of these! Swapping the salon for the farm is one thing, but some people take their personal grooming decisions to the extreme. A farmer on the Isle of Man apparently loved one of his cows so much, he decided he wanted to create a lasting tribute to her. He made his friends ratchet-strap him to a pallet and had them brand her number – 369 – right onto his chest. His brand probably came out beautifully because, unlike a cow, he would have been easier to shave. Each to their own, I say.

After shaving the area, I'd wet it with methylated spirit. Freeze branding works better with meths than on dry skin. I had two sets of branding irons. They were numbered zero to nine, allowing me to make up any combination I needed. I kept them in a big box filled with the purple-brown soup I used to cool them. I used to leave the irons in the box overnight. It was unconventional, but it saved on dry ice, and it meant that I was good to go in the morning.

The nasty side effect for me was that the handles of the branding irons froze too. My gloves were in bad shape, and I couldn't afford a new set. Every day, until those handles warmed up, for maybe the first ten cows, I'd get freeze burned. I always had blistered skin between my thumb and index finger. Even now, if you meet me and remember to check out my hands, you'll see the skin in that area is gnarly and calloused – a reminder of the constant cycle of damage and repair from the cold.

I'd stand behind the cow and push the branding iron as hard as I could into her hind quarters. If I pushed a piece of metal at minus eighty degrees into your butt cheek, I'm guessing you'd struggle. You'd probably want to kick me. The irons had to stay on for fifty seconds. That meant a wrestling match every time but there was no way I could let that iron come off the back of the cow before the time was up. If I lost contact, if I moved or slid even slightly, that meant a badly defined number and that wouldn't do. I'd always been a perfectionist. Now I was literally having to fight to keep my standards up. Just to add to the challenge, I was pushing on one side, so I was trying to deal with a moving target, at an angle.

If that sounds bad, I also had the farmers to handle. Farmers like to extract the maximum value for money out of any financial transaction. It's like an eleventh commandment to them. I'd hand over my stopwatch and ask them to time fifty seconds for me, but a lot of them thought a bit longer meant a better deal. Fifty seconds is the optimum amount for a reason though. Any longer and you'll burn the cow. I explained this whenever I handed over the stopwatch, but a lot of them still thought they knew best. That meant a lot of second guessing on my part. Luckily for me, wrestling three hundred cows a week gave me a fairly accurate sense of how long fifty seconds actually was. I'm pretty sure I did a decent job for every farmer – even if they were working against me.

The comment I always got was that I must have really strong arms. I'd love to say that it's true, that I am actually seriously jacked, but anyone who has seen my videos might take issue with that. I had a trick; an efficient technique of locking my arms straight, then pushing with my lower back. I'd plant my feet on the ground and use a low centre of gravity to get all my weight behind it. After doing that with about seventy cows, I'd have to put my arms through a gate and hang there, for a couple of minutes, just to stretch my back out. You can't stretch for too long though. You're always on the farmer's time. Either they're helping you or one of their workers is, and that comes with extra pressure to move quickly. You need to get on with it.

As well as tight profit margins, I had the added fun of trying to get Davie to pay me. He in turn had to wait until the farmers paid him. That meant a constant tension between us over money. I had, and still have, a lot of respect for Davie. I liked him. I was probably the closest person in the world to him at this point, but he was one of the most disorganised people I ever met. The friction meant that we constantly got on each other's nerves. I'm pretty polite as a person, but like everyone else, I have a line. If someone is impolite to me, they'll know all about it. Davie was impatient and could be really abrupt. That led to some 'heated discussions'.

The novelty of the travelling and the constant changes did eventually start to wear on me. Some days I just wanted to wake up in my own bed. One day I was working on a farm up north, just outside Aberdeen. As always when I was away, I was trying to cram as much into as short a time as possible. It was a tough shift, and I didn't know the farmer very well. He told me he was part of a long farming line, and his family had all fallen out when his parents died. I remember being positive and upbeat. Sometimes these guys don't see people for days, even weeks, on end, and you might be the only person they've spoken to in a long time. I knew he worked alone. When I looked away from what I was doing, I realised he had broken down, right there in front of me. Depression is a big problem in farming. The pressure of the money involved, combined with the isolation, can overwhelm people. I felt terrible for the guy. I really did. But I had problems of my own. I just wanted to finish up and go home. I had no idea how I was going to get out of the situation.

'Hello, Graeme,' chirped a familiar voice.

I looked up to see the face that accompanied it. Robyn was a girl from home, and she was sitting on a high, wooden fence, smiling down at me. She worked for an artificial insemination company, and she'd been in the area, covering someone else's job. She had seen my van and wandered over to track me down. I was pretty glad to see her, and grateful for the diversion from the previous conversation.

A few days later I was rescued again, in an altogether different way. Davie approached me and offered to sell me his freeze branding business for £4,000. I took the deal. I was now in business for myself, at last. I would be able to do what I liked and focus on what I loved. Or so I thought.

Now that I was set up and running on my own, more and more people told me I should become a hoof trimmer. I was starting to seriously consider it, but I decided that if I was to make the leap, I would have to do things differently. Very differently. I'd enjoyed travelling to far-flung parts of the country, but, economically, it just didn't make sense. I would start out in the Dumfries and Galloway area instead, close to home, to keep costs down. Unlike freeze branding, where the cow only needed my attention once, hoof trimming was a recurring gig. That meant more work locally.

I decided there was no way to grow the freeze branding business any further. I felt as though I'd mastered it and taken things as far as I could. I needed a new challenge. I could earn a lot more money hoof trimming, and, if I didn't travel as far, I could make things more efficient. So much of my time had been spent on the road with freeze branding that my true hourly rate was probably less than minimum wage. I'd be getting paid just for hoof trimming now, instead of burning time and money driving. To begin with, I'd trim all four feet on a cow for £11, if I was working with a new customer. I'd charge £10 if I was visiting the same farm every four weeks, and £9 if I was visiting every fortnight. Regular visits made the job easier, so it made sense to price my services accordingly.

I had some problems from the get-go. First of all, I didn't have a cattle crush – the sturdy stall I needed to safely contain the cows while I worked. Even a basic spec of crush cost around £45,000 brand new. A similar second-hand crush would be about £12,000. I didn't have that kind of money. Secondly, I had no experience and no training. Davie had offered to train me in the past, but he had stopped because of the abscess on his spine. And, lastly, I had no equipment. The angle-grinders and trimming disks I needed were well over my budget.

The way I saw it, training had to be the first priority. Without Davie, I needed the right teacher and the best I knew of was Pieter Kloosterman. He taught a four-day residential course, in 'The Dutch Method' of hoof trimming, with a company called Embryonics, in Cheshire. It was, and still is, a recognised route into hoof trimming. Pieter had spent thousands of hours working up close with cattle. I had no choice but to borrow the money from Mum and attend the course.

Pieter is an ultra-Dutchman. He's six feet five in height, and wears clogs. He always seemed to be in a pair of shorts and a tight little vest. An ever-present roll-up cigarette hung from his lips, looking very much like a spliff, although I'm reliably assured it wasn't. I snuck a picture of him on the first day, for McGill. We both love a character, and I knew he would never believe me when I described Pieter to him – he was so chilled out, the total antithesis of someone you'd expect to find delivering an industry training course.

Pieter is now a friend of mine, and I see him a couple of times a year. We usually get drunk and tell each other stories. These days, I know the owner of Embryonics and the people who work there. They sponsor Hoof GP videos and once provided the training for Susan's husband, 'The Craig'. It's funny to think how much things have changed in just a few years. I was almost scared to meet all these people, and now I know them all well.

My social anxiety aside, I enjoyed my time on the course – much more than I thought I would. I came back like a new version of myself. GP 2.0., if you will. I was ready to get stuck into hoof trimming, after all those years of resistance. I sent out letters to twelve farms I'd worked on in the past. Crucially, these twelve farms all had their own crushes. My letter informed the farmers that I was moving into the hoof trimming business and proposed that if I used their crushes, I could trim their cows' hooves at a discounted rate. I also asked the farmers to supply their own hoof blocks in exchange for an extra discount. All twelve were keen, and I still trim for every one of them today.

I could only afford the most basic tools, but I put together what I needed in a bucket, and I was good to go. I remember my very first job. I turned up, on a bitter February day, with my bucket. The farmer was an old Irish guy and he didn't believe in hoof trimming, but his son lived in the twenty-first century and persuaded him he should give me a try.

The most cows I'd ever trimmed in a day, in training, was ten (and that was between three of us!). I had sixty-three to do here. I calculated, or rather, I hoped, that I could get through them in two days. I'd really jumped in at the deep end. I'll never forget the state of their feet. To this day, they're still the worst I've seen. Fifty of them had rotten hooves, totally infested with maggots. I don't think I've seen worse since. I'd been around farming in one form or another for twenty-five years and I've seen a lot of things that would turn your stomach, but this was truly disgusting. I had to do a lot of precision work to make any kind of impact on them. The feet we'd seen on the training course were all in good condition. This was a big awakening.

My videos show me doing a lot of angle grinder work. The grinder has a specialised disk, with three blades – a vital piece of kit for me now. Back then, I was just using knives. I'd never even used an angle grinder on the course, but I knew how much work I had to do, so I pretended to the farmer that my angle grinder was broken, and he let me borrow his. It wasn't easy getting used to it. There was the risk of removing too much hoof horn and making things worse, so I had to take a softly-softly approach.

At the end of the first day, I'd managed to trim twenty-nine cows. I was amazed. That meant £290. I was a happy man. I was done in, but the money almost made it worth the exhaustion. The next day I was back again, working my backside off, through the filth and the maggots and the brutal cold on my hands. I got to the end of the day, and I'd managed the remaining thirty-four cows. That meant a grand total of £630. I was broken, but the money made it seem worthwhile.

The farmer reached for his chequebook. He carefully wrote out the cheque: £630 plus VAT, meaning a total of £756. He was about to hand it over to me when he said, 'Do you mind if I post-date this for two months' time?' I felt like he'd just ripped my heart out of my ribcage. I was tired, cold, filthy, and now, gutted. I nodded, smiled, and said, 'That's absolutely fine.'

I remember that feeling so well; having absolutely no money, looking forward to telling Ashley I was paying a cheque into our account, and that it would clear, then realising I couldn't. I needed that money. Apart from anything else, I had to pay Mum back. Two days of hell and I would have to wait another two months to get paid. I told Ashley when I got home. 'Why did you let him do that?' she asked. 'I had no choice,' I said. If I hadn't accepted the cheque post-dated, the farmer might have cancelled it. It might have bounced. At least this way I had the cheque, and I was fairly certain I was getting paid in two months. It was better than nothing.

Years later, I was at a conference in Bristol. I was talking to another hoof trimmer. We were trading war stories – comparing the worst farms we had been to. I asked about his, and he said, 'That's easy. It was this old Irish farmer just outside Dumfries. All his cows had feet infested with maggots.' It turned out we'd been to the same guy. We agreed neither of us had taken a worse job, and neither of us had been back since.

I still feel bad for that farmer's cows. I wonder if anyone ever went back there and did what it took to get on top of them, or if everyone was so pissed off at the post-dated cheques, they never went back.

# Chapter Eighteen

After I became more established in my new endeavour, I gradually started dropping the freeze branding side of the business. I was now a full-time hoof trimmer, and I had begun to realise how dangerous it was, using other people's crushes. That, and it was much more tiring.

I should point out that most of the crushes I was using were actually built by Davie. He had several side hustles to his main business: building crushes, installing cattle mattresses, and concrete grooving (no it's not a weird European dance craze; it's putting lines in concrete to stop cows from slipping). That was part of the reason his business was so precarious. He did too much. He travelled too much, and he charged too little. He was building decent quality crushes for knock-down prices, doing his customers a favour because he saw them as friends, rather than making a profit.

You might think a crush is a crush, but hoof trimmers, like all other beasts, come in all shapes and sizes and need their own working specifications. I remember trimming one day at the farm I live next to now. I was using the farmer's crush, and I had the cow fastened in place. I was about to trim her front left foot. I was completely focused on what I was doing because I get lost in my work.

Something went bang. I felt a thump, then I was thrown into the air. I couldn't understand what had happened at first. It took a while to realise that the cow's back left leg had shot forward. She was a heifer. Her hoof was small and sharp. She had kicked me, hard, with the point of that hoof, right in the bicep. That might not sound too severe – it wasn't as if she'd kicked me in the head – but she hit me so hard she burst a vein. Within minutes, my whole arm turned black, as the blood haemorrhaged out into the surrounding tissue. The swelling and the pressure were unbelievable. It's up there with the most painful accidents I've had. And as we know, I've had a few of them.

For the sake of my health, I decided I had to design my own crush. It hurt me to do it, but I borrowed more money from Mum – on top of the money that I still hadn't paid back – and for three weeks solid I laboured on the build after work. I cut all the metal to size, welded all the joints neatly and painted everything Massey Ferguson-tractor red. I bought the paint from the local dealer. When I was finished, I was proud of my work.

It functioned really well. Don't get me wrong, it had its faults. All prototypes do. Even Edison had a few goes at the lightbulb before he got it right. With my new crush, it was as if someone had turned the dial up to eleven. My work rate increased exponentially, and I felt like the greatest hoof trimmer on earth. I wasn't just turning up with my bucket anymore. I was turning up with my crush, *and* my bucket. That felt like my turning point. I was a professional, at last. I used that first, hand-made crush for about eighteen months. Then, one day, as I accelerated out of Kirkcowan up to about fifty miles per hour, I heard an ominous bang. I looked out at the side-view mirror. My crush cartwheeled down the road, straight past me, then crashed to a halt on the side of the road. I can't remember how I extracted it from the verge, but that was the end of that.

As per the customary mirroring of our family mishaps, this wasn't the first time one of us had experienced that. When I was young and Davie was still hoof trimming, he was driving along a tricky road that runs round and over the Rocks of Garheugh, between Port William and Auchenmalg. To give you an idea of how dicey this bit of road is, I need to tell you a story about James and Kirsty.

James had just bought a new car, and he was very happy with it. It was a Vauxhall Astra Mark Two. That was when Astras looked cool, and James thought he was invincible. So much so, that he took it flying. He was following Kirsty and I over the Rocks of Garheugh, when he decided he would prove how nifty his new whip was and catch us. There was a car between him and us, and James moved out to overtake it, on a chicane-style corner. He was an inexperienced driver, so he misjudged it. He moved over too far and hit the grass verge on one side of the road, overcorrected, then hit the wall on the other side. The car flipped multiple times, and Kirsty and I saw it all in the rear-view mirror. We thought James was dead. Miraculously, everyone was fine. When we reached his car, it was balanced between the road and the dyke, upside down. James was hanging from his seatbelt.

Once he'd unclipped himself and slumped to the ground, he demanded that we check the boot to see how his golf clubs were. The boot (or trunk) was mangled and resting on a wall. That's when rage overtook fear and Kirsty lost it.

'What the hell's wrong with you? We thought you were dead!'

James was having none of it. 'Never mind that. There's fifteen hundred pounds worth of golf clubs in that boot.'

You can still see gap in the ivy today.

Davie was driving the same stretch one day when he had his own mishap. The first moment he realised something was wrong was when the crush overtook him. Murphy's Law (also known as Sod's Law around here) states that if something can go wrong, it will. I have a slightly different version of this going on: if it can go wrong, it will, and on a road – while driving. For me this usually involves the loss of a wheel. I once heard a loud bang and saw one bounce past me, into a field, but other components have been equally mobile over the years. Davie's crush suffered the same fate.

The loss of my first, very own, hand-built crush was potentially disastrous for me. I had a little bit of money set aside by then, but still nowhere near enough to buy a ready-made crush. Still, I had my original design and eighteen months' worth of solid testing behind me. So, I went back to the workshop every night. I built myself a hydraulic version this time. I was physically and mentally drained by the end of it, but I was even more proud of the result.

The only thing I hadn't done myself was wire up the hydraulics. The first day I took it out, the main part of it snapped off in front of one of my customers. I felt like an idiot, but it turned out to be a small enough problem to fix. After that it was awesome – quicker and much safer to use than my previous version. My life was now much easier. Looking back, I think that was the point I really started to enjoy hoof trimming.

I was working one day with Montbéliarde cattle. They're dual-purpose cows – a cross between beef and dairy. Beef cows are bred for beef, and I suppose the word 'beefy' is the best description for them. They're big, muscly and grumpy to work with a lot of the time. If you lived on a hill most of your life and got dragged in only to be injected, dehorned or branded, you'd probably be a bit suspicious of humans too. Dairy cows are usually slighter in stature. It's all about milk production, so they tend to have a small frame and large udders.

Montbéliardes have an attitude. They're known for it. They have fiery red patches on their coats, a muscular build and a strong urge to work against us, whatever we're doing. In some ways that works in our favour. They tend to shoot into the crush, because they want to get away from us at all costs. On this particular day, we were using the two small gates we'd hang off the back of my crush and tie up to the farmer's crush. That created a race, allowing the cows to come through the farmer's crush and into the back of mine. A simple but effective way of doing things.

Or it should have been.

The gates themselves had another, smaller gate, around nine inches wide, inside them. The mini gates meant I could slip through the race when I needed to. Stupidly, I left one of them open. One of the Montbéliardes spotted the gap. Nine inches isn't a massive gap for anything of bovine proportions, but cows aren't known for their ability to judge distances. She didn't see the potential for embarrassment; she saw only opportunity. She took her chance, made a break for freedom and learned the hard way that she was more than nine inches wide.

She was determined. I'll give her that. She somehow managed to get her head and shoulders into the space. If that sounds bad, it was about to get worse. The gate wasn't properly on. She might have been stuck, but she was nothing if not adaptable. Eventually, she broke free, wearing the gate around her. Craig and I watched on, helplessly, as she careered round the farm.

We waited until we thought she might have worn herself out, then we made our move. We had to try to get the gate off without hurting her, and without the farmer finding out. Most important was her wellbeing, followed closely by our credibility. She came back round towards us, and I made a run for it. Every time we got closer, she made another break for freedom, and every time she did that, the gate slipped further down her body. Eventually it was around her hips, and we were out of ideas. In the end, I had to do the solemn walk back to the pick-up to fetch the angle grinder. Cutting her free from the gate definitely hurt me more than it hurt her.

There's a concept the French call 'débrouillard'. It belongs to the culinary world. Débrouillard means flexible; resourceful; the ability to improvise to get the job done. When I worked in restaurants, we used to refer to it as 'system D'. That has stayed with me all these years. I'm proud of my ability to adapt, to find my way out of situations. It feels like the ultimate empowerment, the opposite of depression. I welded the gate back together as quickly as I could and got back to it.

Crush number three was built by someone else. It was second hand and thirteen-years-old. I saved every penny I could so I could buy it from a friend, and I still had to pay him in instalments. Crushes have a hard life. A thirteen-year-old crush is a lot like a thirteen-year-old sheepdog; it might be hard-working, reliable, even loyal, but it's on the home stretch – ready for the end. And you know when it does go, it'll be pretty catastrophic.

On the fated day in question, we were on our way to a farm called High Three Mark, near a place called Stoneykirk, just outside Stranraer. It's a four-hundred-and-ninety-acre farm with around seven hundred dairy cows. The owner, James, had built up the business in his twenties, along with a friend. Getting into farming these days is quite a challenge. There's a lot of money involved, so seeing someone manage it in their twenties is rare. We were about four miles from High Three Mark when we heard the mother of all bangs. I looked in the rear-view mirror. We were pulling a lop-sided crush. Sparks were shooting into the air where one of the wheels had been, as the axle bounced along the road. I was half tempted to just drag the crush all the way to the farm, trailing a grinding, pyrotechnic wake behind me, until the other wheel fell off. I like to think I'm pretty resourceful, but even I get a bit panicky in these kinds of situations. I phoned James, to explain what had happened.

'No worries,' he said. 'Take your time, but you are still coming, aren't you?'

'Yeah, yeah, yeah, of course,' I reassured him. 'We won't let you down. We'll be there just as soon as we've fixed ourselves up.' I paused for a second or two. Let the thought hang in the air. 'Actually, you might have to give us a lift. If you've got a tractor and a loader and you can drive down here and pick up my crush, then yes, we're still coming!'

Being the all-round good guy that he is, James climbed onto his tractor, lifted the crush from the road and drove it to a local welder for a quick repair job, then drove it back to his farm so we could get to work. We managed to trim a hundred cows that day. It was a tough shift, the kind of workday you would normally finish off by collapsing into the driver's seat of the truck. Unfortunately, we still had an axle to fix and reinstall on the crush.

Back we went to the same welder who'd half-fixed it for us. Then we went back to High Three Mark knowing we had to hammer the thing back into place. The crush weighed a tonne and a half, so we had a big job on our hands. After some pondering, a lot of hammering and some fairly expressive language on my part, we finally had the axle back in position. That's when we realised that we didn't have a castle nut. A castle nut has notches cut into the end of it, making it look like the battlements on a medieval castle. We needed it to hold the wheel to the axle. The notches that give it the turret appearance allow you to stick a pin through the end of the bolt. I realised the welder would be closed by now. I would have to bodge it, go full 'system D', or I wasn't getting home or getting any more work done this week. Craig tried to talk me down. He could see the way my brain was heading, and he is – quite often – the sensible one.

Then I saw a chain hanging from one of our gates.

I took my angle grinder, bolted on a cutting disk and took one link from the end of the chain. Then I welded the link on to the end of the axle stub. It held the wheel enough to get us home and enough to get us through to the end of the week. At that point I knew I'd had a good run and paid someone to fix it properly. It's wise to remember your luck can run out.

There's a central debate in the hoof care community. If you put a bunch of hoof trimmers in a bar, the conversation will eventually turn to one hot topic: Are you an upright guy or a layover guy? (Or girl, although most hoof trimmers are men.) I'm an upright guy. All my cattle crushes have had that in common: they've all been upright. That is, except for a recent exception when Craig did his own 'conversion' on the Appleton Steel we now have, by rolling it sideways off a concrete step. This became a viral video for us. I have used layover crushes, in the past. Once you've loaded the animal into the crush, you can tip the whole thing over on its side. They are a lot quicker to use because all of their feet wind up in the same place, in the air, at an angle, meaning you don't have to keep running around the crush. Unfortunately, their main problem is exactly that: all the feet wind up in the same place, in the air, at an angle. That makes them much trickier to trim evenly.

There's also the added risk that the cow can break her leg when the crush tips back over, hitting the ground at a forty-five-degree angle. I know that has happened in the past and it really puts me off. Don't get me wrong, there are some fantastic tipping crushes. The Double O Flipper is a brilliant feature – a sort of arm that hugs the animal while it's in there. But I like what I like, I guess.

My biggest crush catastrophe, however, was the one I managed to avoid. I knew a guy called Charlie who was selling a second-hand crush. It was state of the art in my eyes – this was well before the days of the Appleton Steel and the KVK I use now. I knew it would be a huge stretch, but I spoke to him briefly and agreed what I thought was a fair price. I would pay Charlie £17,000 in two instalments. He was happy. I was ecstatic. This was a crush I never thought I would be able to afford, and it was within my grasp.

I then went to an agricultural show with another hoof trimmer I knew. We were on a road trip. The chat was good. We were having a laugh, and the conversation turned to the crush I was buying. He seemed happy I'd got such a good deal on it. He was genuinely interested and asked quite a few questions about it. I was due to take delivery of it that December. I double checked with Charlie and made sure we were all good for then. I waited on the call like a kid waiting on the next Harry Potter instalment. If I could have joined a queue somewhere at 5 a.m., I would have. We got a couple of weeks into December, and I still hadn't heard anything. Chasing people isn't something I enjoy;

I hate that side of running a business. Following up on unpaid invoices isn't a nice feeling, and, as you now know, I get massive anxiety even when anyone phones me. So, I really hate it when I have to phone them.

Eventually my enthusiasm for the crush won out and I picked up the phone.

'Oh, I thought you didn't want it anymore,' Charlie said, when I finally tracked him down.

'No, of course I want it,' I said. 'I'm desperate for it.' What on earth had made him think that?

There was a slight pause at the other end of the line. 'Oh. Well, one of your friends phoned me and told me you didn't want it anymore but it's okay, he bought it off me instead and gave me an extra thousand pounds to deliver it, with him living further way.'

Obviously, I was raging. Who wouldn't be? But it was too late to do anything about it. I'd been properly done over; gazumped. I felt like I'd lost out on the deal of the century, but I was wrong. Everything that could have gone wrong with that crush, did. The first day the new owner took it out, the wheels fell off, on the busiest roundabout in the busiest town in the area. Then the electrics caught fire, and that was on one of the rare occasions they were actually working. The rest of the time they were just haywire. From my perspective that crush couldn't have gone more wrong if it had been made by ACME and Wile E. Coyote had been using it to try to catch the Road Runner. Karma's a bastard, eh?

Although I felt stupid for being too trusting, and for losing out in the beginning, I'd lucked out in the long term. In the end, I bought a much better second-hand crush. It was a tough lesson to learn though. I have always trusted people, and it hits me hard when they let me down. I suppose it beats going through life as a cynic.

I have of course, by now, made my way through quite a few crushes. My early days at making my own and struggling to negotiate affordable prices for the right gear are, thankfully, behind me, but that's only a relatively recent development for me, as crushes – especially the really good ones – remain incredibly expensive pieces of kit. One of the hardest decisions I ever made was whether to set up a GoFundMe page for a new crush. At the time I had my second-hand one, a thirteen-year-old Wopa. It had been all the crush I'd ever dreamed of when I'd started out, but that was at a lower work rate, and my back was younger then. Both had seen better days and the demands I was putting on them were only increasing. Everyone commented on this, or it certainly felt that way at the time. I'd reply that I couldn't afford to change it. I was okay with that. I was still in a better position than I had been on day one, with my home-made-crush mark one, and a knackered bucket full of tools.

More and more people suggested I set up a funding page for a new crush, but I refused. And I kept refusing. Never let it be said that I don't know how to dig my heels in. The way I saw it, funding pages were for charities. I couldn't stand the thought that I might be taking advantage of people's good will. In the end, it was my friend, fellow hoof trimmer and YouTuber, Aaron LaVoy, who changed my mind. Aaron, who goes by the name Midwestern Hoof Trimmer, lives in Wisconsin and we've known each other for a few years. He phoned me one day out of the blue. He said that people had been contacting him, asking if he would set up a GoFundMe page for me. I was blown away, but Aaron seemed kind of annoyed at me.

'Graeme, what you don't understand is that these people want to give you money,' he said. 'They don't view you as a charity, but they do want to be involved and give you money and you're not allowing them to do that. And you're actually pissing them off. So, if you want to lose subscribers, then stick to your guns, but if you want to make everyone happy, start a GoFundMe page'.

None of this had occurred to me. But it still felt like a massive decision. I worried that people might see it as begging, that some might find it annoying and others might be jealous, in some way. Eventually I caved. I started a page, but I was honest about my feelings. I explained why I was reluctant and how strange I felt about the whole thing. Regardless, the fund took off. Within a few weeks, I had raised $17,000 to buy a new crush. What I hadn't seen coming was the effect it would have on the channel. It felt like a real turning point, like people were literally buying into what I was doing. Some of my viewers now felt way more attached to the channel as a direct result of the fundraising. I hadn't been wrong about the negativity, but all of it came from locals and other hoof trimmers. That made me realise I'd done the right thing. It was a bit unnerving and quite embarrassing, but in the end, the positivity of the experience vastly outweighed any apparent hostility. It was overwhelming, a real whirlwind of emotions. One lady donated £750. That was incredible and very humbling. She had once been given the same sum, by a local priest, when she was a young, single mother. The one condition he gave was that she paid it forward when she could, and now she was.

That blew me away.

The crush I wanted wasn't $17,000, unfortunately. It was $68,000. Why was the price in US Dollars? That's because the model I wanted was from Appleton Steel, in Wisconsin. That was, as far as I could see, the best model I could possibly own; best for the cows' stress levels, best for my back, and best to make as much of an impact as possible on a daily basis.

I messaged Appleton Steel on Facebook. I said, 'I really want an Appleton Steel crush, but I don't think I can afford it. Can we talk about it?' I hadn't intended to contact them. I'd planned only to buy a slightly better crush than the one I had, but I realised I didn't know anyone at Appleton Steel, so what did I have to lose? They messaged me back straight away, asking for my number. On the phone, I explained everything that had happened. I told them about my channel, that I couldn't afford the Appleton Steel, but might they be able to do anything for me? They asked what I could afford. I told them $17,000, but that I wasn't in a position to bargain. If they could do something, that was amazing, but if not, not to worry.

Incredibly, they agreed to give me a crush for less than a third of its value. The way they saw it, their crush would appear prominently in every video. It was kind of a sponsorship deal, but one that meant I could be honest. No contract, no requirement to do anything. That way I knew I wasn't selling my soul. I did sell my old Wopa though, so now I had the best crush in the world, plus some money in the bank. I could use that to buy better tools.

I was picky about the way I sold the old crush. I'd bought it three years earlier and looked after it meticulously, upgrading and improving it wherever I could. We had a lot of offers, but I didn't want to sell it to an established hoof trimmer. I'd already bought it from one – a man called John, who is now a friend of mine. He'd sold it cheaply because he wanted to give me a helping hand, and now it felt only right that I should pay it forward myself. I eventually sold it to a farmer's son who wanted to take up hoof trimming, but first, I sent it to a welder and fabricator who got it into the best possible condition before I passed it on. That farmer's son got a very good deal, and I hope he has had many happy hours trimming with it.

Now, thanks to Appleton Steel and the amazing YouTube community, I own and use a state-of-the-art crush. I took delivery of it in April 2020, and naturally, I documented the moment on YouTube. I call it The Dark Knight because I got zero sleep the night before I used it for the first time. I was like a kid on Christmas Eve. I tossed and turned like a drunken sailor, but it was worth it. I got used to it quickly – it only took about a week to get up to speed. Now, I'm spoiled. The way it positions the cow's feet, especially at the back, is a game changer. The front feet positioning took longer to get used to, but quickly it become the norm. The access is way better than on my old crush.

The Dark Knight was, as you would expect, primarily black, but, like myself and Craigus Maximus, it had some funky accents to enhance it: red cables and hydraulic pistons; stainless steel boxes and cupboards. All of those really pop against the base colour, like the stripe on *The A-Team* van or red brake callipers on a supercar. I felt like I was turning up in a Lamborghini, even if it was quite a bit heavier.

It was quicker, easier to clean, and most importantly, the cows seemed to be a lot happier. More recently, Appleton Steel approached me and asked if I would become a dealer for their crushes, but I knew that would mean time away from trimming and cows so, unfortunately, I had to turn them down. My new house and my workshop space have made that logistically possible, but for now, the workshop is perfect for looking after and maintaining my own crush. I've installed a steam cleaner, so I can give it a good blast, twice a week, and keep it in the best condition possible. That's the least it deserves, and it's also essential for work safety – an added extra on top of the post-farm-visit cleans we do as standard.

We don't just high tail it straight away when we've finished trimming. We usually take an hour to clean everything before we head to the next farm. The crush gets a good going over, so it looks brand spanking new, and we clean all the tools, gloves, grinders and pads. We even do the eight individual screws holding them on. It's not easy. They need to be soaked and scrubbed with a wire brush. Then we dry everything and wrap the handles of the grinders with claw bandages, ready to go again. Here's my #protip: it's easier to remove dirty bandages than clean stained handles. We even cover the remote control on the crush with heat shrink to make sure it stays clean, and crucially, dry.

Farms are naturally mucky places, but that isn't an excuse to turn up with grubby equipment. There's a real danger of cross contamination. I lived through a period when foot and mouth disease ravaged the whole of Dumfries and Galloway, including the Wigtownshire area. Many farmers lost their livestock to the disease. Cows had to be killed or burned, on the farm, to stop its spread. I remember standing on a hill near Dumfries and counting the fires. Some farmers had to watch as their entire livelihoods were destroyed. It was devastating, and all because of something as simple as cross contamination from vehicle wheels or the soles of people's boots.

A filthy crush would look unprofessional. I restock everything in the crush: about fifty blocks; enough glue and nozzles for those fifty blocks; a gallon of iodine; hoof fix, rope and claw bandages – anything I might need for a day's work. Years ago, when I first started trimming, a local farmer was talking to me about another hoof trimmer, trying to describe who he meant. He eventually said, 'the guy with the dirty crush'. I immediately knew who he meant. I never wanted to be that guy.

And I wasn't.

In that, and in many other respects, I was crushing it. Despite the chaotic birth of my business and the ongoing struggle to afford (and keep) the right equipment, most other things were going well for me. My love life could not have been better, and things were about to move to a whole new level.

# Chapter Nineteen

Ashley and I had been together for three years by this point. They'd been three of the quickest and best years of my life, and we'd become more serious as a couple over time. Ashley's thoroughly unique combination of beauty and the easiest going nature I know, meant that I'd fallen in love with her before I knew it. All of this meant that life on the road had been hard, but now, with hoof trimming being more local, we were able to build more of a life together.

We moved into a rented house, in Kirkcowan, in December 2013; the place where my family had owned the mill all those years before. Later that month, our son Keir was born. I felt so full of pride I could have burst in two. We were continuing the family line. I get that maybe it's a bit old fashioned, wanting a son to carry on the family name. A daughter can of course do exactly the same thing, and Maddie was of course no less important to me after Keir's birth than she had been before, but it is what it is. We gave Keir the family middle names: Milroy Glen – the same as me, my brothers, my father and my grandfather. It helped me to feel this new and positive connection to my family and my past.

I can remember how focused I was on Ashley and how proud I was of her. She got through what turned out to be a tough labour, in true Ashley style, like the hero she is. Keir was born in

Dumfries in the same hospital I was. I have a picture of myself, trying to cheer Ashley up – sick bowl on head, like some kind of budget bowler hat, as if I were my grandpa Nimmo, doing something I really shouldn't be. In it, I'm laughing, and poor Ashley is in the background, clearly in pain.

The main things I remember from that time are Keir's olive skin and blond hair, how quiet he was as a baby and the sense of warmth and closeness I had, spending time with my family, in our new home, that wonderful first Christmas.

If you haven't guessed by now, Ashley is the best thing that's ever happened to me. Since I met her, she's never not been there to bring me back from the brink – from my worst times, from the highs and the lows, the floating on clouds and the black dog days, the tangents and the full stops. She always seems to know exactly what to say and when to say it, whether it's 'shut up', 'grow up' or 'calm the fuck down'. We were together for almost five years before we got engaged, and she spent a lot of that time telling me I should hurry up and propose. She was right then too!

We went on a big family holiday in October 2014. Ashley, ten-month-old Keir, my mum, my sister Susan and her family, all trooped off to Kos. We'd been there a lot, maybe as many as forty times between us all, over the years. Kos, and the Greek islands in general, had become a sort of refuge for my family, with everything going on with my dad and his eventual death. It's a four-hour flight and a world away from your problems. Sure, they'll always be there waiting when you get back, but you'll be better rested, and you'll have a decent tan. Life's always better with a tan.

Ashley had been dropping 'subtle' hints since Keir's birth. In the few months leading up to the holiday, she'd helpfully pointed out a few jewellery shops, just in case I wanted to buy anything sparkly. I'll hold my hands up and say I have no clue when it comes to jewellery. I was also stony broke. I knew I couldn't spring for the kind of ring Ashley deserved, so I deployed my finest débrouillard game, and came up with the best interim fix I could under the circumstances. I bought a ring for £100 from Argos. If you're not from the UK, Argos is a shop where you turn up and buy things from a catalogue. The comedian, Bill Bailey, calls it 'the laminated book of dreams'. Argos isn't exactly known for its quality jewellery, but there I was, ring acquired. I packed it away in my luggage before Ashley could spot it. It would do as a placeholder; something Ashley could wear until I could get her the 'real' ring. One that would last the rest of our lives.

Kos is beautiful. It's a small island in the Aegean Sea. The people there are friendly, and it has a local feel, unlike some of the bigger islands. It has a different vibe from Ayia Napa, with its super clubs and chain stores. We'd been to a lot of the restaurants before, and we knew the same faces. It had started to become a second home.

I had the ring in my rucksack, and she hadn't spotted it. The plan was simple. I'd asked Mum to look after Keir and I was going to take Ashley out for dinner. There's an amazing restaurant in Kos Town, in the shadow of The Hippocrates Tree, the place where the father of modern medicine – the original GP – taught his pupils two thousand four hundred years ago. The tree and the restaurant are in an ancient square across a bridge from the Castle of the Knights, surrounded by ruins and vine trees and bathed in candlelight; it seemed the perfect place to pop the question.

I'd planned it all perfectly. Or at least, I thought I had. I booked a restaurant, and a taxi. Mum was ready to swing into action. All I had to do was casually suggest a date night and we would be in business. What I hadn't factored into my planning was Ashley's ever-present maternal instinct. She didn't feel right about leaving Keir and going out for the night. I tried to persuade her but that just made her more determined. She wasn't leaving the apartment. It didn't matter what I said, she wouldn't budge. The conversation got more and more heated until eventually – and I'm really not proud of this – I snapped and threw the ring down on the bed.

'I was going to fucking propose to you tonight,' I shouted at her. 'How am I supposed to do that if you won't even come out with me?'

I was trying to do romance. It wasn't going to plan. I was furious.

Surprisingly, despite my plot-spoiling theatrics, Ashley wasn't furious. Her stubbornness disappeared. Boom. Back in the room. We agreed to go out, but I told her I couldn't propose that night. I'd ruined the surprise, and the moment was no longer right.

We went to the restaurant and had a delicious meal. Steak, lobster, good wine, a perfect, romantic evening, under normal circumstances. Ashley had obviously been waiting all evening, regardless, for me to reach into my pocket and present her with a ring. I could see her eyes darting around, hunting around for signs of anything sparkly or a tell-tale box. After the meal, I suggested we walk to our taxi and head back to the apartment. I could see she was starting to look a bit unsure. After all, I had told her I wasn't proposing that night.

We walked back towards the Castle of the Knights, over its two-thousand-year-old bridge. It was a warm, summer evening. Crickets chirped in the background. We reached the halfway point, and I dropped some money. I reached down to get it and came back up, holding the ring.

Ashley burst into tears. 'Yes,' she answered, before I could even ask the question.

Just as she said yes, we heard clapping. An old couple had been watching us the whole time.

Result! We were engaged *and* we got a good story out of it. I remember walking along the nearby marina afterwards, arm in arm with my new fiancée, calling our families to tell them our news. It's one of my happiest memories.

The next day we threw financial caution to the wind, went back into Kos Town and chose a more expensive engagement ring – one that turned out to be a rip-off when the stones fell out within six months. I'm relieved to say Ashley now has a very nice third engagement ring.

As soon as we got home from Kos, we got stuck into wedding planning. First of all, we had to try to set a date. We decided we'd get hitched in June the following year, but that didn't suit everybody, so we decided on July. Then that didn't work either. Everyone seemed to have conflicting ideas about dates with summer holidays getting in the way, so eventually we thought to ourselves, 'hang this,' and booked the big day for just four months later, on the 7th of February 2015. Looking back, it maybe wasn't the cleverest day to pick. The anniversary of us meeting is the 2nd of February, and Valentine's Day is obviously on the 14th, so we made it an expensive month for ourselves!

I'd spent years working in the hospitality business. Having served my apprenticeship in the trade, I like to think I know how to organise things well. I also get really bored at weddings. I'm guessing most people probably feel the same way but they're not quite as honest (or rude) as me, so they don't like to admit it.

I decided we would have to figure out a way round the boredom factor.

There's a pre-wedding tradition in Southwest Scotland and parts of Northern Ireland, dating back to the 19th century, called 'blackening'. It's fun for everyone, apart from the person getting blackened. The groom, and sometimes the bride, are ambushed in creative and calculating ways, when they least expect it. They are then stripped to their underwear and covered in whatever their captors have to hand; paint, oil and cow dung are firm favourites in The Shire but if you're inspired to run your own blackening, feel free to improvise.

The object of the exercise, naturally, is ritual, public humiliation, and to have the person on the receiving end rubbing their skin with caustic chemicals and steel wool for at least a week afterwards to remove whatever they've been caked in. The process quite often concludes with the subject in question being tied to some kind of trailer and driven through the nearest town, still half naked, if they're lucky, to the sound of a ringing bell or the banging of pots and pans, in front of a cheering audience.

If you haven't guessed already, you should avoid this quaint tradition at all costs. Nobody is meant to be harmed, of course – it's all in good fun, and in celebration of the upcoming nuptials – but it's a sticky, messy, uncomfortable business. If you grow up in a farming community in Wigtownshire, however, all you'll hear in the run up to your wedding, over and over and from various well-wishers, is that you are going to get blackened. When they caught my old friend, Neil McKinnel, he went willingly. 'If I try and run, it'll only be worse,' he said. He was right.

They got me in January.

Ashley's brother, Kevin, works on a huge dairy farm, near where we live now. He looks after eight hundred cows, and even trims their hooves himself. In fact, he helps me out a lot these days. For anyone who's watched the now notorious Craig crush-flipping video (sorry to mention that again, Craig), Kevin's the calm looking figure on the black and white CCTV footage – the one not holding his head in both hands, like it's going to fall off. He was riding shotgun when Craig had his Thelma and Louise moment. He is, therefore, definitely down for some mischief, happy to play the innocent bystander.

One of the ropes on Kevin's crush needed replacing. He asked me to come round and take a look, and being the good guy I am, I agreed. He wanted advice about what kind of rope he should use. I remember, all too clearly, that it was a sixteen braid-on-braid polyester rope. He'd been going on about it for a while by the time I got round there, and therein lay his genius.

He told me I'd need to be sharp. He wasn't hanging around. If I was there more than five minutes after 7 p.m., he would be heading home. I took Ashley with me. I was in full-on wind-up mode, suggesting that she might be about to get blackened. How did I not see it coming?

When we arrived, we were met by David Montgomery, the farm dairyman. David is six feet two and eighteen stone of rugby player. That was the first time I'd met him, and he certainly made a bit of a first impression. He said he would take me to look at the crush, so I followed on, blissfully unaware. When we got there, he pointed to the area he said the rope was in. I was confused. There was no rope there.

'It's the bit underneath, at the top,' he said. 'You'll need to get in the crush.'

I walked inside, and the words 'GET HIM' rang out around the shed.

I felt a heavy blow to my back as David shoulder-barged me, and I shot forward into the crush. Then they all began to emerge. They were everywhere; behind walls and doors, hidden, anywhere they could be. Everyone was yelling excitedly. I was in a world of trouble, which would shortly turn into a world of shit. They stripped me down to my boxers. They zip-tied me to the crush. Then they began their work.

First came the buckets of iodine. Freezing cold and, of course, an unhealthy shade of yellow. Next came the buckets of cow shit, closely followed by some seriously curdled colostrum – the early milk that comes from a cow when she has just given birth. And on the theme of having just given birth, David next appeared with what farmers call 'cleanings' – the placenta and placental membranes, the afterbirth from a cow, which, as with the colostrum, had been rotting away nicely. There I was, zip-tied and pretty much naked, in front of an audience of about twenty-five people, covered in a hellish brew of god-awfulness. But that wasn't enough. David decided that I needed to be whipped with the afterbirth of a cow.

In my YouTube life, people think I get dirty. They comment about it a lot, and I suppose it's true, but I've been in the farming world most of my life. The muck I experience on a daily basis is just like background noise for me. This was some next level shit (and all the other stuff), but without a shadow of a doubt, the worst part of the whole sorry ordeal was what was still to come.

Uddermint is strong, industrial stuff, like Deep Heat rub. It's a liniment cream containing 35% pure peppermint oil and used to soothe and soften cow's udders after they've been chewed and battered by hungry, newborn calves. I'll let you imagine where my 'friends' rubbed that on me. I could still feel the cool minty pain hours later.

Because this was in January, we were in sub-zero winter temperatures, and maybe that's what saved me. If they'd left me hanging around too long, hypothermia would have got me. When they hit me with the freezing water from the high-volume pressure hose, it was a big relief, even though it was bitterly cold. It got most of the iodine off, which was good. I didn't fancy being Oompa-Loompa orange for a month. I might have been cold, but a warm happy feeling came over me, as I stood there, looking at two of the ringleaders: Dave Old and Kevin. That wasn't because I was overcome with the emotion of the moment, surrounded by my friends. It was because they were both getting married later that year. And guess who was their best man? That's right. Me.

Kevin tried to run away from his blackening – the worst possible strategy. It inevitably leads to more commitment from the blackeners. You might think that's not possible, but trust me, there's always spare blackening energy held back in reserve somewhere. A few of us turned up at the farm he worked on. He's not stupid. He knew the score. He knew karma was coming for him, so he locked himself in his office. Ashley and Kevin come from a big family, so this was quite the event, and he had a bit of an audience.

We couldn't let them down. Could we?

We tried drilling the locks and the hinges on the office door. What we didn't know was that Ashley had nipped round the other side of the office and tipped him off so he could escape through a back door. That was when the real chase started; across darkened fields, with everyone in the back of my pick-up, screaming after him. Kevin's what you might call built for comfort, rather than speed. We caught him after about five hundred yards. I jumped out and rugby tackled him, then we stripped him to his boxers. We hog-tied him with the kind of orange bailer twine you'll see me using to tie heavy gates to the back of my crush in videos. The same kind of zip ties they'd used on me. Then six of us dragged him through the mud, threw him into the back of the pick-up like a bag of rubbish, and drove him up to the farm midden – the place where all the cow manure is collected. Naturally, we then dropped him right in there, before pelting him with more of the same, and, of course, some placenta, with David the rugby player getting in some whipping. I was starting to think he had a bit of a fetish for that.

It was a brutally cold April day, as can happen with contrary Spring weather in Scotland. Kevin had started to turn blue, or at least bluer than he normally is, given that most of us in this country have translucent skin for nine months of the year. That gave me an idea. Farmers use sheep marker around lambing time, so they can match up lambs with their mothers. It has to survive the worst of the Scottish elements and still be legible. It doesn't really come off, and Kevin has pale skin and very blond hair.

The perfect canvas.

I managed to get hold of enough marker to do two hundred sheep and gave him a good dowsing, with the whole lot. He wasn't just blue. He was *blue*. We called him Papa Smurf for about a year, and, for a while, every time he took a shower, he turned the water a different colour.

Eventually we let him go and he got cleaned up so we could hit the pubs. We made sure we went to a good few of them that night, just so everyone could get a good look at Kevin's new hue. There was no hiding that aqua-marine scalp.

If you think mine and Kevin's blackenings were bad, you ain't heard nothing yet. The worst example I know of involved a farmer being stripped naked and tied to a fence, before having his genitals covered in powdered milk. His pals then added a one-hundred-kilogram beef calf into the mix. A one-hundred-kilogram calf that hadn't been fed for two days. Someone was good enough to film the resulting carnage for posterity. I don't know if you've ever seen a calf suckling its mother, but it's not the gentle thing you might imagine. Some of them just about knock their mums off their feet. They couldn't get the calf off this guy. He ended up in hospital. It was that bad. The weirdest part of the story was that someone sent the video to his mother-in-law. She was very happy with it. She showed anyone she could the sight of her son-in-law getting his wedding tackle mangled by a hungry Charolais calf. She thought it was hysterical, which, I suppose, shows how ingrained blackenings are in the local culture.

We must sound like we're all absolutely awful to each other, humiliating each other in this way, and I suppose we are, but it's all done out of genuine love and affection. Southwest Scotland just has a certain roughness and readiness to it. For starters, I'm pretty sure we swear more here than anywhere else on the planet. We use curse words as an alternative form of punctuation. We use some of the very worst ones – the ones people tend to save as their most devastating insults – as terms of endearment. And yes, I am strangely proud of that. Banter, abuse, call it what you will; it's hard-wired into our sense of humour. And we need it. This work is hard, in the old-fashioned sense. It doesn't leave you mentally drained, like you would be if you worked in an office, but it physically assaults you, on a daily basis.

When I'm working with Craig, pretty much every day, I do my level best to abuse the absolute hell out of him, and vice versa. It's how repressed Scottish men express their affection for each other. A recurring theme, for me, is Craig's low centre of gravity: for example, he's always the last person to get wet when it rains because he's the furthest from the sky. Or I might target his lack of understanding of the farming life (he once tried to prank me by filling my coffee with milk straight from the udder, not knowing that this wouldn't bother me in the slightest, seeing as how it *all* comes straight from the udder), or, more recently, his driving. But let's not go there again.

What we put in the Hoof GP videos is toned down, because not everyone will understand the harshness. I don't think it's the norm for most people in life. For me, if I don't make fun of you, it's maybe because I don't know you, or maybe because I don't like you enough!

Craig can't quite reach the top shelves of the cupboards built into the Appleton Steel crush. A few months ago, we were hoof trimming in front of a film crew, for BBC Scotland. Craig was standing on the gate, trying to reach the elusive top shelf. It was just too good an opportunity. I got the crew to film him, but he got embarrassed and climbed down. He told me I wouldn't be able to reach it either, so I reached up and grabbed it. There's a bit of a height difference. Craig looked like a burst ball. I felt terrible. I'm always doing stuff like that. If he's trimming, I'll sometimes tell the farmer that I've let him have a go because times are tough, and I need the extra work – coming back to fix it two weeks later.

I've used that one a few times, which makes me feel like I'm doing my bit for recycling.

Last year I called Craig 'Philip' for a while, because I found out he didn't like me calling him Craigie Boy.

'Can you not call me something else?' he said.

'How's about Philip?'

Unfortunately, this was in a video. For the next couple of weeks, his sons wound him up relentlessly. They were on holiday and Craig and Susan were on their honeymoon, and he couldn't get them to stop calling him Philip. It was bad enough that he didn't like being called Craigie Boy, but I kept that one up for so long he wound up having to use it as the name of his YouTube channel. Luckily, he's grown to love it. And he knows I love him really.

Although my blackening was an ordeal, it was worth it. The man bonding was strong, and it felt right to be part of a community tradition – something that cleansed me of my past before sending me into my future. It was a good omen.

# Chapter Twenty

Whether omens played a part in the proceedings or not, our wedding ended up being everything we wished it to be. We had wanted an afternoon ceremony, and so, on the 7th of February 2015, at 4 p.m., in the little stone-built church where Ashley had been christened, just outside the equally little village of Sorbie, where she grew up, we tied the knot in front of a hundred and twenty of our close friends and family. Sorbie church is beautiful. It's located up a small lane and is surrounded by trees that must have seen some interesting comings and goings over the last hundred and fifty years. It has intricately laid stained glass windows depicting St Ninian, the man who brought Christianity to Scotland.

It was one of those crisp, sunny winter days. There were kids and kilts everywhere. We were married by The Reverend Meade, the minister who had christened Ashley as a baby, and who had come out of retirement to perform our wedding service. I felt awed by both the circularity and the significance of that. Maybe a little too awed, because when the critical moment arrived, I put Ashley's ring on the wrong finger. It could even have been the wrong hand, but I quickly realised my mistake, so hopefully I didn't create any bad luck!

We held the reception in a chocolate factory, because why wouldn't you? This chocolate factory doubles as a kids' play centre. I initially had my doubts about that, but I was wrong, and it turned out to be amazing.

The venue is a good forty miles from the church. The only drawback was that everyone in attendance had to troop off back to their cars and head out along the road that sweeps round Wigtown Bay. It's a stunning stretch of the A75 on any given day of the week, but the sunset, on that special winter's day, was like nothing I've ever seen. The sky was on fire and bathing the sea in the flames. Everyone was talking about this magical sunset when we arrived at the reception venue, setting the tone for the evening. The photos circulated for weeks afterwards.

The chocolate factory in question – The Cocoabean Company – sells quality chocolate all over the world, but they also do kids' entertainment and other celebrations. There's a massive marquee at the side of the factory building that they use for weddings. During my sceptical phase I had told Ashley I would never get married there, but over time I started to see the place in a different light.

Our evening guests arrived at 6 p.m. for a sit-down meal. There were four hundred and fifty of them. A slightly higher number than we could fit in the church! Traditionally, the day guests are the ones who eat and get to listen to the speeches, but we wanted everyone involved in, or rather, subjected to, our speeches. I know it's a cliché (surely the best clichés are exactly that because they're true?) but our wedding was the best one I've ever been to. We had an awesome band, the venue was exactly what we wanted, and the food was amazing. It was a proper, old-fashioned family wedding, with a difference. If you have a midday wedding, there's a big gap between the service and the evening reception. That's a lot of hanging around for everyone else while the newly married couple have their photos taken. With our wedding starting later, we were straight into the celebrations, and everything snowballed from there. There was no killing time, no lag in the middle and no chance for anyone (including me) to get tired or bored.

As is tradition, you would normally expect the best man to get stuck into the groom during the speeches. I decided not to give mine the option. Dave Old was my best man, and I expected him to have some kind of sneaky plan, so I devised one of my own: I would dish the dirt he had on me before he could. I thought I was being clever. I was convinced Dave was the one I'd have to worry about, but I hadn't counted on Ashley's stepdad, Wallace, being the one to watch out for. I did manage to spoil one anecdote I knew Dave would be dying to unleash, however, before Wallace stepped in.

I have a bit of an appetite. I sometimes wind up with the belly to prove it, particularly if it's been an exceptionally harsh winter. I can overdo it when it comes to food, and especially with anything sugary. Ashley and I had been together for a year or two when we went on a date night, to celebrate my thirtieth birthday. As I write this, I'm now past my fortieth so that seems a very long time ago, but the events of that evening are forever imprinted on my brain.

We were out for dinner, and I ordered two puddings, which is something I always do. If you're going to indulge, you might as well get it out of your system properly. Go big or go home. Ashley's eyes were bigger than her stomach. She ordered her pudding but couldn't eat it. Being the chivalrous guy I am, I helped her out. I like a challenge, and I certainly did my best, but crème brûlée, Eton mess *and* chocolate brownie with ice cream are a bit heavy on the lactose for me. Two miles into the drive home I wasn't feeling too clever.

'I think I'm gonna shit myself,' I said, trying to laugh it off, and killing any remaining semblance of romance in the process.

Ashley started laughing.

'No Ash, I really mean it.' I could hear the pleading in my voice, as if she could do anything about my desperation. As if there were anything *anyone* could do about it. Then it happened. The very worst thing that could have. There and then, in my car, at the ripe old age of thirty, I soiled myself. I can't quite believe I'm admitting it here, but there you have it. I suppose it happens to the best of us – we all have that moment that renders us human. I'm still absolutely mortified, even thinking about it, but it's also hilarious. My brother and I have (perhaps aptly) almost wet ourselves laughing at the prospect of other people reading this and being horrified, but I bet at least one person who does has had the same thing happen to them.

And what do you do when something like that happens? In my case, I slammed on the brakes, pulled up at the side of the road and dived out. I had to get rid of the evidence at all costs. So, I pulled off my trousers, and I was in the process of throwing my underwear into a hedge when a car came round the corner, lights blazing, illuminating the whole sordid scene into a stark and unmistakable focus. I've taken a hell of a lot of stick for that one over the years – mostly from Ashley – but I made sure I included it in my speech. Afterwards, talking to Dave, he admitted he *had* been planning on telling that story. I'll chalk that one up as a win.

But then Ashley's stepdad, Wallace, let rip instead. He's a gruff, hard sort of Scotsman. He's the kind of guy we'd call wiry; he's lean and strong, an absolute worker of a man. He's been in agriculture most of his life and has the brown, pitted skin to show for fifty-odd years of toil in the great outdoors.

I've known him a long time. Years ago, he used to help our family out with silage contracting, doing buckraking. Buckraking – packing the freshly cut grass into the silage pit – is a dangerous job, and I've heard of a few people dying while doing it over the years. Wallace would pick up the grass with a fork on the back of his tractor, then load it into the pit, driving over the top of the grass to compact it, and fit as much in as possible. Driving up and down on the unstable surface is what makes it dangerous. You can easily roll a tractor. I remember Wallace buckraking at The Knock and me following him around, fascinated.

Wallace began his speech gently by telling the story of how I used to sit on his tractor. I told you The Shire was a tight knit place. Then he moved on to his more adult material. He remembered, he said, the first time I stayed over at his house. I wondered where this was going. A few people in the room looked a bit nervous at that point. It turned out what I hadn't realised, that first night, was that Ashley's bedroom was directly above the room he slept in. My embarrassment was made complete as he went on to describe seeing the light swinging on his ceiling as he tried to get to sleep. 'I'll give Graeme his dues, though,' he said. 'I realised, that night, that cars aren't the only thing he likes fast, so he didn't keep me awake very long!' Our blushes aside, the other reason for everyone else's nerves was the fact that Ashley's father, a twenty-five stone bear of a man, was sitting, stoney-faced on the other side of his precious daughter, waiting to give his own speech.

Although it isn't traditional in Scotland, Ashley made a speech of her own that night, keeping it classy and raising the tone by thanking everyone, and in particular, her mum, dad and sister.

After the speeches and the meal, I proceeded to get very, very drunk. People kept buying me drinks and I felt I had to drink them. People kept passing me drinks to give to Ashley, and I felt I had to drink them too. I'm still regularly reminded that I'm an awful person for not dancing with her after the first dance. We chose 'Photograph' by Ed Sheeran, a song about life being imperfect, and about relationships being hard work. It's about real love. It's actually about a mother's unconditional love for a child and the longing to come home, but I think the words are kind of universal. We didn't just want a cheesy, happily-ever-after song to kick off our married life. We wanted, and still want, our marriage to be based in reality. I think the song says something about how we both feel about our relationship. You see so many relationships breaking down, after the honeymoon period and the dizzy phase, when there are no complications and real life seems a million miles away. We'd been through the early days, we'd started a family together, and we were in this for the long haul. The superficial stuff might have moved to the background, but we were left with something much deeper, and I wouldn't change that for anything.

After the first song, Ashley danced with Wallace. Her dad had taken Keir home for the night. I danced with Maddie, who had come to the wedding. She was only ten years old then and maybe it was more like carrying her than dancing, but that's a moment I'll always cherish. Maddie stayed until the end of the night, which was amazing. She was really growing up. I remember her, in her little princess dress. I remember looking into her eyes and carrying her around like she *was* a princess.

The guest list was eclectic. My friend Francival, from my days at The Windmill, and his now husband, Pedro, turned up in full Highland dress. It was quite something to see two immaculately presented gay men hanging out with a bunch of rough, heterosexual Scottish farmers. It was a sight to behold. We partied until 1 a.m., then realised it was time to go home. It was the quickest day of my life. We weren't even out the door before Wallace, who, like everyone else, was three sheets to the wind, decided he was going to settle the rest of the bill for the wedding. I protested as hard as I could, but I was hammered and he's a determined man. We were, and still are, very grateful for his generosity. At the time, we really needed it. Money was tight.

Everyone was surprised that we didn't want to spend the night in a hotel, but we really wanted to get home. That might sound strange, but we were happy there, so why not? We also couldn't really afford the alternative, on top of the other wedding expenses. I remember saying to Ashley, before the wedding, that we could either have a wedding and no honeymoon or *no* wedding. The only slight hitch in our plan was that we had forgotten we had to get home from the chocolate factory, somehow. We ended up having to get one of the guests to give us a lift back. Not exactly a traditional way of leaving your own wedding – by cadging a lift!

We did end up going on a sort of honeymoon immediately after the wedding, in the form of a freeze branding trip, to Nairn. We didn't have the cash or even the time for a fancy getaway, so Ashley got the pleasure of sitting in my mucky van, reading magazines, for eight hours a day, while I got stuck into some hard graft. It can't have been an entirely unromantic trip. Our second son, Campbell, was born nine months later on the 11th of November 2015!

Shortly after his birth, Ashley handed him over to her mum, Mary, so she could take a shower. Mary gave him a bottle, just to see if he would take it. When Ashley came back, he'd drained the lot. We were really worried about it. We needn't have been. He's been adventurous with food ever since and has been known to happily chew his way through a blue steak and lick his lips at the prospect of lobster. A lad with expensive tastes! Campbell is his own man. He is, in his own words, 'ginger and proud.' He likes being scared. He'll happily sit in one of my off-road buggies, or on a jet-ski, flat out. He loves it. But he has no interest in driving yet, thankfully.

We still haven't quite managed to go on a 'proper' honeymoon. We've talked about it a lot, and of course we've been on family holidays since then, but not something that's just been for the two of us. Maybe we'll go to Thailand or the Seychelles one day, but the real dream is Bora Bora, the small, South-Pacific island group northwest of Tahiti. It's about as far-away-from-it-all as you can get.

Like so many other couples, the big source of stress at the start of our relationship was money. My early encounter with the old Irish farmer and his cows with maggoty feet, wasn't, unfortunately, my only experience of post-dated cheques and big delays in getting paid. Farmers have cashflow problems like everyone else. It was a relatively common occurrence to wait patiently (or otherwise) for payments to land in my bank account, sometimes from multiple customers. I might visit twelve farms in one week and have to bill each one of those farms separately. The financial pressures on farmers can be truly immense meaning some were unable to pay me for weeks, or even months. That kind of tension can put a strain on any relationship.

We've had three particularly hard periods, financially – long, drawn-out spells where Ashley and I were in a real mess, flat broke and, at times, I struggled to see a way out. A few years ago, things got so bad I had to lay Craig off. I simply couldn't afford to pay him. It was bad enough working without getting paid myself, but the thought of Craig working and me not being able to pay him was too much to deal with. Times could get seriously grim, all too easily. I was working my ass off and I'd never been busier, but it felt at certain points like I was unemployed, that I was a loser, and that I was letting my family down every day. Waiting for money for weeks on end was the worst feeling in the world. It was something I had no control over. It could be eleven or twelve weeks before the cheques started to come in, and when they did, I was so happy I felt like crying. This was a professional rollercoaster, and it often took weeks to get back to anything like normality.

In the past I might have written the whole thing off, dropped my new career, gone away and done something else, but it wasn't just me anymore. I was married now, and I had children. This was also my very own business. I felt like I had a calling, so I stuck with it. I doubled down. I rode the rollercoaster. I built my knowledge and became more accomplished every day, managing the transition from one kind of job into another. I'm so glad I did, because all my hard work, and my decision to stay the course, was about to lead to emotional, professional and financial rewards I could never have dreamed of.

# Chapter Twenty-One

Aside from the financial gymnastics, freeze branding had otherwise been fine as a business for me to start out with, when I took over from Davie. But I was never going to do it forever. My eventual decision to move into hoof trimming wasn't just based on my desire to manage overheads, my need to reduce the country-wide commutes or my inclination to mitigate the ever-present job hazard of being relentlessly kicked by cows. The main reason is that it just didn't give me the emotional rewards I get today, because it doesn't benefit the cow. Sticking a number on a bovine bum is just an administrative procedure, and while I derived some pleasure in the efficiency of how I worked, I never got to go back and appreciate the end result. It takes two and a half months for the hair to grow in white, so you can't even see if the number comes out well.

With hoof trimming, there's an instant result, and that usually means instant gratification. I don't want to overstate my role in the cows' welfare, but hoof trimming can really transform the life of a lame cow in minutes. You get to see her walk away, wearing a block, moving more comfortably. You can see when she's in less pain, and hopefully, on the way to better health. Doing what I do well means helping animals back to full health, and that's the best feeling in the world.

When I was freeze branding the logistics were always too tight – with the management of dry ice in every decision I made. I had to brand multiple cows in one go and I didn't get to revisit any of them. With hoof trimming I can, and do, sometimes visit a farm to work on just one cow in urgent need. I want to help cows, and I want to help farmers. Vets can't do it because they don't have the kind of equipment I do: the crush, the knives or the grinders. Farmers usually have to pay a one-off call-out fee to another hoof trimmer but I'm happy to turn up for the odd one-cow visit. If I didn't, the cow might go lame, and ultimately, it's all about the cows.

I'll admit that when I first started hoof trimming it was mainly so that I could spend more time at home. I was tired of travelling all over the country, missing my family and trying to scratch a living. It was only later that I realised that what I was doing had a genuine benefit, and one I could connect with. If you can reduce suffering, that has to be a worthwhile thing. Freeze branding was feeding my family when the cheques arrived – another worthwhile thing – but it wasn't very satisfying. I wasn't doing anything for the cows, and I wasn't really benefitting the farmer beyond putting numbers on bums. This was real job satisfaction.

As time went on, and I'd acquired my own crush and indulged the geekery of tailoring it to my needs, I became more interested in the structure of a cow's hoof. From the outside it doesn't look particularly complex, and when I first started hoof trimming, I had no idea how far down the rabbit hole it was possible to go. I thought it was just another job, a bit different, but just as straightforward as freeze branding. My stepdad had never really involved himself in the finer details. Even though Davie had been a skilled hoof trimmer, doing the job for the best part of thirty years and teaching others how to, he wasn't particularly interested in the interior anatomy of a cow's foot. He didn't spend time thinking about the subtle mechanics; how a cow's foot moves, how all the components interact. Davie knew how to make the outside of the hoof look a bit better, and importantly, how to get the farmer to pay him, so in the beginning that's all I thought hoof trimming entailed.

I usually get bored easily, but I could happily talk for a week about cow anatomy. I find it hard to get bored when it comes to that. There's always new knowledge out there. New discoveries are made every day. These days, I get a lot of comments and questions on my videos about this evolution, and people ask me how hoof trimming was done years ago. There has been a progression over time, but, maybe surprisingly, the biggest developments have been in the past ten years. And no, that's not because I started roughly ten years ago!

For one thing, the use of social media has sky-rocketed in the last decade. YouTube, Facebook and TikTok are not something I would ever have expected to affect my profession when I started out. After all, we work on farms, in the middle of nowhere. We're about as disconnected from the wider world as we can be, but the democratisation of knowledge has been a powerful thing everywhere, so why should hoof trimming be any different? In that regard, social media has been instrumental in driving up the standards of hoof trimming.

I was pretty green when I started but it didn't take me long to realise how much knowledge and skill was needed to make a cow more comfortable. I started thinking carefully about the importance of the expertise I was acquiring. I felt like there was a need, and a responsibility, to pass on as much as I could to farmers. Some farmers and farm workers, like Kevin, were looking after their own herds' feet. To me it just made sense to help them wherever I could. In the end, it's all about the cows. Given that I once struggled to make ends meet, it might be tempting to take a cynical view of things and say that training or educating people reduces some of your own business, but I've never been stuck for work in the hoof trimming world. I want to add as much value as I can for my customers.

A farmer might just see a lame cow, but experience will tell someone that she can be lame in different ways, for different reasons. The key is getting to the root cause and sorting it out, and quickly. If I can tell the farmer what the problem is, he can help the individual cow, but he can also then spot the same problem in other cows. Better still, he can stop the problem even occurring in other cows, and that has to have a wider reaching effect on the health of the herd.

When I trained under Pieter Kloosterman, I learned the Five-Step Dutch Method. It was created by a man called Toussaint Raven, a professor at the Veterinary University of Utrecht. Summarising it wouldn't do it justice here, but you can simply think of it as 'hoof trimming 101'. It's pretty much the gold standard these days; the one most hoof trimmers on the planet follow. There are other styles, but they're all derived from the same origin. The basic principle is that in a healthy cow, the two claws on each foot should be the same size. They should also be flattened uniformly, so the weight bearing is equally distributed between both claws. In practice, the rear outside claws take more of the weight. I'm guessing the outer edges of your feet would take a bit more weight if you had to make room for a heavy udder swinging around between your knees.

If you watch my videos, you'll hear me talking about 'modelling out'. That involves taking away a small, dish-shaped section from the inside of each claw, so it winds up looking like a quarter of an avocado with the stone removed. By taking that part away, more of the weight goes on to the inner claw, relieving pressure on the outer one, and hopefully stopping an ulcer developing there.

In the 1960s, lameness became a big problem in dairy cows in The Netherlands – home to the most recognisable dairy cow: the Friesian. Friesians are the black and white cows you probably think of most when asked to imagine dairy cows. Most of the cows we see here are American Holsteins. They carry more weight but have less fat in their feet, meaning they have less cushioning, and that leads to more problems. Most of the problems in modern farming come from the pursuit of greater yields, or in this case, the drive for more milk. Toussaint Raven researched the lameness farmers were seeing. He then studied the techniques of as many hoof trimmers as he could, and he discovered that most of the lameness originated in the cows' hind legs and mainly in the lateral claw – the one on the outside. The claws in question can bear up to about eighty percent of the weight on the feet, so they can take a real battering.

Raven also noticed a height difference between the two claws on each hind foot, with the outside one being taller. It makes sense if you think the cow's foot is at an angle, with the udders pushing it out to the side. He experimented with trimming the outer claw down to size and discovered that it reduced lameness and cut down on the occurrence of ulcers. By trimming away the excess sole, he made the cows' feet stable and spread the load. He also found that modelling out the inside of both claws allowed muck to pass between them and took away the weight from the area most prone to ulcers. As you can imagine, not having to walk around on infected feet makes a huge difference to the cows' wellbeing, and for me, that's what my job's all about.

The Dutch simply call it Functional Trimming. The first thing Pieter Kloosterman said in the training I attended was, 'I know you all call it the Dutch Hoof Trimming Method, but the Dutch call it Functional Trimming'. I like that way of describing what I do. The real job of hoof trimming isn't to create the perfect foot. What we want is for any cow feeling uncomfortable or sore to go into the crush, and for the hoof trimmer to make her feel better. I can't always completely restore a cow's foot but if I can make her feel even ten percent more comfortable, I'm doing an important job, and I've made a real difference to that cow's life.

A cow's entire weight is in contact with the ground at eight distinct points: eight little bones, called distal phalanges or pedal bones. The equivalent in humans would be the bones at the end of each finger, thumb and toe – the ones that shape the nail. Humans usually have a total of twenty distal phalanges. Cows have eight – two per hoof. Each digit has a pedal bone within the structure of the hoof. The cow's whole skeletal structure – and weight – bears down on these eight tiny pedal bones and they're only about five centimetres long. If the cow's walking on soft grass, it's cushioned. Imagine walking on all your fingers and toes on concrete!

The single biggest factor affecting cows' feet is, in fact, concrete. Cows simply haven't evolved to stand on it. Their ancestors walked on soft ground, and grew small, vestigial hooves, further up on the backs of their legs. They're called dew claws, and they stop cows sinking too far into mud. Cows, and especially dairy cows, live in an unnatural environment, at least part of the time. When they're not out in the fields, they walk on concrete in and around farm buildings, and they don't have Nike Airs to soften the blow. The concrete is easy to keep clean and provides a solid surface for cows to walk on, but it also bruises their soles, and that can lead to sole ulceration. That's because the base of a cow's foot allows it to flex into the soft ground, but when she walks on concrete, all the force that would normally be flexing through into the earth goes straight onto the corium, making it bruise and bleed.

Then there's those tiny pedal bones I mentioned, which rest on top of two important structures. One is called the digital cushion. It's like the insole in a shoe, but it's made of fat particles. Three tubes of fat run across the underside of the pedal bone and dissipate all the weight from the cow's foot. They're just like Frubes, the kids' yoghurt. The digital cushion presses down on top of the corium, which is what produces the hoof horn. The corium is only about a millimetre thick and, as anyone who watches my videos or knows anything about cows' feet can attest to, it's a very precious thing. Pieter calls it 'the quick' – the old-fashioned word for the human nail bed, and the origin of the phrase, 'cutting to the quick.'

The way the cow's foot deals with dissipating the pressure is incredible, as long as the hooves are well maintained. If there's even the smallest break in one of the hooves, the dissipating forces don't work the way they should, and they just run into that break. You could think of the hoof capsule like a cartoon bicycle tyre. Evolution has engineered it do a job: holding everything inside. It dissipates the weight perfectly, but if you have a crack, a hole or a break in there, everything pours towards that break, in the same way that if there's a weak point in that tyre, all the air pushes towards that, trying to find the exit, resulting in an unsightly bulge.

A hoof is a fantastic thing when everything is as it should be, and it's my job to try to keep it that way. The major problems happen when there's a break in the hoof capsule, and it's not just as simple as sticking a cartoon patch on it and hoping for the best, because the integrity of the structure has disappeared. The Dutch call the hoof capsule the 'horny shoe', which might sound like a euphemism but it's a nice description. That's what I trim – the outside of the shoe, not live tissue. If you had a hole in your shoe, and you had no way to change it, that would hurt a lot, and you would also put more pressure on the other one, because it would be more comfortable. But in the long run that's going to give the second one a beating – so then you would have a problem with both feet.

Here's where it all gets mind bending, though. If you have the weight of the cow bearing down on the pedal bone, that in turn dissipates all those forces through the digital cushion and those three tubes of fat, which in turn sit on top of the corium. Where it gets really weird, is that the pedal bone is actually being held up by the *top* of the hoof. It's suspended. Every time a cow takes a step, the inside of her hoof is pulling down from the top, and not the other way round. Strange, eh?

There are also little lines called laminae that connect the foot to the inside of the hoof wall. They act as the suspension, stretching every time a cow steps and the pedal bone sinks down. Humans don't have hooves, obviously. It would be good for business if we did. All the pressure is channelled through our feet, on to our soles, but cows are completely different. All their load is spread round the hoof capsule, because of the way the interior part of the foot is attached to it.

This all means that *a lot* of things can go wrong in just one hoof. It's not all bad news though. Simply by trimming a cow every four months, you can head off any potential problems. Modelling out the sole gives the pedal bones room to move. That's a thirty second job on a healthy foot. Taking the time to do that and making sure the surface of the foot is at the recommended 50° angle should be all you need to stop bruising and ulceration. It's a quick, simple and effective preventative treatment. I'd rather spend time preventing problems than fixing them, although I realise it would mean my videos were a bit less interesting. 'HOOF GP does NORMAL ROUTINE trim on HEALTHY cow' isn't exactly click bait, is it?

So, if the problems we see are easily preventable with regular visits, does that mean that when a cow's foot does get bruised or ulcerated the farmer hasn't looked after her properly? Not at all. Most of the cows I look after are cared for by accomplished farmers and dairy people. They really care about these animals – in the same way I do. They want to have them in the best condition possible. Apart from the laws and ethics of livestock welfare, it just doesn't make any business sense to have sick animals. Whatever the motivation, the end result is still the same and that's alright with me, as long as it leads to happy cows.

The number of regular customers I have is proof of how much these farmers care about the welfare of their animals. If they didn't care I wouldn't get any phone calls. And yes, the examples I've given you are only from my own personal experience, but I've lived in a farming community for a long time, and I can hold my hand up and say the vast majority of the cows in Wigtownshire are well looked after. A lot of the farmers I know show a serious and genuine affection for their cows. It's the kind of thing that noticeably goes well beyond any financial gain. It's like my dad and his herd of pure-bred Charolais. There's a lot of pride involved in this business.

In all seriousness, if you were a dairy farmer who didn't love working with cows, you'd be in the wrong job, because it's not just a job. There's no clocking off at 5 p.m. It's a twenty-four-hour gig, a vocation and a lifestyle. I'd guess about ninety five percent of the cows' feet I trim are perfectly healthy. The extreme cases I see are few and far between. These are, of course, the ones that end up on my social media videos, but that's the nature of online content, and it's important to make the point for educational purposes. They are the exception, rather than the rule. These farmers are doing their very best to keep their animals happy and healthy. And they are generally succeeding. We trim around fifteen thousand cows a year, and Craigie Boy and I don't see that many lame cows between us. Most of our working life involves the routine treatment of healthy hooves, but I can see how I might give people the wrong idea.

Shamefully, however, the lameness rate in the UK as a whole is a much darker picture, averaging at twenty-five per cent. It's a ridiculous situation that a quarter of all cattle in the UK are lame and that it's entirely preventable. If the average cattle herd lameness rate is twenty-five percent, and it costs an estimated £2.20 per lame cow a day, for a herd of four hundred cows, that results in an £80,300 loss per annum! So, hoof trimming is cheap, by comparison, and a necessary investment.

At the time of writing, I've trimmed the hooves of about two hundred thousand cows. That's eight hundred thousand feet and 1.6 million individual digits, and I've done all that on about sixty farms. My customers keep me busy, with return visits to treat the same cows, either by tackling chronic conditions or carrying out routine maintenance. I'm just one hoof trimmer in a small, hammer-shaped corner of Southwest Scotland, and

I'm very busy. So, as much as I'd love to, I can't help all the cows in the world needing their hooves taken care of, but I can share the knowledge and techniques required to do so with others, to ensure it's done in the right way. Being able to use social media to impart valuable information and experience is something that really excites me. It's empowering to contribute to animal welfare by talking to other hoof trimmers, by seeing what we can learn from each other, and by sharing those insights for the greater good.

This is where my YouTube channel can really help farmers and would-be hoof trimmers. I often come across cows with painful problems on their left back foot, for example, and the farmer will say, 'Oh yeah, yeah, we picked her up, we trimmed her a little bit and ... she's not going that well, but she is slightly better'. Knowing that, I'll go to pick up the other back foot to check it, and the farmer will invariably say, 'No, she's just lame on that left foot, don't bother with the rest'. Nine times out of ten, I'll check the back right foot and she's either got a significant problem or the start of one, but she'll still favour it because it's not as painful as the one that the farmer spotted in the first place, so this is where my knowledge and experience comes in, and I can pass that on to the farmer.

When I rock up at a farm with my crush, I always know the animals I've worked on in the past. Naturally, I want to follow up on them. In a big herd of cows – a typical farm might have four hundred – it generally won't be me who makes the judgement call on which animals need to be treated, so the farmer's keen eye and knowledge is important. If the farmer knows what to look out for, I can get in early and treat the cows before they develop a more serious problem, but I can only treat the ones that are brought to my attention. The key to winning the hoof care game is to spot the cows that need help before they become visibly lame.

Having the chance to educate people on something I feel so passionate about, to pass on my expertise, is massive for me, but of course, I do still get questioned about my right to pass that knowledge and experience on. One of the questions I'm most regularly asked is, 'What qualifications do you need to be a hoof trimmer?' Unfortunately, as in Davie's day, the hoof trimming industry is still entirely unregulated. You can be at high school one day and then decide the next that you want to become a fully-fledged hoof trimmer, pick up some knives and get stuck in. You'd technically be free to start up your own hoof trimming business, potentially maiming and killing perfectly healthy cattle in the process. There's nothing stopping you, other than your own common sense and the word-of-mouth of your customers, but people have been tricked into crazier things than employing unqualified hoof trimmers, especially if they come at a knock-down rate.

Madness, isn't it?

Legally, I don't have to be checked. No one does. And while that's disturbing and potentially disastrous, from my perspective, it's not the point. To keep our trimming skills up to date and on-point, Craigie Boy and I regularly put ourselves through voluntary checks. I'm confident in our skills and that we're doing everything as we should be. I go out of my way to stay up to date on the latest research, and by using the best, safest and most suitable equipment and techniques, but it's nice to have someone else confirm we're doing everything correctly, in line with the latest knowledge. It's one of the reasons we're so active on social media. It's yet another check and balance, and we do, in fact, have a YouTube video specially dedicated to this very issue. You can see us being grilled on the subject, and Craigie Boy being formally examined for his hoof trimming diploma, by watching 'THE HOOF GP is NOT a REGULATED HOOF TRIMMER!!! *THE TRUTH REVEALED*' – a video I posted on 10th May 2021.

Testing days are not the easiest thing we do and I'm happy to admit that I get nervous every time, which is probably a good thing. It means I'm in no danger of becoming complacent. There are other hoof trimmers present, and there's professional pride at stake, especially when you've put yourself out there, in the world of social media. You really don't want to mess it up and look like an idiot in front of your peers. I also worry what the examiners think. Is testing in a video for the channel sending out the wrong signal to them? It's the same on farms. I have to be mindful not to let filming take priority. The cows are why I'm there. I don't want to be messing about with a GoPro when there's an animal in discomfort waiting to be seen.

Most of the farmers I visit seem to be fine with it. Maybe some of them secretly think I'm taking the piss or that I have ideas above my station, but everyone seems to trust me to get on with the job. I hope that my emphasis on the educational side of filming, combined with an element of entertainment, shows both my professionalism and my overriding love for the animals. After all, that's why I got into this. I'm always conscious not to film anything too sensitive. I want to be authentic, but also unobtrusive. I could be filming the most interesting hoof in the world, but if the camera gets in the way or I get distracted by filming, it just gets thrown to the side. The absolutely most important thing is trimming the cow's hoof.

I may be nervous at the prospect, but I quickly get into the flow of the test days. I've done a lot of them now and know their rhythms. I don't *have* to attend these sessions, but it's good to meet new people and it keeps me on my toes, which is important. It's like driving. The more you do it, the better you get – in theory – but you can also pick up bad habits. These days are important to keep me doing the best job I can for my customers, and, most importantly, for the cows. I wouldn't resit my driving test every year though. I'd probably fail.

On a typical testing day, there'll be six or seven hoof trimmers. There might be three old hands like me, and three newbies, getting their diplomas, like Craig. There will be four or five crushes set up. It's an impressive sight and gives me the opportunity to geek out a bit and check out what everyone else is using these days, how the different systems operate and which ones I might be interested in. After a brief introduction we get down to some trimming. You're there for the whole day and the examiners take it in turns to walk around and scrutinise everything. We'll explain what we've done and why we've done it. Sometimes the examiners won't have seen the foot before you get to work so it's important to explain everything that's relevant.

On the day we filmed the testing video, it was fantastic to watch Craig. He was full of confidence and easily held his own, in amongst the old hands. Later on, he had his oral inspection, delivered by the two examiners. They gave him a thorough grilling, but he knew his stuff and came out of it well. He was able to talk authoritatively about anatomy, and he described clearly and concisely, step-by-step, what he'd done and why he'd done it. It was a proud moment for both of us. I know all of the examiners – Celia, John, Craig, Pieter and Nick – well. I've known them for years, which makes me all the keener to impress them.

The examiners give most of their feedback at the end of the test day. We trim about half a dozen cows' feet each, and the two examiners then look at everything we've done separately, so we have two individual takes on it. If you ask them for feedback, they'll give it to you there and then. Otherwise, they'll wait until the end of the day to go over the good and bad points. Either way, it's a leveller. It keeps you humble.

When the practical part of the day is done it's time for the exciting part – the theory. We're given a multiple-choice exam to get through. Who doesn't love an exam, eh? Once that paper's out of the way, we move on to the oral part of the day, which, as you can imagine, being the chatty lad I am, I really enjoy. We examine photographs of trims done by other people and we talk through how they could be improved, what's happening in the photo and how we might do certain things differently.

We look at both the internal and external anatomy of a cow's hoof. That's when you can really disappear down the rabbit hole. You're down to the raw mechanics of hoof trimming and I really enjoy this part. Yes, I know – I need to get out more. But I love what I do, and I love taking an in-depth look at the anatomy. It's fascinating how many different factors can come into play to impact a cow's feet, her mobility, and overall comfort.

One of the best things about the examination days is that I get to meet a bunch of new people on a new farm. That's like a day out for me. I don't really take on new customers these days. My schedule is pretty rammed looking after the existing ones, but there are always exceptions. I recently took on a herd half an hour away from my house. I'd heard the farmers were nice people, and they really needed my help. Their herd's lameness rate was at seventy eight percent, meaning eight out of ten cows had a problem. Craig and I made a few visits to start making as much of an impact as we could. We worked on the cows, and we trained the staff. Within eight months, we managed to get the lameness down to twenty four percent – one percent below the UK average. Since then, the farm staff have kept on top of the hooves and maintained the health of the herd. We couldn't cure every single lame animal – we can't expect to – but we did at least make every cow more comfortable. For the lame ones, it's sometimes about making them more comfortable until they leave the herd. Some of them didn't make it. They had to be put down, and, sadly, that's part of the process in situations like these. That's why it's vital to catch these things early.

If I can treat a tiny ulcer and get a block on early, it's more than likely we'll have a complete recovery, but if you let things slide, without the right management, you can quickly find yourself with a herd of lame cows. And if they're your herd, that can feel like an insurmountable problem. It's a bit like keeping your house tidy. Do a bit of housework every day and you'll have a clean and tidy house constantly. Let it get out of hand and before long you'll have so much dust and clutter that you won't know where to start. Or you will, if you're not married to Ashley, who is the tidiest person I know.

The other thing that piques people's curiosity is whether cows' feet are the same as horse's, but they are about as similar to them as they are to human feet. They do share a lot of foot anatomy terminology, but a horse only has one digit on each foot, rather than two. It is a similar enough digit, but these basic differences mean the ailments and the kinds of wear and tear vary, as do their repair needs. Horses also generally have healthier feet. They wear iron shoes, and they spend their lives on grass, rather than concrete. They're most often pets, or performance animals, kept for sport in limited numbers. Their owners therefore tend to be people who are prepared to spend a lot of money on them, unlike cows which are viewed as less prized commodities, unfortunately. I couldn't just pivot to trimming horse's hooves, or call myself a farrier, unless I specifically trained to do it.

I do, oddly enough, know a bit more about giraffes. In fact, I regularly have people working in zoos who contact me about their giraffes' feet. They're actually very similar to cows' feet, it's just that everything's on a bigger scale. As with sheep, goats, deer and pigs, there's no giraffe hoof trimming society where zoos can go for an update, although I genuinely wish there was. I would definitely join, just for the laugh. I love that my YouTube channel can help when it comes to taking care of other animals with similar feet – especially the giraffes. It's a happy by-product of what I do.

Just don't ask me to help you if you're a horse.

# Chapter Twenty-Two

Being the cow aficionado I am, this book wouldn't really be complete without dedicating an entire chapter to one particular cow – a cow who also happens to be the subject of one of my favourite ever YouTube videos. The video follows the story of Cow 812, now one of the most famous cows on the planet. The very first Cow 812 video has been seen by more than twenty million people. That's a staggering number.

I first met her in January 2020, and I thought she might be unfixable because she had problems with both of her back feet. Even worse than that, she had problems with both claws on one of those feet. She was in a really bad way. She was struggling to walk because her feet were so sore. She was drastically underweight and dirty. But – and I can't stress this enough – it wasn't because she had been neglected in any way. The rest of the herd on the farm were in fantastic condition, and very well looked after.

Cow 812 was wasting away because she had a serious infection: E. coli. That made her lose weight, and, as anyone who has ever tried to lose a beer belly will tell you, fat loss happens everywhere. That meant those fatty tubes between the pedal bone and the corium had faded away along with everything else. A lack of fat padding meant there was no cushioning in her hoof capsule, which in turn meant less movement, less eating and a vicious, spiralling cycle that was only heading one way.

She was dirty because she couldn't get outside. She'd been put in a straw-bedded pen to recuperate, but she spent most of her time lying down because of the pain that any movement caused her. When she did walk, the straw stuck to her sides and her head hung low. She looked like she'd given up, but the farmer was doing everything he could to keep her comfortable. When I started treating her, she was on a course of non-steroidal anti-inflammatory drugs in an effort to relieve the pressure on her feet, and a course of antibiotics, to fight the E. coli infection. I was brought in to do whatever I could to save her. It looked like it was going to be a struggle. She seemed dangerously close to the end.

I started this particular series of videos because I knew anyone who wasn't from a farming background would think she was being neglected, and that just wasn't true. I wanted to show how cows can look neglected, even when they're well looked after. It was a real tug of war. Would it backfire, showing a cow in such an emaciated state? I took a couple of weeks to upload the first video, going back and forth in my mind over whether I should just delete it or not.

On my second visit to see Cow 812, I glued blocks onto two of her rear claws, one on each foot, then I gently wrapped the other two. I was back again five days later. I was disappointed to watch her, as she walked through the shed, still very obviously in pain. When I got her back into the crush, I peeled off the bandage and the block from the back right foot with a bit of trepidation. The digital dermatitis she had been suffering from was gone from the right claw, thankfully, so that was something, but then I discovered a lesion on her left claw, underneath the block I'd stuck on. I was gutted.

First, I had to take away the block. Then I cut away the overburdening hoof horn. I had to expose that lesion to fresh air, because if I didn't, I knew it would never heal properly. I still had the option of an 'iron block' – like half a horseshoe. I attached that round the outer edge of the inner claw – the bit of the claw that was still properly intact. That took the weight off the injured parts on both claws, allowing them time to heal. When we visited again later, I had to file the block down to stop it digging into an ulcer. Like the old saying goes, no plan ever survives first contact with the enemy. You have to learn to adapt in this job.

I'd done what I could with the right foot and moved on to the left. I unwrapped the bandaging on the right claw. I could see that the dermatitis was gone there too. The right claw didn't look so good. There was a white line spot. Five days earlier, it had looked minimal. Now I was here again and looking at it more closely, contrasted with the claw that had been healed, I realised it was worse than I'd thought. The crack ran all the way up, between the inner and outer wall horn, to the hairline, where the horn grows. Back to square one with the left claw.

I had to remove every little bit of overburdening horn. It didn't flex. In this case, the inner portion of the foot was swelling because of the infection. The lack of flex meant there was a build-up of extreme pressure and, as a consequence, pain. By taking away some of the horn I could allow room for the swelling and stop most of the pain. That should normally promote the growth of fresh horn, and eventually, hopefully, a good recovery. I couldn't put a block on that back left foot, but I'm a glass half full type of guy, or I would be, if I didn't drink everything in one go.

I felt hopeful that we could get her to come good. She was on a clean, straw bed and the cushioning surely helped. The next week was critical for Cow 812. I'd done what I could. Now it was her turn. She had to feed herself up and build some fat reserves to help her feet and boost her immune system so she could fight off her infections. I really believed we could get her back on her feet, functionally, and return her to the herd, within the next couple of weeks.

It took twelve months of treatment, with me and Craiga-saurus-Rex visiting her every two weeks to get her better. In the end, she looked like a different animal, like someone had cloned a fresh version of the same cow and done a switch. She was almost fully recovered. She was pain free. She had regained her weight, and given birth to a healthy calf, and she was producing milk. By the time we got to the end of her treatment, I had made a few videos, documenting her progress. She grew a following. There was huge interest in her recovery among my subscribers. We gave her a proper name – Gracie, as in 'by the grace of God', and we named her calf Lola.

So why do white line defects take so long to heal? I did a demonstration in one of my videos, using a welly boot and some crazy glue. Conveniently, my welly had a crack, running up the side, simulating a crack in a hoof. I glued it back together and it looked smooth, but there was a bead of glue there. Then I ripped it again and used more glue. That left more beading, and the effect was like scar tissue, seeping into my boot. If I walked around in that for an hour it would cause some irritation. I'd get a blister, and I'd moan about it, a lot. It's similar when the crack in a hoof heals. Projections of horn grow into the underside of the hoof capsule and aggravate the flesh underneath, leading to pain, just like the glue on the inside of my boot. Every time the cow puts her foot down and walks, those projections will be causing pain. In the long run, she's also much more likely to suffer from lameness again.

Hoof horn takes about nine months to grow fully, from the coronet (where the hair on the ankle meets the hoof horn), to the base of her sole. With that slow regeneration time, and the horn actually sticking into the cow's foot, it's not hard to see how healing can be a tricky process. And then there are the complications to factor in – sometimes dermatitis will become part of the equation, which further compromises the healing time. Working with those feet can be like trying to bake a cake while someone tries to eat it.

I passionately believe that lame cows and bulls should be treated as emergencies, and sometimes I worry that we're sending out the wrong message on my channel. We show ourselves fixing a lot of defects and the ones we show tend to be major. My worry is that we might accidentally be suggesting it's okay for these cows to get lame, or that it might even seem routine. After all, we can fix them, can't we? It's never as straightforward as that, unfortunately. Outwardly, we may appear to fix those cows, but they'll never be as comfortable as they were before the lameness set in.

White line problems are down to cows' environments, and concrete. Turning sharp corners on a hard surface, for example, isn't something they have evolved to do. Simple measures, like putting rubber on the floor, especially around corners, is a nice way of stopping those white line problems from ever happening. Cows would never have to turn sharply on the grass out on a field or if they lived in the wild, and if they did there wouldn't be the same level of damage. Turning on concrete puts huge forces into the white line. It tears it away from the sole of the cow's foot. So, we end up with low level white line defects that evolve into full-on white line disease, and, if she's really unlucky, dermatitis sets in and causes real problems. We can fix a lot. Gracie is proof that there's always hope, but a lot of what we're fixing is on the surface.

The fresh, healthy horn might look good on the outside but those jagged projections lurking underneath will always hurt and the cow will never be quite the same again. When she's lame, or there's an internal problem in the foot, her body will send more blood there, to try to deal with it, and that causes calcification of the bone. The pedal bone should be a triangle, all sides of which should be nice and smooth, but when blood is pumped to an extreme, it causes calcification, and bone spurs, like spikes, stick into the corium. The foot ends up bruised and ulcerated and that can't be cured. I've seen bones five or six times the size they should be, and nothing like a healthy triangle.

It's horrible to see.

The only way to guarantee that a cow's life is as comfortable a life as possible, is to stop these problems happening in the first place, and if they do happen, to treat every case as an emergency. And no. I'm not just saying that because I want to fit a blue flashing light to the top of my pickup – although, and this may not surprise you, I do have a set of blue lights, and some livery, with the words 'Hoof GP Emergency Response Team' to fit to my Polaris off-road buggy.

I sometimes have to take away a huge amount of detached hoof horn. You'd think you'd be down to the bare bone of the foot, doing that, but if I can get my knife in behind a fragment of horn, even just the tiniest shard, it has to come off, for the good of the cow. Every cut with my knife is assessed before the next one and experience has taught me enough to allow me to do that quickly. Sometimes I get down to a thin layer that flexes and wrinkles as I run my thumb along the surface. It looks like skin, but as long as I glue a block onto the other claw on that foot, I can elevate the one I'm working on, keep it out of the way, and protect it until it heals.

When I'm doing the more precise cuts, I crack out the grinder, with its whirring bladed disk. It may look like an implement of torture, but it's a neater, safer tool for the job. After trimming hundreds of thousands of hooves, it's like an extension of my arm. Don't get me wrong. It has the potential to be dangerous. I wouldn't recommend anyone trying to use one without training.

The story of Cow 812 caught the imaginations and captured the hearts of people across the world, and Gracie's become a mascot for us. Her story became a bit of an emotional roller-coaster for me as people everywhere became invested in her struggle and eventual recovery. People sometimes ask if the cows remember what we do for them. I don't know for sure, but if any of them do, Gracie seems the most likely candidate. My repeat visits meant I spent a lot of time with her. When I first met her, she was in too much pain to relax, and she hated the crush. She didn't want to be anywhere near it. I suppose you wouldn't either, if you didn't know what it was, all black metal and moving parts. It's what I imagine Darth Vader's home gym would look like. But, over time, she got a little bit better, a little friendlier with each visit. She started to like being petted and clapped when she was in the crush with us. It was as if she started to see it as the means to her recovery and equated it with feeling a bit better afterwards. By the time we'd healed her, she let me stroke her face and give her a hug when she was in the crush. She was comfortable and she trusted me, and that meant a lot.

She's now completely over her crush fear, and we're old friends.

When I trimmed her feet and filmed her again, in early July 2021, after eighteen months of treatment, I was seriously happy for her. I felt a great sense of pride at what we'd achieved. We managed to get Gracie through life-threatening problems and out the other side. It wasn't just about curing one cow and making her more comfortable. It was about proving what we can do for these animals, if the right amount of time and effort is put into any cow in need. It was a big learning experience for me, and hopefully for some of the people who watched the videos.

I'm often asked now how Gracie is and if she's doing well, and I'm happy to report she's still going strong. Not only that, but her celebrity cow status has grown beyond YouTube infamy. Among the millions of people inspired by the story and the reaction to Gracie, was local author and illustrator, Shalla Gray. Shalla wrote and published a picture book called *Saving Gracie*, which tells the story of a cow living in the peaceful rhythms of the dairy farm in green and bonny Galloway until one day she falls ill and needs help from the Hoof GP to fix her sore feet.

I'm a bit biased, but I think it's an awesome book – and no, I don't make any money from its sales, I just happen to love the fact that I'm sharing space on the page with one of my most rewarding work projects. It's both Gracie and I's first outing in an illustrated picture book, and yet another totally random and unexpected offshoot of my almost-never-happened career trimming hooves.

# Chapter Twenty-Three

My inadvertent career started to have other impacts too, and not all of them were positive. The columnist, Mary Schmich, once wrote that, in life, 'the race is long, and in the end it's only with yourself', shortly before Baz Luhrmann quoted her in song lyrics. I agree with both of them but maybe I've maybe been coming from a different angle. For years I felt I was on the run, but I was trying to escape from myself.

There were things I was perfectly happy with. My family, for one, and work itself. I loved the instant effect I could have on the quality of life of a lame cow. That never gets boring for me, and bringing an animal like Gracie back from the brink of death was a real privilege and a massive buzz. Being paid for my work and being able to look after my family is another reward. That said, I can't pretend that alone made me blissfully happy, and I'd be lying if I said I didn't appreciate having my efforts and skills acknowledged by the farming industry.

In October 2017 they were, when I won UK Contractor of the Year at the British Farming Awards. I was thrilled. I couldn't believe how far I had come, from not knowing what I wanted to do with my life to finding a real vocation and becoming successful and recognised for my efforts. It was a big moment for me, and confirmed how far I'd grown my skills, to the point

I was now at the cutting edge of my profession (pun fully intended).

The award itself was very unexpected. I had been nominated and I'd even been interviewed about it, but at no stage did I actually think I could win it. That's not false modesty. In fact, I was so sure I hadn't won, I'd booked myself a holiday that clashed with the awards ceremony. The call from the organisers came the day before I was due to fly out to Majorca. It wasn't normal protocol, but in the end, they had to tell me that I'd won, because of the circumstances. They wanted to know if I was planning to attend the ceremony, so I cheekily told them that I would if I won the award. I didn't want them to give it to someone else, just because I couldn't get there to receive the prize. Thankfully that wasn't the case. I ended up flying off on holiday, and someone else collected the award on my behalf.

I should have stopped to enjoy it more. It was a real high point. But like a lot of high points, the only way from there seemed to be down. Over time, despite my life growing happier and more settled in many ways, I continued to battle with my mental health. Looking back, I now realise how oblivious to it I must have been. A lot of what I now know to be symptoms, I wrote off as annoying character traits. One minute, I would be hyper – laughing and joking around, the life and soul, drunk on my own enthusiasm. I was full of energy but there was always this feeling in the background, like a nagging doubt, not dissimilar to the anxiety I'd experienced as a child. The energy I projected was like a mask I wore for the world, as if I wasn't good enough without it. In a lot of ways, I hated this version of myself. Then, the misery would come, like when the sun disappears behind the clouds, and everything just seems to go grey. I'd start to feel like I'd done something wrong, even if I hadn't, or that I was the worst person in the world, and that something awful was going to happen. Those waves of uncertainty used to floor me regularly. Sometimes they still do. Those episodes are horrific. Unbearable. So bad they have pushed me towards considering suicide more than once.

There's no rhyme or reason to it. My mood can completely alter in the space of five to ten minutes. I can be stupidly high – annoyingly high – and then someone can say something trivial, and I come crashing down. It's like being in a state of mania, then someone slaps you and you wonder, what is the point in all of this? I started to over-analyse. It didn't matter if big things or little things happened, it was as if I was just sitting on a couch, waiting for something that might never happen, and even if it did, what was the point?

I was working, doing something I enjoyed, becoming successful. I'd made a home and family life with Ashley, but underneath it all, I was still struggling, somehow. I had been for a long time. I was starting to have moments just as concerning as my not-quite suicide attempt years earlier.

I jumped into my car one lunchtime and drove deep into a forest. I parked up and just sat in the car for hours. Ashley was at home, wondering where the hell I'd gone. I'd abandoned my phone on the coffee table. That's how quickly I'd left. She couldn't contact me, but she could see my search history. It showed that I'd been googling 'easiest and most efficient ways of suicide'. Ashley called the police. I'd been clinically logical. I'd sought out something that couldn't be reversed, once I'd started the process. Ashley and the rest of my family would endure a night of hell before I eventually arrived home at 4 a.m. There was no specific trigger, no cause or reason for my disappearance. We hadn't had a row or anything like that. I was in a lot of debt because I hadn't been paid in a while, but that was something we'd gone through before, so there was nothing, other than the awful illness I would discover I had.

It's only with hindsight and my now daily dose of Fluoxetine that I can see the signs of what was going wrong for me, and the difference between my life then – even though I was often happy – and my life now. That was a painful time, with some hard truths to face up to, but I had to go through it. I had to figure out what was happening with me. I needed to speak to someone about it.

My brother Bob and I were at Agri-Scot, at the Royal Highland Centre in Edinburgh. My three-year-old nephew, Jack, was busy, climbing on tractors of all shapes and sizes, the way we would have done at the same age. I was on and off those tractors with him for a solid hour. They were about to leave, and I realised I couldn't put it off any longer.

'I think I've got what Dad had,' I said, matter-of-factly.

We talked about it and agreed that my symptoms sounded like manic and depressive episodes. My doctor subsequently told me that years ago, they would have called what I have manic depression, but they don't use that terminology anymore. Talking about it openly and facing up to the unknown was maybe the most important part. Guys are pretty hopeless at that, especially in Scotland. But once it was out there it was real, not something hiding in the shadows, waiting to attack, and not something to be ashamed of. Everyone in my family agreed that I needed to talk to a professional, and that, I am happy to say, is what we did.

We had an awesome family doctor and it's partly thanks to him I was very quickly diagnosed with rapid cycling bipolar disorder. It had a name. That was my epiphany moment. When the doctor explained the physical element to the mental illness that I had been fighting most of my life, I understood it, just like I understood the physical elements of what I do. I could rationalise it. It's all to do with the serotonin levels. Serotonin is a neurotransmitter. Its job is to transmit signals between the nerve cells in your brain. It also regulates your mood. Low serotonin means weaker signals and unstable moods. The meds I take now regulate my serotonin levels. Someone with depression would have low serotonin levels, permanently. My levels are more like an ECG reading. They're up and down like a yo-yo in a lift. What does that mean in real life? When my serotonin levels are high, I'm hyperactive. Other times they dip, and I feel low, and stressed.

I was also diagnosed with ADHD – another explanation for my restless impulsiveness and issues with concentration. It was totally obvious with the benefit of hindsight. It all made perfect sense once I knew what was happening to me. It was a massive turning point. I understood that I could be treated with tablets, to reverse the physical effects. That in turn improved my mental state. I had a way forward, a way to navigate the peaks and troughs. I wasn't becoming my father, after all.

I've said before that my memory used to feel cloudy. People used to comment that I looked glazed at times, like I was looking through them. After three weeks of Fluoxetine (otherwise known as Prozac) and Sertraline (otherwise known as Zoloft), every day, I noticed I was thinking more clearly. People told me I didn't have that 'look' anymore. Seven years down the line I have a focus and mental clarity I never want to lose. If I do forget to take my tablets, I very quickly start to regress back to the way I was before and I realise what I've done.

Before I was diagnosed and started to receive treatment, I couldn't deal with stress of any kind. My brain went into a sort of lockdown, like a self-preservation thing; there was too much going on in my head so the trip switch would go, like a fuse box overloading or a car going into 'limp home mode' to protect itself when it's on the blink. I stumbled over my words, and I couldn't think straight. Even now, with my medication, I have to be careful to avoid overstimulation. If there's too much happening at once it messes me up. I love kids, but we can't have too many people in my house. When we do my head gets so busy I'm quickly overwhelmed and regress into myself.

Prior to starting my medication, I often acted impulsively. You might have guessed that if you're this far into the book! One brutal manifestation of this was my spending. When I was manic, I spent money I didn't have on crap I didn't need. I got toothache one night and couldn't sleep. I spent £7,000 I didn't have shopping online, as a form of distraction. I ended up owing HMRC £37,000 in income tax, on top of what I owed Mum for setting up the business. That sat heavily with me. I felt like I was a drain on everyone. But once I could think clearly, I knew I needed to get my shit together.

I met up with my brother James for lunch in The Golden Cross (a pub in Biggar), on the way to Edinburgh. We spent two hours looking at my finances, to try to sort everything out. James is a wizard when it comes to money, and he'd agreed to look at my bank statements and tell me where I could make savings. When we'd finished, we went up to the bar to pay. We'd both had three-course meals and a few drinks. I wanted to pay my share of the bill.

'I'll get this,' James said to the barman.

'No, I'll pay,' I said. I felt if anyone should get lunch it was me. He'd just given me a bunch of much-needed advice. James glared at me. He'd just spent two hours telling me how to stop wasting money and now I was turning down a free meal. 'And that's another thing,' he said. 'When someone offers to pay the bill, it means they want to and secondly, it means you're not paying the bill, so just shut the fuck up and take it'.

He was angry, which, to be honest, sometimes feels like his default setting, but it was justified. I needed to learn how to fix the mess I was in. Neither of us could have predicted that in a few short years, all my money troubles would be over, and I wouldn't need to lean on him anymore, but in that moment, he was helping to carry the load I'd created for myself.

There's a song that really got to me recently: 'I Can't Carry This Anymore' by Anson Seabra. I feel as though the song's creator must have suffered from the same kind of depression that I do. The first time I heard it, I was driving my Jaguar F-Pace SVR, an absolute beast of an SUV, along the achingly desolate road that runs between Glentrool and Straiton. We drove through the Scots Pines of the Galloway Forest and climbed up over heather-strewn moors, along a perfectly smooth, single-track road. It was a happy family day. My life was as close to perfection as it could be for me then. There I was, in a Jag. *My* Jag, with Ashley and the boys, a big V8 engine underneath us. I drove for fifty miles and started to wonder, 'How on earth did I get here?'

That song came on and I was in tears.

'What's wrong with you?' Ashley asked. I couldn't explain myself. The lyrics just resonated so much. I was overcome with emotion that someone felt the same way I did. Happiness at knowing I wasn't alone. Sadness that I felt this way. It was a big moment in my life, which is weird, because nothing was actually happening.

My own road had become a lot smoother, and I no longer needed to outrun myself.

# Chapter Twenty-Four

Now that I was more focused I began to realise I could channel my energy and enthusiasm in a more productive way. Even better than that, I could put it into anything I wanted. I was doing well with the hoof trimming. I loved it and still do, but I felt like I still needed a challenge; something to keep me engaged. The mental clarity the medication had given me meant there was nothing stopping me from doing that, and so I decided to set myself a goal: to start a modest little YouTube channel.

Ever the fool, my first video went up on 1st April 2019. I'd made videos before that – stuff with my family and my cars, but they were for fun. They didn't have any real direction or purpose, but it turned out flunking both a photography and an IT course at college wasn't entirely wasted. I had learned some skills, after all, and I understood what made images work and pop. Now I could put that knowledge to work. If I was able to pull a still photo composition together, I knew I could do the same with the shots for my videos. My early attempts meant I had the basic know-how needed to work out how to edit videos. I also had years of customer experience. I knew how to talk to people. I felt a sense of things coming together.

When I'd worked in the restaurant trade, some of the most loyal customers I had were the ones who started out by complaining. You can take a complaint and turn it into a positive experience, if you're able to handle it well. If you go the distance to make that happen for someone, they'll come back, and you'll have a better relationship with that customer, because they trust you.

These days, I actively look for ways to turn seemingly bad situations around. A prime example would be when we receive comments about cows being kept in bad conditions on farms. I'm able to reply to those comments and explain that, actually, these cows live out in green fields most of the time. They're only inside because I'm trimming their feet. I can give context to rebut people's misconceptions, and I can provide useful information to change people's minds.

Back in my pre-diagnosis days, there's no way I would have had the concentration and focus needed to produce all the videos I do, or to run my YouTube channel – with everything else that involves – along with trimming hooves. Without everything that happened prior to making videos – my worsening symptoms and contemplating suicide again – I wouldn't have gone to see a doctor. It was an extreme time but once I'd ripped off the plaster and confronted the worst of the problem, things started to get much better for me, and making YouTube videos has been a fundamental part of my recovery. It settles me down and gives me somewhere to channel all my obsessive drive and excess energy. It's something tangible, something I've created out of nothing but my own life and experiences. It feels strangely like everything happened in exactly the order it needed to. People sometimes talk about ADHD as being a superpower. If the focus is channelled correctly, it can be a massive advantage. Looking back, I can see that happening all the way through my life. I get obsessed with everything I get into, and sometimes I worry that if I'm 'fixed' it will remove the elements of 'me' that have made me good at what I do.

People talk about flow – a mental state that means you are absorbed in whatever you're doing. There's nothing else. You're not thinking about the peripheral stuff, the day-to-day odds and sods of life that float around the back of your mind. Some psychologists believe that's the state you should aim to achieve. I'm not a psychologist, but I'd agree with that idea, on the basis of my own anecdotal evidence.

The first YouTube channel I set up was just for me, and I got a bit lost in it. Around the same time, I was becoming much more visible on social media. I'd been posting about my life and work on Facebook for a while. I'd go to conferences and people would comment on the things I'd been posting. They seemed to like what I was doing. That made me want to do more, and I wondered how I could up the ante. Maybe I should make some videos about my work instead?

The reason I first started making videos was to make extra money. Farmers were still paying me late and I would miss my own payments as a result. Then I'd get fined by my bank. I'd always be able to make my payments in the end, but I'd still be in debt because of fines. I was also carrying the massive HMRC debt I'd racked up, plus the money I owed to my mum, and I didn't know how I was going to keep paying Craigie Boy. I'd already had to lay him off once before. It was a simple calculation. If I could get £30 a day from YouTube, that was £900 a month. That meant I could pay my bills. I feel embarrassed to admit that this was the initial drive to do everything I have, and it might be a bit of a let-down for people reading this, but I was focused on the survival of my family. I either had to go and do something else, or I could subsidise my income with money from YouTube and keep doing what I loved. All of the positives of my channel are real but none of it would have been put in motion without that initial spur: the hunger to provide a good, stable life for my family.

The first videos were an excellent way to highlight the potential problems with bovine hoof health. They were educational. They were made to help farmers. I could send the links to my customers. It was a nice little extra that added value for those clients. If I could educate them on hoof health, I'd maybe prevent some of the issues instead of just fixing them all the time. I tried my hardest to look professional and sound concise. This was my business. I had to be business-like.

Then something weird happened. I started looking at the analytics on my channel dashboard. It was addictive. There were some crazy stats in there, but the views I was getting were not the views I was expecting, and they weren't from the viewers I was expecting. In my head I'd pictured grizzled agricultural types clicking on the links, getting into the technical detail of what I was doing, but my main audience wasn't from rural communities in the UK. They were from cities, in America. Most of my viewers had absolutely nothing to do with farming, other than the window on the world I was giving them.

That made me stop and think.

I then did what everyone does in the beginning. I watched a bunch of other YouTubers: Casey Neistat, Peter McKinnon – the people I really admired, and still do. I watched what they were doing, closely. I saw what I thought worked and I tried to adapt it, to fit with what I was doing. Eventually, I started watching more agricultural stuff, but that was another world. I told myself I had to behave professionally, in a buttoned-up sort of way, to prove my credentials somehow. All I really needed to do was let my passion shine through.

In the end it kind of happened on its own. I slowly morphed from the 'me' I thought I had to be on camera, to the me I really am, except bigger, louder, and 'out there' enough for the world of social media. That's when things really took off, and my channel grew exponentially. At the same time, I developed the content range for my videos and started sharing my love of all things cow, this crazy little country, and the life I lead. I threw in the odd bit of stupidity and insanity and made things as entertaining as possible. The biggest change I made in front of the camera was the same one I made when I first left home and went to college – I let my guard down and stopped hiding.

It worked. The more views I got, the more people saw the videos, and the further I spread my message about healthy cows and hoof care. Somehow, doing it for the cows gave me a higher sense of purpose. Then the more the videos encompassed my daily life, the more I involved my family in them. It was always their choice whether to appear, but they're such a big part of my day I felt the boys needed to feature. They've always been keen to come to work with me, so it seemed like a natural progression. The more people warmed to the videos, the more relaxed and confident I became. It really did feel like everyone was winning, especially those cows. That seems to be the crucial 'secret' to my success, although I went into it all in a video titled 'The Secret of my Success', on my other YouTube channel, 'GPS Everything', so it's a badly kept secret!

I'm sure there are people out there who watch my videos and think, 'What the fuck? This guy's an idiot.' I know there are. I've seen some of the comments! That doesn't really concern me. The people who matter most to me are my family. Their opinions are the ones that count. It's funny, because growing up, that was one of the positive messages my dad used to drum into us constantly.

I'm just not sure I got it until I was an adult. Up until a few years ago I used to really worry what people thought but these days I only care about what my family and my closest friends, the Daves and the McGills of this world, think. They come first.

Aside from the hoof trimming questions, people often ask me how I got so big on YouTube, and the answer is I don't think I am. It's the Casey Neistats and Peter McKinnons who are massive. They're the people I started out looking up to and still do. But I don't want to be them anymore, no matter how many subscribers or views they have. I just want to be me. That's the thing I've loved so much about the whole YouTube adventure – the fact that people buy into the channel, into me, for just being me. That's an awesome feeling and one I'll always be grateful for. There's an Oasis song called 'Little by Little' that has the line: 'true perfection has to be imperfect. I know that that sounds foolish but it's true'. That's how I try to live my life these days, to recognise the beauty in the little imperfections, the uniqueness and the quirks that make life that bit more special.

That's not to say I never had a sense of personal ambition. I knew the more subscribers I got, the more money I would earn. My first target was one thousand subscribers, and four thousand hours of watch time. That was, and right now still is, the minimum you need to monetise your channel. That took me six weeks. If that sounds quick, it is. So, I zeroed my beady eye in on another target: I wanted to catch Olly's Farm. Olly is a farmer from Norfolk, and at that point he had eighteen thousand followers. (At the time of writing, he's up to one hundred and eleven thousand followers.) Once I'd done that, like Forrest Gump, I kept on going.

Cody Creelman was the next target on my list. Cody runs a veterinary practice in Alberta, Canada. He had thirty-two thousand followers back then (and is up to almost sixty thousand now). I was competing in an international game now. I felt like I was really going for it when I set my sights on Tom Pemberton and his Tom Pemberton Farm Life channel. Tom runs a family farm in Lytham, in Lancashire, four miles from The Windmill, and my old life. He had fifty-four thousand subscribers then (now edging towards six hundred thousand), and I was determined to catch him. By the time I did, we were both on a hundred and twenty thousand, and we'd become good friends. These days, we like to appear in each other's videos.

I became obsessed. Surprise, surprise! I did everything I could think of to try to boost my audience. I commented on the videos of other YouTubers as soon as they went live, so my comment would be at the top, with my channel name. I commented on their live feeds. I paid to do superchats on their live feeds. I was relentless. In the beginning, I spent eight hours a day on YouTube, on top of the day job. I'd be up editing videos until one or two in the morning. Every. Single. Day.

I registered my channel in the US because it was a bigger market, and I could grow more quickly. My YouTube bio still says I live there. I started uploading on an American schedule, releasing videos around 11 p.m. BST, and I did (and still do) live streams at 11 p.m. or midnight UK time, all so I could fit in with my biggest audience, in the good old US of A. It's funny to think I grew up watching TV shows from across the pond, like *The A Team*, *Knight Rider* and *MacGyver*. (He was my favourite by country a mile. He could enter a room with a couple of rubber bands and a tube of UHU and he'd fly out the door on a device of his own invention). It's still weird to think that I'm now getting most of my views from the country of my TV childhood.

Another trick I used was meta tagging. When you release a YouTube video into the wild, you are asked to add tags. I added the names of top agricultural influencers. That meant when people searched for them my name would pop up at the same time.

The next target on my list was the Funky Farmer – a dairy farmer in Gloucestershire. He was at that point up to a hundred and thirty thousand subscribers. I kept setting myself bigger and bigger goals and used them as bite-sized staging posts along the way. If I broke it up, it felt like I was winning with every step. Bite-sized they may have been, but the numbers were steadily growing. There was Larson Farms (a fifth-generation corn and soybean farm in west central Minnesota, which currently has four hundred and ten thousand subscribers), Welker Farms (third generation farmer, Bob Welker, and his two sons, Nick and Scott, in North Central Montana, currently on five hundred and eighty thousand subscribers).

When I started writing this book, I had six hundred thousand subscribers. That sounds insane, doesn't it? But my channel was growing by roughly thirty to forty thousand subscribers a month. I earn a decent amount from hoof trimming. It's a skill, and one that's in demand. Now though, I'm able to earn several times what my hoof trimming business brings in, through YouTube monetisation, sponsorship and merchandise. I'm up to over two million subscribers. It's nuts. All that from making videos about my unusual job and the life I live.

In 2022, I overtook the top agricultural YouTube channel in the world: the Millennial Farmer, based in Minnesota. He's currently sitting at just over one million subscribers. We were now the biggest agricultural YouTube channel (try to imagine this being said in an important TV announcer's voice) ... *in the world.* It blows my mind to think we're at that point. No one else in the world of agriculture has that kind of reach. That sounds big-headed, and I have to check myself just writing it down, but it's not bad for a guy that didn't finish college and nearly never made it out of his twenties. There are magazines and TV shows that don't have that level of circulation. And it's not just about the subscribers on YouTube; I have just over two million followers on Facebook, too. My videos are viewed approximately one hundred million times a month, between Facebook, TikTok, YouTube and Lad Bible. I might speak to 1.6 million people in just one day.

How do I know all that? I have an app on my phone that gives me the numbers as they happen. I might seem comfortable with that, but I'm still a bit of a nervous wreck. I'm still the guy who needs medication to manage health issues, and I'm acutely aware that the whole thing could keep going or end tomorrow morning. Potentially because of ... me. A while ago I started a bonfire with some petrol and blew myself up in the process. I remember thinking, *I've just accidentally killed myself.* I could get cancelled for saying the wrong thing (which I frequently do). Or people might just get bored of my chat. All these are very real possibilities. I'm only ever one screw up or change in the online breeze away from everything vanishing into thin air, so I feel a huge sense of responsibility.

We have a main channel sponsor – EasyFix. They sell mattresses, among other things. It's a sign of how things have changed that I used to fit those mattresses for minimum wage. We have sponsorship deals for a lot of the products we use, but I don't want to milk that either. I'm ambitious for the future of the channel and I wouldn't want to ruin it by getting greedy. I can see how easy that would be. I can also see that growth needs to be manageable, and the content should be driven by quality, above all else.

I've always set myself the target of three videos a week. Ideally, they should go out on Tuesdays, Fridays and Sundays, and I've stuck to that. I usually tell people I have three types of video: first up, the car-crash style video – click bait in the extreme. It should grab you by the eyeballs and make you want to click on that thumbnail. It should be short and sharp, and produced to bring people into the channel. The format owes a lot to Dr Pimple Popper, and the car-crash videos are actually some of the most satisfying visits, from a hoof care point of view. These are the ones where I can make a real difference, making a cow more comfortable in a matter of minutes.

Next, we have longer videos, personal ones that introduce people to my family and my lifestyle, what I've been up to lately, what else I see on my travels, that kind of thing. There might be drone footage of where we've been, or some kind of daftness, usually involving Craig and I – like the time I turned the back of my pick-up into a makeshift hot tub and His Craigness decided it would be a good idea to open the door.

The third type of video is a medium length revisit of a cow, a follow-up to check on her progress and a sequel to her first starring role. Gracie's videos are good examples of this. People care about these animals as much as I do, so it's important to follow up where we can.

People are often surprised when I give them a look at my life behind the scenes. I made a fly on the wall video for my members – or 'moombers' as I like to call them – called 'SUNDAY FUNDAY ... A VERY BUSY VLOG!' (16th August 2020). I filmed a typical Sunday in my house, and I'll admit that it shocked me when I realised just how busy I am these days, even on a day 'off'.

After getting up early and making bacon bagels for the family – which gives Ashley a rest and hopefully keeps me in the good books – I slide through to my study and get in a few hours of video-editing. It takes me about eight hours to edit a full video, so three videos a week adds up to around twenty-four hours, or more, as I'm a perfectionist when it comes to editing. It's taken me years to pick up the skills I have, and I think I've refined the process down as much as I can. I use an Apple Mac, as for me, it feels like the best kit for editing videos and photos. The retina screen makes all the difference. It's also what I'm used to and that counts for a lot, especially when you're in a hurry and trying to do things as well as you can. Casey Neistat, the original vlogger, says it's more important to make things 90% perfect than to never film something that's 100% perfect. It can always be better, and that's fine. He also has a tattoo on his arm that says, 'do more'. I think that's an excellent mantra and it's something I try to live by.

Next up in my Sunday Funday video, I have to stop work and help Keir pull out a wobbly tooth. It's his first one so he's understandably nervous, but he puts on a brave front. It's a childhood milestone. The boys are growing up fast.

I'm back to the editing after that. I get the video finished, export it – which takes even more time when you're shooting in 4K – and then post it on YouTube. I love clicking the *publish* button and seeing what happens next. There's nothing quite like putting something you spent time producing out into the world. It doesn't matter what it is: a meal; a photo; a YouTube video; a book. It only feels like it exists when it's properly out there, taking on a life of its own. That never gets old. People usually start commenting straight away, telling me what they think and where they're from. It's great to watch the action in real time.

Then I film myself opening a parcel that arrived in the post. I'm excited because I'm sure I know what it is, and I'm right. It's a set of Hoof GP decals for the roof of my crush. They'll look seriously cool when I get them on. I carry on filming as I get to grips with a couple of freebies someone has sent me from Ireland – some awesome grinder pads with my name and logo on them. I'm lucky to be sent some amazing things: fan mail, flags that I now have all over the walls of my workshop, and some crazy gifts. One of my favourite gifts is a walking stick a long-time subscriber of the channel carved and sent to me. It's the most beautiful walking stick you can imagine, all twists and gnarly turns, with a perfectly carved hoof at the top. I'm almost looking forward to getting old just so I can road test that bad boy.

Then Mum comes round for coffee. She knows that the price of entry on a Sunday is pastry, so I get stuck into a croissant or two. Fixing on the decals can wait. After lunch, I have a bit of a cleaning backlog to get into. I finished late on Friday night and Craig wasn't there, so I didn't have time to clean all the equipment, like I normally do, and you now know how important equipment hygiene is in my job.

Even though my actual Sunday Funday was now only half over, I had my footage for the next video. How can a fifteen-minute video take eight hours to edit? You'd be surprised how quickly the time adds up. There's usually about two and a half hours' worth of footage to get from my GoPro on to the iMac. That takes a while to do. I'd get a bit bored just hanging around staring at the screen while it uploads, so I find something else to do. Usually that's shower time.

Once I have everything on my iMac it's time to start cutting. I stick everything together in a big timeline, then go through the footage. I cut out anything boring or superfluous. There's always lots of dead time in the footage I have as the GoPro is quite often just running in the background, so the vast majority of what I film ends up on the virtual cutting room floor. Once I have the basic video done, I jazz it up a bit, merging all the clips together with nice transitions, adding music tracks and voiceovers, as well as the now very much expected drone footage. I usually film my aerial shots in batches at the weekend. My working days are so action packed I just don't have time, even if it does look like I released the drone on my way between farms.

The videos are ultimately about entertainment. I need people to be captivated and entertained so that YouTube promotes my videos, and that they filter them out to farmers so I can teach people what I need them to know. I need people to be interested, so it's important I include new things my audience haven't seen before. That said, I do sometimes make a point of including a mundane trim, or the odd speeded-up montage of me trimming healthy cows' feet – which is the majority of my farm footage – just to remind everyone that lame animals are the exception rather than the rule.

Then there's the people (and things) other than Craig and I who feature in the videos. A lot of people get stressed when they get a camera stuck in their face. They'll say to me, 'I don't know how you can talk to a camera.' They feel awkward, as if someone will eventually be judging them. I never feel that way when I watch anyone else. I just watch it and then move on. But there are a *lot* of outtakes. Even though we've been doing this for a long time, one of us will inevitably talk at the wrong time, or someone (Craig) will drop the camera, or someone will appear round the corner. I get tongue tied and lose my train of thought every day and that old adage about never working with children or animals exists for a reason. Cows love to make a racket at just the wrong time.

Perhaps the most counter intuitive discovery I've made, over time, is that smiling on camera is all wrong – or it is in my case, anyway. It's not that I never smile on camera. Anyone who's ever clicked on one of my videos knows I regularly give people a flash of my pearly whites, but a constant, fixed grin is a big no-no for me. A lot of presenters do it on TV, but it's not realistic. They're only on screen for a few seconds, trying to maintain the energy and probably being told by the director to keep smiling. I'd just feel fake, grinning away like I have a coat hanger in my mouth. I'd rather concentrate on what I'm saying, keeping the content entertaining and letting my passion for my work and my life shine through. That way it's more like having a conversation with a friend.

I still shoot my own videos. I sometimes let Craig hold the camera, like he's a child who's won a competition on an 80s kids' TV show, but even then, I have to set it up myself. I'm a control freak when it comes to setting the scene. I'll film from one angle, and then film the same shot again from a different angle, giving a more layered effect, like a two-camera set-up. It could be something as simple as me walking, but the detail has to be right. I've been filmed for TV a few times lately, and I wasn't surprised to learn they do it the same way. Filming in a TV environment can take even more time. The problem there is that you have too many perfectionists around.

While I use drones for the aerial shots, it's mainly GoPro cameras for the stuff on the ground. They're discreet, uncomplicated and bullet-proof. That counts for a lot, even if we do get through four or five in a year.

I love to film the wildness and beauty of the landscapes we drive through between farms, towing the crush along at a relaxed pace. The drones make that easy, although there have been a few fatalities. One Boxing Day I was three sheets to the wind, telling Mark, my brother-in-law, how amazing the drone I had at the time was. It had an autodetect mode, to stop it crashing into things. Drunk me had it in sport mode and flew it at my neighbour's house to prove how it couldn't possibly hit it. We watched as it hit the house and smashed into pieces. Mark said, 'Oh well. That'll be that then.' He's a master of understatement.

Autodetect doesn't work in sport mode, incidentally.

I try to make videos I enjoy watching. For me, that means a fine balance. I want a mix between entertainment and education. If I go too crazy with the detail, or if I get too technical or too preachy, that's going to bore people rigid. Selfishly, it's going to bore me rigid. If I start to get bored when I'm editing, I start deleting stuff. If I don't want to watch it, why would anyone else? On the rare occasions I miss a scheduled upload, you can safely assume my boredom switch has been tripped, and I've scrapped the whole thing. It's better to post nothing at all than a whole load of nothing.

The unseen parts of my videos are also some of the most important elements. The music is crucial. A lot of people ask me about the song in my intro, and, of course, the singer. It's called 'Fall Into You' and the group performing it are Houses On The Hill, but with one special addition. The voice that colours the track belongs to a featured singer – a Swedish songwriter called Ebba Bergendahl. She went to university to study music. I read in an interview that she had to work four jobs to keep going.

I found the song on the royalty free music website, Epidemic Sound. I was looking for something that spoke to me. Something that conveyed the romance I felt about my job, my way of life and the landscape I lived in. That song, and Ebba's voice, seemed like the perfect fit to me. And most people I speak to seem to agree. I use other songs, in different parts of videos, but that one blows everything else away. As of now, I don't think she's signed to a record label, but I hope millions of people have heard her music through my videos. I tried contacting her once, but I didn't hear anything back. I really hope she finds the success she deserves. Her haunting, bittersweet voice deserves to be heard far and wide.

The most important thing we need to remember when we're filming is that it's secondary. We need to make sure it stays in the background, and we need to be on the farm for as short a time as possible. Anything else is a nuisance. We'd be like clingy house guests, with cameras. That does sometimes mean the cameras run while I focus on trimming, which can mean a lot of dead air to edit out. But crucially, it doesn't interfere with the process of hoof trimming, or adversely impact the farmers, or, more importantly, the cows.

And, at the end of the day, no matter how big my modest little YouTube channel gets, it's still all about the cows.

# Chapter Twenty-Five

Gracie might have ended up being the best known non-human star of our videos, but she certainly isn't the only cow that has required intensive or prolonged treatment. There have been plenty of others that have tested our skills to the limit and given us more than a few headaches in the process.

A video from 17th July 2021 titled 'PEELING BACK A BANDAGE from this INFECTED COW'S HOOF!', documented another monumental struggle we had. We went all out on this particular cow's foot, cleaning it as thoroughly as we could. But when I started to trim, I hit a wall of problems, literally. She had a white line defect on the axial wall of her inside claw. That video got graphic, very quickly.

We wanted to film it as an example. The cow in question was the first, out of an entire herd, that had any sign of lameness. She was the exception that proved the rule, and she was extremely lame. I trimmed both toes back to the right length, then made sure the soles were all completely level. Then I got down to the hard-core stuff. I had to take away all the loose and disconnected horn. There was a lot of it. It was a delicate process, and in the end, I'd uncovered a whole load of trouble: the double whammy of digital dermatitis and a vast, open wound. On a cow like this, you're never sure if the infection is undermining the whole sole. She would almost certainly have been in pain twenty-four hours a day, and while that's hard to see, it gives me the satisfaction of peeling back those layers of horn, knowing I'm making a real difference to her quality of life.

Perseverance is crucial with cows like these. You need to keep going if you want to make a real difference. We took our time and did the best job we could. We attached a rubber block, then sprayed the lesion with a vivid blue broad spectrum antibacterial medicine called Oxytetracycline, to attack the dermatitis. Then we covered the infection with salicylic acid paste. Salicylic acid is an organic compound found in willow bark. It's the precursor to acetyl salicylic acid, otherwise known as Aspirin. That eats up the exposed, infected flesh and makes way for fresh, healthy skin. We wrapped the infected claw with a bandage – tight enough so it stayed on, but not so much it cut off the circulation – and she was off. We could see she was walking well, straight out of the gate, but we were keen for the follow up. Things can look deceptively good sometimes. You can have all the confidence in the world, but nothing is an exact science. Mother Nature has a way of second guessing you and there are times when I have everything crossed for our return visit.

We were back six days later. I wasn't expecting a miracle. On one level, I was confident that the trim was good, and the salicylic acid was doing its thing. We were about to find out.

I unwrapped the bandage and gave the hoof a good wash, so we could see what was really happening in there. Things were healing well. As I checked the foot out, I couldn't resist shaving off just a bit more excess horn. The blue remains of the salicylic acid and the oxytetracycline still clung to the hoof, so I hosed everything down, looking for the lesion underneath. It hadn't healed completely – far from it. She was going to need a few more visits, but I knew I could get a flatter, more even surface, so I took off as much loose, raggedy horn as I dared. I wanted to give her as good a chance at a full recovery as I could.

I sprayed her hoof with green Repiderma and wrapped it in a red bandage. I love the way these videos document how well cows recover from different conditions, but more than that, I love seeing them walk away from the crush. A lot of the time, they're in a much better state than they arrived, walking straighter, more confident with every foot-strike. It's amazing the difference you can make in just a short space of time.

Every single foot teaches me something new.

It's not always about perfect recoveries, though. There is a video on my channel titled, 'THE WORST COW'S FOOT ON THE HOOF GP ... AND I FAILED'. That one first appeared on 1st June 2021. It tells a different story to the one my audience are used to. Four weeks before I made it, I'd featured a cow with a badly infected foot in another video. That was – and is – one of the most graphic trims I've ever shown.

Blood seeped from the back of the cow's heel, even though the horn itself looked in decent shape. Sometimes a completely normal looking foot quickly turns into a horrific mess, when you start removing the damaged and detached layers. That's where a lesion can be lurking. I worked away with my knife, paring back the loose horn. Slowly, the full, grim picture emerged. As a minimum, she was going to need a block to get this claw off the ground. Once I glued that on, I started trimming on the other side. That's when things got serious. The whole of the horn was detached from the foot within. As I trimmed further and further back, it wasn't long before I was dealing with a pus-and-blood-drenched mess. I kept going, removing anything that wasn't attached to the internal structure. I realised this cow had started out with a white line injury. That had progressed into dermatitis, and the dermatitis had gone on to attack the corium. No wonder her foot was a mess.

In the video we posted, it was important to stress that the cow was from a herd of six hundred. Imagine a village of six hundred people. You're obviously going to see common health problems in there, and yet she was the only one with any real lameness. The farmer kept up her pain medication. I'd already seen her twice, so I was hopeful for an improvement next time around.

Four weeks later we were back. She was walking surprisingly well, and I was feeling confident. This was visit number three, and she was getting used to us. She headed into the crush, seemingly unconcerned. I was keen to get her foot in the air and see how she was progressing. I unwrapped the bandage. The putrid smell hit my nostrils as a congealed, brown paste, a mixture of blood and medication, hit the air. It was a sticky mush, so I cleaned the area with water. Her foot hadn't healed. It was slightly better than it had been, but we needed to move things on. We needed to see progress. I wanted to get her walking the way she should be. I was hopeful about that, right up to the point I realised the corium was infected. She had digital dermatitis. Any new horn would be eaten as it grew. On the plus side, she hadn't gotten any worse.

On my first visit, I'd wrapped the wound with Embryonics Magical Paste. It normally does an amazing job, but this time it just hadn't been strong enough. It's a mix of salicylic acid, iodine and an antimicrobial clay. I was going to have to bring out the big guns. Pure salicylic acid, again. It's not as harsh as people might think. It's used on warts and verrucas, and even as a face cream. That said, I'm sure it sounds like battery acid when I describe it.

Viewers regularly ask me why I strapped a particular foot or why I left one unwrapped? It's a tough one to answer. There are a lot of variables when it comes to bandaging. If it's a particularly dirty farm, a wrap will help more of the paste to seep into the claw. On cleaner farms, iodine will clean out the wound and help heal the lesion, without the need for any bandaging. It's always good to let the air in when you can, if you can. Iodine was used in the Second World War, sometimes instead of bandages. It dries out the wound and creates a sterile barrier.

Now I was faced with a glue dilemma. If I glued a block on the other claw, there might not be enough of a height difference between the two claws, if I added a bandage. That meant the injured claw would come into contact with the ground again. That would put pressure on it and invalidate the whole point of the block. If I'm not treating dermatitis, I probably won't wrap anything. Even when I *am* treating dermatitis, I'm really just trying to buy some time and fend it off for a couple of days to let the cow's own immune system catch up.

Before I started using YouTube, I saw a Russian viral video of a huge farm. Lame cows crossed the road, between buildings. It looked horrific, but I realised that maybe there was an infection that had gone through the whole herd. I always remember how terrible it looked, how everyone was horrified, and then realising there was no context.

In the same way, you're probably wondering what exactly happened to this cow? Did the farmer neglect her? Did he just not care? Had she never even had her hooves trimmed? Well, actually, none of the above. If I was forced to hand over money and take a bet on it, I'd put everything on her having had an accident, and not a major one either. All it takes is for a bruise to form behind the hoof horn, for the pressure to build, and an abscess to grow. It's a perfect storm in there. The abscess has nowhere to go, so it bursts through the top or bottom of the hoof capsule. Then our old friend digital dermatitis pops up, like Whac-A-Mole. Problems like this are pretty much unavoidable. But when they do happen, it's my job to nurse these girls back to health.

From time to time, we all need to accept a bit of failure. In life I'd argue you have to embrace it. My job is no exception. It's just that the stakes feel pretty high – not for me, but for the cows. Sometimes, no matter how much effort you put in, you just can't get a hoof back to perfect condition. There will always be cases where too much damage has already been done. There's a video I posted on the 7th of November 2020 called 'THE BONE FELL OUT OF THIS COWS FOOT!'. Subtle, eh? I like to tell the audience exactly what they're getting. To date, thankfully, this is the worst foot I've ever had to deal with.

A month beforehand, I'd trimmed a cow with a sore back left foot. It wasn't a filming day. Not every day is, but I'm a twenty-first-century digital boy, so, of course, I had my phone with me. I filmed a fair bit around a foot that would turn out to be a lot worse than I thought.

The cow was new to the farm we were on, having been brought in from another herd. She'd arrived very lame. Someone had already been treating her and she had a block on the foot we were looking at. We have a protocol for these situations. If we're looking after a cow and she has a block on her foot, we'll remove it as a matter of course. The thing that jumped out about this block was its placement. Whoever had been working on the hoof – it could have been a professional hoof trimmer, a farmer or even a vet – had glued it on to the wrong claw. We went ahead and removed the block, and when we did, we lifted the pedal bone from inside the cow's hoof. It was poking straight out of the hoof. Imagine ripping the sole off a shoe and seeing the sole inside, except the sole is the pedal bone. Cows feel an enormous sense of relief when it's removed. What we saw underneath was bad. Really bad. We pulled the bone straight out of that claw, and it wasn't difficult either. We didn't have to dig around or cut or snap anything. I just reached into the claw and picked it out.

There was also toe necrosis, which stinks. It's the worst smelling thing we ever deal with. A lot of the time when people say, 'Oh, that smells so bad', it's something I don't notice any more. When it's toe necrosis I do. That smell stays on your hands for at least two days, no matter how hard you scrub. I don't need to tell you this cow was in a bad way – clearly in pain, fighting serious infection and badly in need of our help. We glued on another block, this time on the outer claw, to keep the weight off the damaged one and ease some of the discomfort. We did our best with the trim. It was never going to be a shining example of the hoof trimmer's art, but I was hopeful. We poured some iodine on the open wound and caked on the salicylic acid. That at least made her more comfortable.

When we went back, she looked a lot better. She was walking a lot more naturally. She'd put on weight and her coat was shining up nicely. When I got her in the crush, I could see she'd managed to lose the block I'd put on. That meant the pedal bone still within the hoof capsule had started to decay. The possibility of a full recovery had just been rendered null and void, but you need to adapt. It's important to remember the 'why' of what you're doing. In this case, I shifted my focus to making her life as comfortable as possible. I could still do that. If I put the work in, I might be able to get the end of the toe to heal over to produce some solid hoof horn and protect the internal structure. I examined her foot more closely. It was doing well. I was happy with her progress. I got to work with my knife and pared back all the loose, cracked horn. It was unbelievably hard because of the iodine and the straw she was walking on – sucking out the moisture. I worked slowly and carefully. The worst thing I could do at this stage was to cut into that delicate, new horn – the only thing protecting the inside of her foot. I'd been doing this for years, but it still made me nervous. I had to keep pressing the sole. If it started to flex, I'd gone too far. I had to be extremely precise with my knife.

I get asked a lot if I have a favourite brand of trimming knife. For me, that's an easy one, but it's all about personal preference. Just like the debate about tilting versus upright crushes, this one could go on for hours in the bar at a hoof trimming conference. I always used to use Aesculap vc110s, vc111s and vc112s. They were the best I'd seen or used. But now we've developed a new brand of knife, with Bovibond, one with all the features I need.

I always use double-edged knives. A lot of people are dead against them – people who seem to have problems with cutting themselves, instead of the horn. Craig and I love them, though. The double edge speeds the trimming process up. That gets the cows through the crush quicker, which means less stress all round. Plus, you don't have to swap the knives over as often. It's all about time and making it hard to take short cuts. If you're using a single-edged knife and you cut down the hoof, you might decide there's a bit that would be better cut with an upward stroke. If you have a single-edged knife, you should really swap it over, but most people won't. They'll just bodge it. Double-edged knives mean you have everything you need to get the job done in your hand.

I'm not a vet, so I have to be very careful when I add medicine into the mix. In the UK, only a veterinary surgeon is permitted to diagnose, advise on treatments, and prescribe medicines under the Veterinary Surgeons Act (1966). This act, and the written guidance of the Agriculture and Horticulture Development Board states: 'Professional foot trimmers must follow the guidance of the local (prescribing) veterinary surgeon to be legally compliant. In practice this means using the products provided by the farmer, who in turn has had them prescribed by the vet'.

When we get down to the detail, I'll generally know more about the condition of the feet of cows in a particular herd than the local vets. I'm happy to say I have a good working relationship with them, but I have to make sure I don't overstep my bounds. My knowledge is highly specialised, but, as we know, hoof trimmers aren't regulated. Maybe if we were, we could do a lot more.

I didn't see the point in criticising whoever dealt with this particular cow. Yes, they put the block on the wrong claw, but the main thing was that we all learned from what happened. The video meant I could educate people on the importance of using blocks for the right reasons, and in the correct way to place them when they do. It was my job to fix what I could and use it as a teachable moment. That's what hopefully makes my videos useful and entertaining. I would never discourage anyone from trying to help the cows and ultimately that's what this person was trying to do. The way I look at it, these revisit videos are a living record. They document the progress of different cows with different conditions. They are a demonstration of the effects, complications and likely recovery rates for different diseases of cattle feet. I love making them, because often they show the difference we can make in a short space of time. It's always valuable to revisit your decisions, the work you've put in and the outcomes that arose.

It's how we all move forward with everything in life.

# Chapter Twenty-Six

Life seems to have its defining moments. That's been my experience, anyway. Having bipolar disorder has surely impacted my life in certain ways. I'll never know exactly how much and I'm not sure if I want to. But, even with its ups and downs, my life is mainly all about hard work, day to day, putting in the hours, staying consistent, and that makes the big events stand out.

Even recently, with the YouTube channel really taking off and everything that's involved, my lifestyle has stayed pretty much the same. It's all about trimming, filming and editing videos, and running multiple social media channels. The watershed moments – the one hundred thousand subscriber mark and the silver play-button plaque from YouTube, then the one million mark and the gold version, even being able to buy a McLaren – these things are incredible, but they're not the everyday grind that keeps me on an even keel, and they're nothing compared to my family life.

One of the biggest defining moments for me was what eventually happened to Davie. He and Mum grew apart over the years. In time, they agreed it was best to go their separate ways, and they split up. Mum moved into my granny's old house and Davie moved to a flat in Glenluce – a nearby village. The name Glenluce roughly translates as 'the valley of light', a fact

Davie regularly told people, along with other edited highlights he'd picked up over the years and liked to dish out with his trademark frequency.

I think Davie was happy in Glenluce. He had diabetes, and his eyesight had failed. That meant he couldn't drive any more, but he mastered the local bus timetable and regularly toured the countryside. He was in a sort of enforced semi-retirement by this point and usually popped up in Mum's coffee shop a couple of times a week, talking to the customers, distracting the staff, and telling stories. Davie loved a good story, and he'd get maximum usage out of every single one. He once spoke to a tourist who mentioned Ireland to him.

'My ancestors came from there,' the man said.

'Mine too,' Davie told him. 'They were driven out of Rathness Island.'

'For religious reasons?'

'No! Sheep rustling.'

The man went away, laughing. That was Davie in a nutshell, and these were exactly the kinds of conversations he liked to have.

Now that we no longer worked together, and he wasn't married to my mum, we had started to get on pretty well. He wasn't my dad, but he had, in many ways, been the biggest influence in my life. I just don't think either of us would ever have admitted it to each other, being the bull-headed men we both were.

I dropped in to see him most weeks in those days, just randomly, whenever I could. I was working with a nearby farmer called Gary Mitchell every week, so I'd stop in at the local store then call in for coffee with Davie afterwards. Maddie, the boys and I would take him out every so often. I remember taking him to The Waterline in Stranraer for lunch one day, and how happy he was to be out. He wanted to treat his grandkids whenever he could. He had a habit of spoiling them, when he wasn't obsessively measuring them. Somewhere in my mum's house, there's still a stick, with all their heights marked in pen, representing different stages in their life. It's good to still have that reminder of him.

One Tuesday, I stopped in to see him a bit earlier than normal. I was about to knock on his door, and then for some reason I thought better of it. Maybe I thought he wouldn't be up, or maybe that he wasn't home. Two days later, however, I got a phone call when I was working at High Three Mark – the place the farmer had to rescue me with the tractor. Someone, I can't even remember who now, phoned to tell me that Davie had been found dead. Could I go? I was the closest. It was like being stabbed in the stomach. I downed tools and drove to Glenluce.

I don't know what I was expecting when I got there, but the police were in his flat, and they wouldn't let me in. I stood there in the damp-smelling hallway, talking to them. Trying to persuade them. But it was too early to say what had happened and this was potentially a crime scene. I was desperate to get through that door. All I wanted was to see how he was sitting, if he was comfortable. He had died three days earlier, on the Monday. He'd been sitting there, dead, in his chair, when I pulled up that Tuesday morning for my coffee. I obviously couldn't have done anything for him then, if I had discovered him. He'd already have died. It's just a desperately sad and lonely way to think of him. It still haunts me that I was right outside his door, and he was lying just a couple of yards away from me, dead and alone.

It's Davie's life, the manner of his death, and his funeral, that are probably the biggest lesson I've ever had in my working life. Davie thought he was friends with all of the farmers he worked for. He *was* friendly. He was that kind of guy, but a passing sense of humour, or banter, or good customer relations, aren't the same thing as being friends with someone. Davie never looked at it that way though. He went out of his way to help people. I'm not saying that's a bad thing, but you have to have boundaries. You need a bit of self-preservation. He'd make things cheaper for people, stretch things, do jobs that didn't make financial sense. He built cattle crushes at a loss, just to keep his 'friends' happy. And yet, when it came to his funeral, only a handful of them turned up. Of the ones that did, I'm really proud to say they are still my customers now.

Davie had a catchphrase: 'Nae bother'. He loved to help people out – not just at work, but in life, and that's an admirable thing. You'd thank him and the response was always the same, just a self-assured smile and a 'Nae bother'.

No bother. No problem. Not for Davie.

At his funeral I stood in front of the crowd. And there *was* a crowd, after all. I was able to tell them how we'd argued, how we'd never seen eye to eye on anything, and also that he'd been the biggest influence on my life. In the end, I knew that he had become proud of me, and that meant a lot. He'd come along hoof trimming with me. He told me the WOPA 51 crush I had was pointless, that he thought it just meant you could set things up quicker. I later heard, through other people, how impressed he was with it. That was typical of the man, saying nice things about you behind your back.

Later, when we were thinking about an inscription for his

tombstone, it seemed only right that it should include the words, 'a man to whom everything was nae bother'. It wasn't my place to decide, but I hope one day to see those words on the stone.

It was around the same time Davie died that my sister met a new man. I was sitting in my mum's living room, on the floor, drinking coffee. It was a standard Friday evening really, with people dropping into mum's house just to annoy her. There are five of us, so she doesn't get many breaks. This guy walked in with a mohawk, and, worse – a South Ayrshire accent. Enter, The Craig. This was my first encounter with the man who now works with me, and who I relentlessly take the piss out of – fondly, of course. I wasn't sure about him at first, though. For starters, he was going out with little my sister, and that never endears you to anyone.

When Davie died, Craig was a massive source of support. He helped my mum and Susan clear out Davie's flat, while a whole crew of us, including my brothers and Davie's nephew, all cleared his garden. None of this was easy. He was the biggest hoarder I've ever met. Craig was working at the time as a sort of handyman for his brother-in-law. Eventually he got laid off, and feeling like I needed an extra pair of hands, and that I could help him out, I asked him if he wanted to come and work for me. He said he'd worked on farms before so I thought he would know his way around a cow. It turned out he'd been working with ducks and chickens.

Knowing where to stand, or how to move a cow in a particular way, is an ingrained skill. If you're a farm boy (or a proud slack-jawed yokel, like me), you pick it up without knowing you're doing it. This wasn't Craig. If there is a worst possible place to stand near a cow, Craig would make a beeline for it. Even now he regularly tries to move cows along with stock phrases like, 'Come on boy. Up you get boy. Come on fella.' He still hasn't quite accepted the fact they're girls.

In the beginning, he couldn't understand the concept of beef cows and dairy cows. His standard opener was, 'Are you getting much milk out of your cows?', which he'd say to bemused-looking beef farmers. He was constantly getting stuff wrong, but he's nothing if not keen, and he asks a lot of questions. You can trust what Craig says. I mean, you can't trust him not to break stuff, but you *can* trust him to tell you what he's broken. These days he's slower at trimming than me, but it's because he cares, and he's become a very accomplished trimmer, despite his initial wariness around cows.

I remember him claiming he'd been kicked once or twice and me saying, 'not yet you haven't'. One day we were working away, and I heard a rasping behind me.

'I've been kicked. I've been kicked!'

My head shot round to see Craig, doubled over, barely able to breathe, a full, brown hoof print on his chest. I tried so hard not to laugh.

'NOW you've been kicked.'

I've given the poor man a hell of a teasing over the last few years because he's so trusting. My brother-in-law Kevin was talking a while ago about moving house. He was planning a moving-in party afterwards, and he told Craig it was guys only. This made no sense anyway, but also because we were all guys, so surely, we'd be invited. Craig took no notice of this implied slight, and said, 'You'll send us photos though?' Then he thought about it for a second and said, 'Send them to Graeme and I'll have a look on his phone.'

I'm not sure what photos Kevin would be sending from a

guys-only party Craig wasn't going to, and I didn't like to ask, but he was still trying to think of everything!

Everything supposedly happens for a reason, and Craig's a stand-up bloke who came into our lives at a difficult time after Davie's death, and really made a difference. He's probably the most trustworthy guy I know, and he's brilliant for Susan.

Taking Craig on was one of the best business decisions I've ever made. Working alongside him makes the days quicker and a lot more fun. Having to lay him off at one stage for a few months was one of the hardest things I've ever done. I'm just glad I could bring him back as soon as we started to see money again.

My defining moments have involved people entering my life at key points, and they didn't stop here. I was about to have another one. One that meant we wouldn't have to worry about money for quite some time.

# Chapter Twenty-Seven

I'm guessing most people reading this have had issues with money at some point in their life. But have you ever been flat broke? Completely and utterly skint? Totally penniless? I have. And I don't mean not having quite enough money to go on holiday this year, or to buy some new Nikes, or go out for dinner. I mean the kind of skint that involves letters from the bailiffs telling you they are coming round to your house to collect your goods and chattels.

If you've been there, you'll remember that sick, miserable feeling only too well. I doubt it ever truly goes away. It's pretty momentous knowing that you can't pay your bills even though you desperately want to and feeling the gut-wrenching inner conflict as you bury your head in the sand, ignoring your bank balance and avoiding the letters from the tax man reminding you just how much money you can't afford to pay. It's both character building and terrifying.

Growing up on Barmeal Farm, and especially later on, at The Knock, I knew there wasn't a huge amount of money floating around. Living in the Knock Cottage, I was acutely aware that everyone on the school bus and everybody who passed our lonely, little house could see us far too clearly: our lack of money; our hand-me-down clothes; the absence of family days out and the deteriorating condition of our home. The signs were all around us, in neon lights.

When Mum and Dad split up, and we moved to number 93 Main Street in Port William, we were living in Mum's friend's house. I can still vividly remember feeling like a charity case. I probably never considered the fact Mum was actually renting the place. I wasn't embarrassed or angry or anything like that. But I felt pitied, like everyone in the village knew what had happened.

We weren't just incomers, with vague back stories and invented versions of ourselves to make the transition easier. This wasn't a clean slate. We were locals, and everyone knew the ins and outs of our lives. Or at least it felt like they did. Don't get me wrong, there's nothing bad about being less well off, and nobody gave us a hard time about any of it. No one really talked to us about it at all, in fact. Maybe that's part of the reason there was always this cloud hanging over my head. I was always expecting them to, and I was ashamed of the path my life had taken. I felt like we reeked of poverty and misfortune.

Looking back, Mum did an incredible job of bringing us up. She provided everything we ever needed, even when she had to cut the odd corner to save some pennies. Overall, life in Port William was good, even without much money. And it set a precedent for a future life at college, in Dumfries, trying to budget around the inevitable lack of funds.

It's not as though I had nothing. I was entitled to a bursary. I had a student loan. Mum even topped me up with cash once a week. But being so young – I was only fifteen when I started college – and having access to my own money for the first time, was never destined to work out for the best. I did what all students do and got myself an overdraft. I maxed that out every time the slightest whiff of cash hit my account. I'd go to the local supermarket, buy a couple of chocolate bars and ask for fifty quid cash-back. For some reason there was a glitch in the system. I might only have one or two pounds left before hitting my overdraft limit, but the supermarket always allowed me that crisp fifty, and the cycle would continue; bank charge after bank charge after bank charge.

When Beth and I were together, we both had ideas beyond our means and were pretty terrible with money. I had good jobs, running The Windmill, managing The Royal Hotel and welding at Houghton-Parkhouse, but, predictably, we were always short of money. It wasn't even that we spent it outlandishly; we just had no grasp on our finances or how to manage money properly. By the time we had Maddie, the responsibility of parenthood imposed a much-needed, tighter rein on our finances, but we never seemed to move far enough away from the breadline.

When I moved back to Scotland and met my wonderful, future wife Ashley, I felt the real burden of financial problems for probably the first time in my life. Until then, money hadn't really mattered that much. Yes, I was always skint, but I was used to that, and I wasn't being chased for money I didn't have. It's one thing to have no money and to worry about that. It's a completely different thing to have no money while owing a whole load to somebody scary, like the tax man.

As I sit here, writing this and remembering those fears, I feel physically sick. The guilt, the desperation, the water hitting the back of your mouth, the churning in your stomach, knowing the problems you're ignoring are only getting worse and will never go away until you truly face them – that sensation never quite goes away.

Before tapping into the potential of YouTube, I was working every hour I possibly could, freeze branding or hoof trimming.

On paper, my business was successful, work was plentiful and technically I was earning a lot of money. But payments were slow. To keep my business running, I needed to buy supplies. I needed to spend money almost every day I worked, and I could still sometimes go for months without being paid consistently. It took its toll, on me and on Ashley. Thinking about it now, I'm surprised she's still here.

In October 2018, I had no money in the bank. I was living in social housing. I'd been spending all of my money on fuel, going to visit Maddie, trying to maintain a relationship with her. I was still over £37,000 in debt. I was drowning. *We* were drowning. Something drastically needed to change.

From small acorns grow great oaks. I never truly understood what that meant, until I got involved with YouTube in 2019, just to make ends meet, and my journey towards becoming The Hoof GP began. My prospects exploded after that, in ways I could only ever have dreamt of, and more. I've never been driven by money, but the lack of it has at times defined me, or at least, it has defined specific points in my life. You need it to survive in this world, unfortunately. That's the only real reason I've ever pursued it. But things changed when I had children and married Ashley. My family are my priority. Their security is my reason for being, and I didn't just want us to survive; I wanted us to thrive.

My growing success with YouTube has allowed us to do just that, and in a relatively short space of time, I went from having nothing to having the kind of financial security I'd only ever imagined for me and my family, all thanks to my wonderful subscribers. YouTube has taken me all over the world, but one place stands out more than most, because of the colossal impact it's had on my life: Los Angeles, The City of the Angels.

It isn't somewhere I ever thought I would find myself, never mind somewhere I'd end up enjoying so much. I've now visited California three times, and I've found myself in some of the most surreal situations, which, for me, is saying something.

I first went there to attend a meet-and-greet in Tulare County, where hundreds of incredible fans of The Hoof GP made the journey to see us. Some of them had travelled for seven hours. I stood in the blistering San Joaquin Valley sun, greeting friends and herd members I'd never had the privilege of meeting before. I felt completely and unexpectedly at home. It was genuinely humbling.

Over several visits, things just got better and better. On one occasion, I sat in the beautiful, manicured terrace gardens of the Beverly Wilshire hotel, at the end of Rodeo Drive, surrounded by my family, in a meeting with high flying Hollywood TV producers. I distinctly remember wondering how on earth a once-poor shit kicker from Southwest Scotland had wound up in this astonishing hotel, made famous by the movie *Pretty Woman*. We had a magical experience. We sailed through Newport Beach Harbour on a chartered yacht, drinking crisp Grey Goose vodka and cranberry juice, over ice. A school of dolphins darted around the boat as I chatted to our hosts, Dwayne and Brent. I had no idea that would be the start of a friendship, and a business arrangement that would bring about the launch of Hoof Grip Pro, our very own brand of hoof glue. As the sleek yacht cut through the calm waters off the Californian coast, I was in a super happy place. Ashley chatted with Dwayne and Brent's wives. Kier sat at the helm of the boat wearing a captain's hat, and Campbell lay on the aft of the yacht, drinking in the sun, staring in wonder at dolphins chasing alongside. This would turn out to be one of the most incredible days of my life thus far, spending time with people who are now close friends.

We visited Brent's hillside mansion. A team of private chefs catered for us in candlelit gardens. We were surrounded by laughter, swimming pools, fairy lights and future memories. At one point during the evening, I leant over to Palle Fjord Thomsen, the Danish CEO of KVK – the people who make my bright green crush. Palle is one of the most considered speakers I know. He pauses before each sentence; his words are deliberate. On this occasion, however, alcohol was involved. The softly spoken Dane leaned forward. With rosy cheeks and a glint in his eye, he whispered, 'How the fuck did two hoof trimmers end up here?!' It was so unexpected and so on point that the pair of us were in stitches.

These three very different moments in California all created meaningful memories, but it was a company in Silicon Valley that properly changed our lives forever.

When you have any sort of social media presence, you are inundated, every day of the week, with emails from all sorts of companies from all over the world. Companies with random names and fake profile pictures – which are usually female, presumably to look more trustworthy – promising sponsorships, partnerships, and untold riches. As you can imagine, I ignore ninety-nine percent of these emails. I'm not even sure how many of them are scams. It's hard to tell when I don't have time to read them. In the past, I've flirted with the idea of doing sponsorships in videos, but I was concerned they would detract from my enjoyment of the video-making process, which in turn might affect the enjoyment of the viewers watching them. I have done sponsorships, but I don't like to do it, so generally I avoid them. It takes something unusual, something special or quirky in the title of an email, to capture my attention and actually get me to read them these days.

Back in the summer of 2021, my email inbox pinged just as it does every morning. I receive anywhere between a hundred and two hundred emails most days. I usually try to browse my inbox at some point in the working day, to stay on top of things. I don't remember what it was about the title of the email Spotter sent me, but something caught my eye.

In the ever-evolving world of social media, there are always new forms of monetisation. And that means there are always new companies, formed specifically to tap into emerging markets. Spotter is, in essence, a company that bets on the future earnings of YouTube channels. Spotter's online bots scour social media outlets, hunting for rising channels, diving into analytics, and running projections on future earnings. If I upload a video to YouTube, the vast majority of the views that video receives – and the revenue they generate – happen in the first seven days. There's a real spike you can literally see on a graph. From there, that spike normally dissipates over the following month. Views and money dwindle with time, but the fantastic thing about YouTube is that for the entirety of a channel's life, those videos keep generating views *and* cash. A year after being uploaded, each individual video's views are fairly insignificant. In combination however, a library of videos on one channel can generate significant amounts of revenue over weeks, months – even years.

The Spotter team sent me email after email, rammed with pie charts, line graphs and projections for my channel. They told me they'd pay 'a significant sum of money', upfront, for the revenue from the videos I had already uploaded, for the next five years. After those five years, any continuing revenue would come to me. The deal was simple. From the 1st of June

2022, the income from any new video would be mine to keep. Then for the next five years, any money generated from videos uploaded before the 1st of June 2022 would belong to Spotter.

But what on earth *was* a significant sum of money? Were they talking tens of thousands? Hundreds of thousands? A million? I hadn't a clue. All I did know was that they'd done their homework in an effort to convince me. That's why they were sending me so many analytical emails, showing their workings.

Finally, after a lot of back and forth, we set a date for a Zoom meeting. Spotter were going to reveal their offer. I was nervous. Ashley didn't want me to take the offer. She was sure there was more in it for them than for us, which made sense. She worried we were being duped. YouTube had given us a life that we could never have hoped for. I'd worked incredibly hard. I'd been doing one-hundred-hour weeks for years by then, and still do. After struggling for so long, not feeling as though I had a grip on my finances, I now had full control over everything, and it was working for us. Understandably, Ashley was worried we were about to make a big mistake.

Mrs Hoof GP is, for the record, incredibly supportive. She's an integral part of how our business works – the one who keeps everything working the way it should, the fixer, the glue that holds it all together. There's no one I'd rather go on this mad, mad journey with. But Ashley's also my wife and mother to our two young sons. She's stood by me throughout difficult times and dealt with the consequences of decisions that hadn't worked out well for us. She – quite rightly – worried that me doing this deal could have an incredibly negative impact on our lives and the future for our boys. With one simple yes and one quick signature, I could be throwing it all away.

I sat in the bedroom I was using as an office, in an un-ironed, baggy white T-shirt and scruffy shorts, staring at three representatives from Spotter on the large screen in front of me. What was I going to do? How might this affect my wee family? I get a bit nervous in some meetings. That usually means I end up trying to deflect the nerves with shallow attempts at humour. Today was no different. I began by apologising that I wouldn't be able to generate subtitles to help them understand what I was saying. I think that joke was lost on them.

I've no idea what we talked about for the first twenty minutes. I vaguely remember them getting into the detail; more graphs, more projections, more analytics – everything they'd been studying for the previous month or so. What I recall most of all is the feeling that they were showing me all this for one reason only. They were justifying the extremely low offer they were about to hit me with. Whatever I was about to be offered, I had to remember that my YouTube earnings from then on out would reset to zero. I'd have to rebuild my channel. It would be just like starting out again, back in 2019. Whatever they offered me had to be substantial.

The man with thick glasses stopped talking. He sat upright and dropped his pen on the table.

'So, here's what we are willing to offer you,' he said.

He flicked the slide in his PowerPoint deck.

It said $590,000.

I stared at the number, then at the three strangers looking back at me, expectantly. I wanted to shout at the screen, 'Yes! Yes! I'll take it!' The figure on the screen would pay off our mortgage and leave us some money as a nest egg – something to fall back on if YouTube simply switched off tomorrow. At that stage, all I was interested in was the future security of my wife and children.

But Ashley's voice rang in my ears. 'Don't you dare agree to anything on the call; we'll need to discuss it.' Just in case it's not obvious by now, I'm the child in the relationship; the impulsive one. Wearing my best poker face, I thanked the Spotter team for their offer. I ended the meeting by telling them that this was a very important decision and one that I would have to talk over with my wife.

Ashley told me the offer was far too low, that Spotter stood to gain far more from it than we did. I understood what she meant, and I agreed to an extent, but I'm a realist. This was business, and for the deal to work, they needed to be able to extract their pound of flesh. Over the next few weeks, I openly discussed my position with the guys from Spotter by email. I pushed as hard as I could, for Ashley's sake. I was on the cusp of achieving real stability for my family; stability I never felt I had as a child; stability that would mean I had achieved what I felt a father should for his kids.

I went to war. I threw out drastically inflated figures and expectations, willing them to meet me halfway. I wanted to extract as much from Spotter as they wanted from me. But I had to be careful, I knew the whole thing could blow up in my face. I couldn't push too hard for too long, or the offer would expire.

In April 2022, we reached a mutually agreeable figure, and I signed a deal with Spotter that gave my family the security I had always wanted to achieve for them.

They paid me $960,000, which at the time was around £780,000.

I had all the security I could ever have wished for.

# Chapter Twenty-Eight

The financial stability given to me by the Spotter deal, plus my ongoing work with YouTube and my hoof trimming business, was a dream come true for me and my family. I should have been elated. I *was* elated. Everything about this was amazing. But, despite my newfound success and happiness, something was missing. *Someone* was missing.

As you know by now if you've been paying attention (and if not, how on earth did you get this far in?), I have three children, but you'll only have seen two of them in my videos. When I do live chats, one of the other regular questions I'm asked is, 'Where is your daughter?' It doesn't matter how much I've come to expect it, that one always throws me, because in reality, I'm constantly asking myself the same question. If I google myself, the third result in the search bar is 'Hoof GP's Daughter'. I don't even know how to feel about so many people looking that up online.

The problem with live chats is that you don't have time to pre-screen what you're reading, otherwise, I would completely avoid the question. I'll often find myself reading out 'where is your daughter?' without realising what I'm saying. I'll stutter and stammer and not know what to say, then get a lump in my throat as I try to keep going. It's an incredibly difficult subject to talk about.

Around the time of publication for this book, Maddie will be twenty years old. I'm not even sure how that happened. How did she get so big? Obviously I'm completely biased, but she's the most stunning young woman you've ever seen, with big, beautiful eyes, dirty blonde hair and smooth olive skin. While Bob and I were writing this book, he mentioned that she popped up on his Facebook feed. It had been so long since he last saw her, that he didn't recognise her. That's heartbreaking. Even more heartbreaking is that I haven't seen her since the summer of 2018.

How did we lose touch? I'm still not sure I understand the answer to that.

Beth and I had eventually split up for good when Maddie was five years old. In the end, it had been a conscious decision for me. The relationship had its good side. Most do. We didn't stay together for years because we hated each other. No one does. Or I certainly hope they don't, anyway. In the end though, we had to admit there was only one realistic outcome. Our relationship was toxic, and we weren't right for each other. No matter how much we both loved Maddie, that's not the right situation in which to bring up a child. We'd had blow-ups, trial separations and reconciliations, but I knew it had to end, for all our sakes, and especially for Maddie's. I didn't want to leave when she was too young to remember me, but I didn't want to hang on to the point where she would be hurt and then miss me too much. There's no good age for a child's parents to separate, but five seemed like the least awful compromise.

I was up in the very north of Scotland when everything came to an end between Beth and I for the last time. The call to come back to Wigtownshire and help Davie came when I might just have made the decision to give things another go. That would undoubtedly have been a mistake. It would have ended in tears, yet again. I needed to put some distance between Beth and I, but more than anything, I needed to maintain my relationship with Maddie. We'd always had a strong bond, since our first days together – wandering the streets, testing out all the latest Windmill creations. She was, and still is, the absolute apple of my eye.

We had a very close relationship for years after the split, despite the physical distance between us. It was just Maddie and me again, like the old days. I'd finish just after eleven every Friday morning, get cleaned up, climb into my pick-up and drive to Preston to collect Maddie from school, before bringing her back to Scotland for the weekend, with us. It was a real trek – I've already quantified it in overall distance – but it meant we could be together every weekend, in Wigtownshire, and that meant everything. That arrangement worked for eight years and in all that time we only ever missed two weekends: the first because I had swine flu, with a temperature of 40.5 degrees (which meant I probably should have been unconscious), and I couldn't leave the house without throwing up; the second because I had a broken arm and couldn't drive. On Sundays, when we did the whole thing in reverse, dropping her off was incredibly hard. The drive back was pretty difficult for both of us, and I would try to keep her spirits up by getting us matching, mint-flavoured hot chocolates – her favourite.

I always knew I had to be careful. I didn't want to cross Beth. She could still be very difficult around me. I'd had concerns about a number of things she'd said, over the years – versions of events that didn't quite add up for me. I was still certain she had lied to me in the past, but I was extremely wary of challenging her and suffering the consequences. I'm not normally very good at keeping quiet, but I kept my mouth shut, for the sake of my daughter. I couldn't bear the thought that I might say the wrong thing, and that might be the end of me seeing Maddie.

It had happened before, after all.

That didn't mean it was easy. I found Beth incredibly unreliable. There were worrying gaps in the information she gave me, leaving more questions than answers. At one stage, I had real concerns and had to contact Maddie's GP to verify something I'd been told. That was one of several episodes where I didn't feel appropriately involved in decisions. There was a lot of mistrust, and it was hard to ignore. I always felt as though I was being set up to fail in front of Maddie. I worried that she was being pulled back and forth between us, in some sort of ego-based power struggle driven by unresolved resentment. I didn't want any part of it, but it lurked in the background, regardless.

It was an incredibly difficult time but thank God I had Ashley. I could talk to her openly and honestly. She was amazing, through all of it, even though she had her own anger and frustrations. She was desperate for Maddie not to get hurt.

In June 2018, Ashley, Maddie, Keir, Campbell and I all went on holiday to Majorca. I love everything about the island – the heat, the atmosphere, even the roads, which are some of the best in the world to drive, with their twists and turns, glorious hills and the epic views. You have to get up early in the morning to experience them in all their empty perfection, under a red Balearic sun, but it's worth it, even on holiday. In years gone by I would have been more interested in the neighbouring island, Ibiza, for the clubs and everything that goes along with that, but the thing I love most about holidays these days is spending time with my family.

We'd hired a small villa, with a swimming pool. All five of us trooped up and dumped our bags by the door. Ashley never likes to get in a mess, and she hates getting dirty. As soon as we arrived, she started running through the house. We wondered what she was doing, and then we all joined in. We ran, fully clothed, into the pool. It was amazing. It felt like the ultimate freedom, and it set the tone for the rest of the holiday. That's partly why it will always stand out in my mind. That, and what happened next.

After a glorious week's holiday together, we flew home. I drove Maddie down to Blackpool and dropped her off at her mum and stepdad's. The need to use our passports to travel abroad had led to some awkward questions from Maddie, resulting from a separate family trip abroad she seemed to have missed out on. Her mum, stepdad and siblings had all travelled to New York the previous New Year, when Maddie was in Scotland with us. Or so they claimed. I'd been sceptical at the time. Why would they do this kind of trip without Maddie and then tell her about it. Was it to punish her for spending that part of the Christmas holidays with us? Later, Maddie said that her siblings didn't have their own passports. How could they have gone to America? Maddie was confused and hurt, and that led to me dropping my guard. She seemed to have figured out the truth of the situation herself, so I ditched my usual pretence of upholding her mother's story. I didn't take sides, but I wasn't going to lie to her, anymore.

It was a huge mistake, and I will always regret what happened next.

We dropped Maddie off, as usual, and started back for home. Ashley and I were in the front of the car, with the boys – who were only four and two years old at the time – sleeping soundly in the back. I know from experience that it's ninety-two miles of M6 motorway, followed by seventy-two miles on the A75 Euro route – the main road to Ireland. That's how familiar I am with the journey. I used to feel like I could nod off myself, and the car would somehow know the way.

I really hope the boys were asleep when Beth phoned.

She immediately launched into me. She accused me of trying to poison Maddie with lies. Normally, I would have tried to pacify her. I would have taken the bollocking, no matter how unwarranted, and said as little as possible. But this time, no way. I explained what Maddie had figured out for herself, and how. Then I pointed out that it was a situation of Beth's own making. It was the wrong approach. My experience of Beth is that the worst thing you can do is to confront her or point out when she'd lied. My own faults aside, when she was the one in the wrong, I was never able to contradict her, because somehow, by a process of manipulation and gaslighting, I always came off worst. It seemed pointless, so, rightly or wrongly, I took the path of least resistance.

But now she appeared to be telling Maddie lies, and that was a problem. I was an adult and old enough to make my own choices about what I believed, but Maddie only knew the world around her – the one shaped by her parents. If one of them was lying, what was she supposed to believe? I knew I was in the right, but telling Beth to clean up her own mess had catastrophic results.

She started shouting. Then her husband joined in. We were driving along the motorway, Ashley's hand on my lap, trying to comfort me, while they screamed at me on loudspeaker. I could tell Ashley wanted to defend me. She was fuming, but she bit her lip, stayed calm, and focused on me and the boys. Then

Beth's husband told me I was getting what I deserved because I'd physically assaulted her during our relationship.

I couldn't believe what I was hearing. I felt like I was sinking. I'd never had any problem with him. If anything, I would have preferred that we got along well, for the sake of my daughter. I'd never even really met the guy, but I'd seen him a lot. Or as much as I could. He always seemed to be wearing a big pair of sunglasses and a week's worth of stubble.

I tried to join the dots in my head to make sense of what he was saying. I'd dropped Maddie off at her house one Sunday and he'd been there. He usually made himself scarce, so that in itself was unusual. Beth was acting strangely. Ashley sat in the car, and I went to the door. I normally spoke to Beth, to make sure everything was okay. This time, her husband peered out the door at me, as if he was keeping an eye on things, as if Beth were scared or upset. When I got back into the car, Ashley asked me what was wrong. 'Nothing,' I said because I had no clue. 'There must something wrong,' she insisted. I was unsettled, and Ashley could sense it.

If Beth's behaviour hadn't added up at the time, it was starting to make sense now. She'd obviously created an impression, for his benefit, based on a hurtful and damaging lie. A lie about the very kind of behaviour I'd tried, and failed, to protect my mum from, all those years ago. A situation she well knew. I couldn't wrap my head around it. What had brought this on, years after our split and all the time Maddie had spent in my care? She surely knew how painful and cruel that was.

I was devastated, but I phoned Maddie the following Wednesday, as normal, at 7 p.m. I checked in with her like that, every week. It was part of our routine. There was no answer. I rang again. Still no answer. I tried again, and again, and again.

Nothing. I phoned every Wednesday night at 7 p.m., for six weeks. Still nothing. I was in hell.

And yet somehow it was about to get worse.

A couple of days after my final attempt to call Maddie, I got a message on my answerphone. A policeman from Blackpool asked me to call him back. I dialled the number as soon as I got the message. He told me that Beth had reported me for harassment. We talked for a while. He listened to my side of the story. He was nice enough. He said that I'd done nothing wrong, but that now we'd spoken, if I tried to call again, it would likely be treated as a police matter.

I had no options. There was no realistic way for me to see my daughter. Beth clearly didn't want me having any contact with her and was prepared to resort to drastic measures to ensure that. It was brutal, but while Maddie was still legally a child, living under Beth's supervision in Blackpool, there wasn't a whole lot I could do about it. I was broke and up to my eyeballs in debt in 2018, and for quite a while after that. I didn't have any money to mount a legal challenge to clear my name against the harassment allegation or go to court to arrange visitation rights for my daughter – a process that would have dragged her into it and placed her firmly in the middle of her warring mother and father. And there was Ashley and the boys to think about, and how any potential consequences might affect them. We all tried to get in touch, as creatively as we could, but I was at constant risk of attracting the attention of the police.

I haven't tried to call since that day.

I hoped that Maddie would find a way to call me instead, and that when she was sixteen years old, and perhaps a bit more able to decide for herself, she would get in touch. I dread to think what version of me she thinks is real, but I'm always trying to come up with ways to let Maddie know we're thinking about her. More than anything, I want her to know that we love her and that I think about her all the time. Without being able to get in touch directly, I've gone with what I know. Every month or so, I upload a video to YouTube, talking to Maddie about what's going on, what I'm thinking about, asking what she's up to. Yes, that's right. I have a secret YouTube channel that's only for my daughter. I don't think she watches those videos, but I've done it for years now and I have no plans to stop. She will know how to find it if she ever wants to.

I've never told anyone about that channel until now, except my family. We all recorded messages for Maddie's sixteenth birthday, and I put them together in one big video and uploaded it on the day. There's nothing crazy in there. No joking around with Craig, or turning him into a chicken, no theme tune or drone footage; just a Dad, talking hopefully, to his daughter.

All I want is for Maddie to know that I think about her all the time. Every. Single. Day. I love her. Ashley loves her. Keir and Campbell love her. Her entire Scottish family love her. More than anything, I want to see her again.

I'll be here whenever she's ready.

# Chapter Twenty-Nine

Life in the last few years has flipped from miserable lows to epic highs. The irony of this isn't lost on a bipolar person. The journey from devastating parental alienation in the summer of 2018, to the attainment of long-term financial security in the spring of 2022, was one of polar extremes. And of course, wedged right in the middle of that, was the small matter of a terrifying global pandemic.

In February 2020, when the idea of Covid shutting down the world still seemed like the fevered imaginings of a conspiracy theorist, I went to visit my friend, Aaron LaVoy, in Wisconsin. I stayed there for a couple of weeks. Aaron had stayed at my house in The Shire and joined me in a spot of hoof trimming. I still remember taking him for a walk across the wild lands of the Galloway hills and him ducking his head every five minutes, thinking he'd get shot for being on someone else's land. Not everyone is familiar with the lack of widespread gun ownership here in Scotland, or the right of responsible access to almost all of the land.

Ashley and I had largely gone to Wisconsin to check in with Appleton Steel, who were busy at that point, building The Dark Knight for me. As usual, I got restless. I asked Aaron if I could go and see some of his clients, and that led to me asking if I could do some trimming. It was a weird sort of busman's holiday, but I loved it.

Wisconsin is vastly different to Scotland, with its wide plains, small trees and big roads. People are really friendly, but the sense of humour is very different. It took me right out of my comfort zone, which is always good. Aaron runs his own hoof trimming school and that really fired my imagination. I'd love to do that myself one day. I mostly try to pass on as much education as possible, in Trojan horse form, disguised as infotainment, but that trip inspired me to put together my own digital course, and I released that online. Over seven hundred people have taken it up so far, which is amazing. And, let's face it, that's way more than I could physically train in a year!

My YouTube videos give you the broad strokes, but the course is a proper, deep dive into the latest science and techniques in my world. It's a structured system to help farmers make a real difference, save lots of money, and do the very best for their cows. I don't want to put myself out of business, but I really believe I can improve the lives of cows by sharing my knowledge. The course is just another way to do that.

We had another opportunity to highlight the importance of hoof trimming, when we were shadowed by a film crew recently, as part of a BBC documentary series, *This Farming Life*. One of my favourite customers featured in the series they were making, and Craig and I just happened to turn up on the day they were filming, and then again, by sheer coincidence, the next time the cameras were rolling. When they asked if they could follow us too, we managed to squeeze in some time for them. That was an amazing experience.

As I look around where I am now, under a massive, changing sky, in what is, for me, the most beautiful place on earth,

I marvel at the life I've somehow created for myself and my family, and I think of the daughter I long to see again in time. Other than my lack of contact with Maddie, life has been pretty rewarding all told. I'm the luckiest man in the world – living where I live, doing what I do, with the ones I love, and my own, perfect woman by my side.

It wasn't all that long ago that I found myself on the run from the police, or alone, in my bedroom, contemplating ending it all, or totally broke and struggling to get by. I had, as I saw it, lost everything: my job; my home; my daughter; my money; my mental health. And yet, in spite of all that, I hadn't totally lost myself.

'This above all: to thine own self be true.'

I know for sure it was Shakespeare who wrote *that* one. I looked it up! It's a lesson I've had to learn a few times, but whenever I *have* lived my own life, it's ended up working out okay. When I went to college and opened up for the first time; when I ran a restaurant and chased awards; when I became The Hoof GP and had the courage to face up to who I am, where I'm from and what it all means – it has all paid off in the end, and it has surprised me too. I started to like myself. I grew into my life, and my purpose, in ways I could never have imagined.

When I took the leap and started hoof trimming, I fell in love with my new life. I had a real drive for it. It got me out of bed in the morning (sometimes too early), but I wanted to share my passion. And when I let other people in, on social media, on YouTube, I found my tribe – my herd – and everything sort of fell into place. I'm not saying it wasn't hard work and I'm not saying my life is perfect, but on a warm, sunny day, staring up at that big, blue sky, watching the clouds roll over the top of my little piece of paradise, it's pretty damn close. I now have

Ashley and the boys by my side for it all. I love having the boys at work with me. It's like a journal of their lives. More than once, I've watched clips back and just stared in awe at how small they once were. Now Campbell bursts onto the screen and shouts 'WE'RE BACK' when I'm recording, and Keir gets stuck in, helping me.

So, what does the future hold for me now? Do I have any big announcements on the horizon? Will I still be making the same content in five years' time?

I have some plans. Who doesn't? There's that honeymoon that Ashley and I never quite managed, of course. I'd also love to keep some animals of my own. Not on the scale my dad did, not agriculturally, but for me and for the kids. I grew up surrounded by animals. It gave me a sense of responsibility, taught me about something outside myself, grounded me. I'd like the kids to have a taste of that life. I know what it would mean for them. We've already started small, with a couple of rabbits, one of which promptly headed off to the pearly gates, but thankfully we found a quick replacement. Ashley's desperate to get her hands on some horses. Not to ride them – just to pet them and do their hair. And we'd love to buy the field behind our house. That would open up a whole load of possibilities. It would give me the option of turning the notion of setting up a hoof trimming school into a reality. That would be a hell of a lot of work, but it would also be awesome.

But for now, I'm right where I need to be. I've positioned myself in what seems like the best place on the concrete floor. I've got it right first time, for once. I'm in the workshop and everything is coming together beautifully. I'm surrounded by my rewards to myself for doing alright in life: my pick-ups, a McLaren 600LT, a BMW M6 in a 'tasteful' shade of green and a Porsche

911 GT2 RS, a dream, all turned into reality. There are two cattle crushes, one in black and red and another in a garish shade of green. My work bench sits in a corner, surrounded by a full range of red Milwaukee power tools – part of my sponsorship deal. Fast cars, trucks, power tools and a haven from the world.

All good things for me, still.

The walls of my workshop remain lined with flags people have sent me. I'm still keen to get as many as possible into shot, to acknowledge all that effort. I've got my perfect starting point, but I still do one last, mental check. I know what I'm going to say. With my checklist done, I take a deep breath, click on the *create* button and then hit *live*. The rush is still there. I'm not worrying about anything. I am present. In the moment. Will tonight be the night I choke? Will I dry up and say nothing? Will it be the night I say the wrong thing and get cancelled? Probably not, and if it happened, I'd survive. I have everything I need. My world is right here. Ashley and the boys are in the garden, and one day Maddie might return to see us again. Our doors will be open.

The tattoo on my arm reads, 'he who wanders is not always lost.'

I've lived in thirty-seven houses. I've been lost so many times and spent too long feeling like I never fitted in. But now, it really feels like I'm home.

# Acknowledgements

Writing this book, with the help of my eldest brother, Bob, has been a journey of rediscovery and healing – one I didn't know I needed to go on, until we were well underway. I wouldn't have reached this point if it hadn't been for the incredible people I'm blessed to have around me.

First and foremost, I want to thank you. This book is for YOU, the people reading it. It's my attempt to unmask some of the truth about social media. What we see of the people we follow online is curated, the edited highlights. If I can lift the lid, even slightly, on the inherent fallacy about most people's social feeds, I'll have achieved some of what I set out to do. And if I can help anyone facing the kind of mental health challenges I have, that has to be worthwhile. Above all, this is a thank you: for all your support over the last few years, and for being The Herd. Without you, there would be no Hoof GP.

My life wouldn't be my life without my incredible family – Susan, Kirsty, James, Bob, and my mum, Christine, who are all (thankfully) still here. I've lent on you all at times. I've asked far more than a lot of people would, and you've always been there, exactly when I needed you. Thank you all for sticking around and for being present when you were needed most. I feel indebted to you all.

I want to thank Davie, my stepfather – for teaching me the

things he didn't know he was teaching me, for being uncompromisingly 'Davie' and unwittingly leading me into the world of trimming cows' feet; but, most of all, for being a man to whom it was always 'nae bother'.

I need to say a heartfelt thank you to my dad. Without knowing it, you taught me so much. At times, it wasn't a conscious or deliberate effort, but your life's path and your decisions created a want in me – to be better, and to make better choices. I will always love you.

To my brothers by choice, if not by blood: Dave Old and James McGill – I don't have the words to express the gratitude I have for you being in my life. The things you've helped and guided me through have been an immense weight at times. You've both been inspirations to me; my moral compasses, surrogate uncles to my kids, and dependable constants in my life. I am eternally grateful.

Thank you to Gillian Hamnett, our brilliant editor, for guiding us through the publishing process, for keeping us on the right track and for kicking our collective behinds when we needed it!

Lastly, thank you, my princess. Thank you, Ashley, for being the continuous, beautiful centre of my world. You and the kids are my reason for existing; you're the strength that lifts me up and the force that pushes me to dream, believe, and achieve. I love you.